Psychotherapeutic Intervention
in Hysterical Disorders

Psychotherapeutic Intervention in Hysterical Disorders

William J. Mueller, Ph.D.
Albert S. Aniskiewicz, Ph.D.

Jason Aronson Inc.

Northvale, New Jersey
London

Library of Congress Cataloging in Publication Data

Mueller, William J.
  Psychotherapeutic intervention in hysterical disorders.

  Bibliography: p. 279
  Includes index.
  1. Hysteria—Treatment.   I. Aniskiewicz, Albert S.
II. Title. [DNLM: 1. Hysteria—therapy. 2. Psycho-
therapy. WM 173 M947p]
RC532.M84   1985   616.85′24   85-15075
ISBN 0-87668-913-6

To Louise and Pam

Contents

Therapist Reactivity • Therapist Reactivity as a Diagnostic Guide • Sequential Analysis of an Initial Interview

Themes in Early Sessions • The Contents of the Session: Preludes to Therapy • The Contents and Associated Affects: Dissonance • The Emergence of Conflict • The Escalation of Anger • Significant Female Relationships: A Crucial Development • Reenactment of Conflict • The Theme of Sexuality • Developmental Themes and the Sexual Orientation • Effects of Premature Remarks • Genuine Concern for the Client: Containing "Acting Out" • The Formative Stages in Psychotherapy • Progression and Regression: The Process of Working Through • Identity Conflicts: A Critical Stage in Psychotherapy • Working Through the Identity Crisis • The Client Comes into Her Own

Initial Impressions of the Client: Hysterical Style • Themes in the Client's Development that Shaped Conflict • The Male Therapist as "Oedipal" Father • Risking the Therapeutic Venture • An Analysis of Two Critical Sessions • The Fathers and their Phallic-Narcissistic Organization • The Client's Sensuousness • Therapist's Reactions as Reinforcements of Core Issues • Sex: the Roadblock to Need Satisfaction • Displacements: Guides to the Emotional Conditions of the Therapeutic Relationship • Displacements and the Isolation of Affect • The Client's Needs and Submerged Features of Personality • Final Observations

Preface

Psychotherapy with the hysterical personality is difficult, but the rewards of observing change and being a participant in the process of bringing to life the submerged substance of character overshadow the frustrations. Despite its deceptive overlay of shallowness, the character is one of substance and beauty. Only after a therapist has become aware of the hidden strength of character and developmental struggles can he or she truly appreciate and respect the hysterical personality. Too often, the therapist responds to the undesirable surface traits and treats the hysteric with the same shallowness for which she is condemned.

Both authors have been interested in hysterical disorders for an extended period of time. Some years ago, one of us gathered vignettes of cases from a sample of trainees in an attempt to study family patterns and variations in symptom production. That informal study was followed by a grant from the Michigan State University Foundation in 1978 to gather diagnostic and psychotherapeutic data systematically on a large sample of female hysterics who were in therapy with male and female therapists. Those data provided background information and verification for some of the theoretical and practical considerations that were developed in a third study about the processes of psychotherapy with the hysterical personality. The third study was partially supported over a three-year period by Michigan State University's All-University Research funds.

Acknowledgments

The authors wish to express their appreciation to the many persons who have agreed to participate in our studies with no personal gain. Their contributions have made this book possible. Of equal importance, the authors thank the many trainees whose work they have supervised over the years. It is in observing the psychotherapy of others that one gains significant insight. Otherwise, one is left wondering whether it is all simply countertransference.

The contributions of those who have written about psychotherapy with the hysterical personality before us must be mentioned. In the references, their works are cited. But particular mention should be made of certain writings which influenced our thinking. We have been guided by the work of Sullivan, Thompson, Fromm-Reichmann, and the interpersonal school of thinking. Wolstein's work on transference and countertransference from an interpersonal framework is noteworthy. Alexander, Erikson, and Rogers are significant figures. Herman's work on father-daughter incest is compelling. The writings of Paul Chodoff reflect a depth of understanding of hysterical disorders and their psychotherapy that is unparalleled.

We have learned immeasurably about hysterical disorders from our colleagues at the Counseling Center. Their ideas and their critical evaluation of our concepts have become an integral part of our view of the developmental and psychotherapeutic process in hysterical disorders. Dr. Imogen Bowers' understanding of father-daughter relationships has been particularly helpful.

We would like to thank the many interns and trainees at the Counseling Center who have tolerated our preoccupation with the hysterical personality and who have contributed to our ideas by testing our hunches in their own work. Appreciation is also expressed to Richard Genirberg for administering the diagnostic testing associated with one of our projects. Mention must be made of Dr. Michael Sherry and Dr. Nancy Egan who critically reviewed very early drafts of portions of this manuscript. Cathy Hargrove monitored the project, helped in the preparation of sensitive materials, and oversaw the work of others. Cheryl Manning did a superb job of typing materials and verifying bibliographic work.

Psychotherapeutic Intervention
in Hysterical Disorders

Part One

Developmental and Dynamic Themes

Chapter One

The Hysterical Personality Disorders:
An Overview

The concept of the hysterical personality has evolved over centuries of interest in persons whose emotional makeup and behavioral characteristics define the boundaries of the diagnostic category. Its history (Veith 1965, 1977; Lazare 1971) is as colorful as are the personalities that define it. Perhaps no emotional problems have historically received more attention, been the subject of greater controversy, suffered more diagnostic confusion, and been defined more globally than the cluster of behaviors, feelings, attitudes, thought processes, and symptoms that exemplify this diagnostic classification. Although this confusion still exists to some degree, a recent flurry of writing has provided some useful distinctions within an otherwise chaotic syndrome.

During the past few decades, the concept of hysteria has undergone successive revisions. Through continuing reevaluation (Easser and Lesser 1965, Chodoff 1974, Blacker and Tupin 1977, Krohn 1978, Baumbacher and Amini 1980), investigators have attempted to account for dynamic and behavioral variations in manifest conflict and in the strivings of an oral nature (Marmor 1953) that are observed in hysterical clients. Using the work of Zetzel (1968) to exemplify the redefinition of hysteria, a continuum can be sketched, with one end defined as "true good hysterics" (p. 256) and the other the "so-called good hysteric" (p. 259). The continuum ranges from those exhibiting a relatively mature personality structure, genitally oriented, with paramount oedipal conflicts, to those who exhibit defective ego structures and preoedipal fixations as paramount features. Such a continuum seems accepted by other investigators (Blacker and Tupin 1977, Tupin 1974, Lazare 1971, Sperling 1973) and appears to be essentially similar to the "hysteric character" and "hysteroid" distinctions proposed by Easser and Lesser (1965) in which the hysteroid personality is viewed as a more severe character disorder.

The revisionists who contend that oral phenomena are predominant features of the hysterical personality have redirected attention to the preoedipal determinants of the hysterical personality. These investigators suggest that maternal deprivation, with consequent preoedipal strivings of an oral character, contributes to a pregenital organization of the hysterical structure (Marmor 1953, Blacker and Tupin 1977, Hollender 1971, Halleck 1967).

Krohn (1978) proposed an alternate, more classic model to account for variations within the syndrome. In his tripartite model, the hysterical personality is considered a nonpathological entity, with true hysteria defined as the manifestation of neurotic conflicts within the hysterical personality. This distinction is in accord with the theories of Alarcon (1973), who concluded that whereas hysterical symptoms are associated with conditions of the hysterical personality, hysterical personalities may not "present or develop symptoms of hysteria" (p. 273). In Krohn's third category, personalities exhibiting such characteristics as impaired ego functioning and ego-syntonic maladaptive behaviors are considered to exemplify hysterical character disorders. This category seems closely associated with the so-called good hysteric of Zetzel (1968) or the hysteroid personality described by Easser and Lesser (1965).

On psychodynamic grounds, Baumbacher and Amini (1980) differentiate the hysterical personality disorder from borderline states and hysterical character neuroses. They consider the hysterical personality disorder to be at a higher level of organization than borderline conditions, with conflicts deriving "predominantly from phallic stage developmental issues" (p. 510). The hysterical character neurosis, which approximates Krohn's hysterical neurosis (1978), is construed as a regressive phenomenon from a later oedipal developmental stage.

The contributions of Baumbacher and Amini (1980), Krohn (1978) and Blacker and Tupin (1977) have provided a comprehensive, dynamic-oriented view of the hysterical personality. Blacker and Tupin (1977), for example, have provided dynamic links in current understanding of the hysterical disturbance by tracing theoretical contributions that, taken together, yield a definition of the hysterical personality. Those authors cite the contributions of drive theory, character analysis, ego psychology, the interpersonal-social-cultural school, and cognitive style as providing the groundwork for a definitive syndrome.

Nomenclature has changed rapidly. Perhaps symptomatic of the state of the art is the preoccupation with definition. Krohn (1978) likened Zetzel's "so-called good hysteric" (1968) to the hysterical character disorders and to the "hysteroid" personality of Easser and Lesser (1965), which in turn he considered conceptually close to the "hysteriform" (Abse 1966). What has been called the "hysterical personality" (Horowitz 1977) has taken a nonpathological twist (Krohn 1978) and found its pathological substitute in a disorder termed the "histrionic personality disorder" (American Psychiatric Association [APA] 1980) or the "hysterical personality disorder" (Baumbacher and Amini 1980, Chodoff 1982). And the hysterical character neurosis appears to have much in common, developmentally and dynamically, with the "hysterical neurosis" described by Krohn (1978).

Despite comprehensive efforts at understanding the interpersonal meaning and intrapsychic dynamics in hysteria, the character traits and defenses of persons so diagnosed have received undue attention. The pejorative attitudes about hysteria that Chodoff (1982) addressed seem associated with reactions

to those highlighted traits. Although it is true that such behaviors as emotional lability, histrionics, dependency, excitabil-
ity, egocentrism, and self-dramatization (Alarcon 1973, Chodoff
and Lyons 1958, Lazare and colleagues 1970, Blacker and Tupin
1977, APA 1980, Halleck 1967) are intrinsic to hysteria, their pre-
dominance has overshadowed dynamic considerations, and psychotherapeutic efforts toward amelioration (Allen 1977, Krohn
1978, Chodoff 1982) have received less note.

PRESENT APPROACH

The main focus of the book is intensive psychodynamic psychotherapy with the hysterical personality, and the use of the
term *client* does not presuppose a particular attitude or approach
toward psychotherapy. We view the client/patient distinction as
a semantic issue and not a substantive one, and, accordingly,
the concepts presented are intended for a broad spectrum of
mental health professionals who are engaged in the practice of
intensive psychotherapy.

Our theoretical orientation to therapeutic work with hysterical disorders is psychodynamic. Many have observed that the
hysterical personality is a relationship syndrome. Thus, the conditions of the therapeutic relationship are of great importance
in effective psychotherapy. More than those of any other client,
the hysteric's productions during sessions are often indirect expressions of her experience of the therapist and therapy. As the
past and present merge and find expression in the therapeutic
hour, the dynamics of therapist–client interactions become complex, subtle, and powerful preconditions for change.

The book addresses psychotherapy with the female hysteric.
The process analysis is based on the female hysteric in interaction with the male therapist. That decision in no way reflects
our belief that hysteria is a female syndrome. On the contrary,
we are in accord with those (Luisada and colleagues 1974,
Blacker and Tupin 1977, Andrews 1984) who have reported hys-

terical personalities in men. In fact, we have often observed hysterical males whose family patterns and dynamics are mirror images of those of hysterical females. Such phenomena, however, are the subject of extensive treatises in their own right.

A major focus of the book is on the *processes* of change in psychotherapeutic work. In the first section of the book, the groundwork is laid through discussions of the developmental scene, the shaping of conflict, and the outcomes in adult functioning. Only through a sensitive understanding of the turmoil of the hysteric's youth can the therapist tolerate the turmoil that must appear during sessions if change is to occur. Based in that understanding, the second section of the book addresses the guidelines for productive intervention. Those guidelines are translated into the processes of change in the final section. Throughout the book, the concepts and intervention strategies are highlighted through clinical material.

In the next two chapters, the neurotic conflicts in the hysterical personality are traced from their developmental roots to their manifestations in adult functioning. Setting aside the question of their oedipal or preoedipal origins, we describe the interpersonal themes in development that shape the adult's conflicts, defenses, and character traits. In Chapter Two those developmental themes are considered from the perspective of the intrafamilial dynamics that activate conflict and necessitate the defensive maneuvering that characterizes the adult hysteric. Six developmental stages within the family constellation are considered critical determinants in the formation of the hysterical personality.

In Chapter Three the outcomes in adult functioning are considered from several vantage points. The dynamic motivating forces undergirding the disturbed relationships of the hysteric, and the displacements characterizing those relationships, are elaborated. Repetitive themes in the adult hysteric's interpersonal relationships are then evaluated in terms of their developmental source and their dynamic functions within the personality. The character traits of the hysteric are stripped of their pejorative overtones and seen to reflect a mixture of conflict, defense, and ego-integrative efforts at communicating.

The guidelines for therapeutic intervention are considered in the second part of the book. Those guidelines are based in an assessment of the intrafamilial dynamics and their outcomes in the functioning and interpersonal behavior of the adult hysteric. The dynamics underlying those familial interactions and the residue of those conflicts in adult functioning are the carrier waves for the transferential and countertransferential themes so characteristic of work with the hysterical client. In Chapter Four the bases of a productive therapeutic relationship are considered.

In the following chapter the therapist is guided in the intervention process through an understanding of the hysterical mode of communicating. Through her many stories, and reports of her experiences and relationships, the therapist receives a running account of the processes of conflict in the client and, of greater import, a fully orchestrated account of the client's experience of the therapeutic relationship itself. The repetitive themes in the hysteric's interpersonal relationships are reintroduced, and their role in understanding the client and in providing further guidelines for intervention is discussed. In the final chapter of Part Two, the interlocking of therapist–client conflict is considered, along with its effects in creating impasses and impeding therapeutic progress.

The last section of the book is reserved for an integration, and the focus is the psychotherapeutic interview. In Chapter Seven the dimensions of the initial interviews are outlined. In those sessions the therapist begins the search for the conditions in development that gave rise to conflict, searches for the modifying effects of maturation, and attempts to assess the sustaining factors of conflict in the client's current interactions. Content is important, but crucial features of personality are gleaned from the interpersonal-experiential aspects of the interview. Among other things, it is in the therapist's accurate experience of his own reactions to the client that the formulation of a hysterical personality gathers diagnostic force and therapy is set on a productive course.

The case material in Chapter Eight allows us to follow the progress of clients during therapy. Particular emphasis is given to the ways in which developmental conflicts are activated and replayed in treatment. In the final chapter, concepts are integrated through case material and commentary.

Chapter Two

The Shaping of Conflict: Developmental Themes

In this chapter a thesis is proposed about the interpersonal themes and intrafamilial dynamics during development that shape the hysterical personality. After a discussion of environmental conditions, a composite picture is drawn of the developmental themes that shape the hysterical personality. The genetic theme is then recast as a series of critical incidents in the developmental process that affect the formation of the hysterical personality. Throughout the chapter, developmental conflicts are related to the conflicts of the adult in a general way. A more extensive treatment of the outcomes in adult functioning is reserved for the next chapter.

ENVIRONMENTAL CONDITIONS

In recent years clinical data about the environmental conditions favoring the development of the hysterical personality have been reevaluated. Some investigators hypothesize that conflicts in the hysterical personality are rooted in preoedipal stages of development. Marmor (1953), noting the oral phenomena present in hysterical personalities, suggested that oedipal phase fixations are *"outgrowths of preoedipal fixations, chiefly of an oral nature"* (p. 662), thereby lending a pregenital coloration to the ensuing Oedipus complex.

That argument has been buttressed by others (Blacker and Tupin 1977, Halleck 1967, Hollender 1971) who contend that maternal deprivation and the self-indulgent mother (Celani 1976) are predominant features in the developmental histories of the hysterical personality. In this vein, Halleck (1967) and Hollender (1971) have proposed that maternal deprivation is a motivating force in the child's turning to the father as a substitute mother, giving rise to the potential sexualization of affectional needs. Dynamically, that event purportedly energizes the hysteric's provocative behavior when in fact nurturance is sought (Hollender 1971).

Krohn (1978) countered the preoedipal argument, interpreting the oral phenomena noted in the strivings of the hysterical client from a different perspective. Drawing on classical theory, he denoted as oedipal the point of libidinal fixation. Using Nagera's topography (1975), he related differing hysterical pictures to the positive and negative stages of the oedipal phase of development. In particular, he noted that the absence of the heightened oral longings characteristic of an oral fixation implies higher-order personality integration.

These differing formulations raise many questions about the psychotherapeutic efforts appropriate in helping the client whose problems reflect a hysterical personality. Depending on whether the therapist considers certain oral phenomena to represent preoedipal fixations, the contributions of the object-relations theorists as they relate to borderline conditions may apply.

The consequences of a preoedipal construction, however, may contribute to errors in psychotherapy unless the assessment is solidly supported by clinical data that refute the oedipal hypothesis. The developmental picture presented in this chapter and later discussions of intervention guidelines are consistent with Krohn's observation (1978) that the misdiagnosis of orality in hysteria simply reinforces hysterical defenses. For example, if a male therapist construes his female client's reports of her mother as representing maternal deprivation, he may tend to the client in nurturant, sensitive, and supportive ways. Krohn (1978) suggested that, in assuming orality, the therapist can reinforce ego-syntonic passive fantasies. A complementary dynamic construction in our example is that the male therapist symbolically colludes as the father did in undercutting maternal authority, thereby perpetuating and exacerbating the client's oedipal conflicts, inducing guilt, reinforcing her defenses, and delaying movement during therapy (see Kell and Mueller 1966, pp. 50-53).

On the surface, the cluster of traits that the adult hysteric attributes to the mother may be construed as supporting the preoedipal hypothesis. Such traits as "cold," "distant," "rejecting," "preoccupied," and "remote" (Blinder 1966, Halleck 1967, Hollender 1971) have been ascribed to the mothers by hysterical clients. Those observations are, however, in direct opposition to the reports of Easser and Lesser (1965), who found the mothers of hysterical clients to be "consistent and responsible" (p. 395) women who seem to foster a nonassertive posture in their daughters. Those investigators construe maternal deprivation as a central feature of the hysteroid disorder, a more severely disturbed personality whose family dynamics reflect greater turmoil. Such intensely negative attributions, therefore, seem an unduly harsh indictment of the mother.

Viewed another way, one would expect a client with an oedipal orientation to distort the relationship to the mothering one and reject her as intruding into the fantasied exclusive relationship with the father. Although made in reference to his thesis about borderline hysterical states, a comment by Semmler (1977) seems appropriate here. He notes that "the overly intense bond to one of the parents and the rejection of the other reminds one...of unsuccessful domination of the oedipal conflict" (p. 272). From the perspective of the developmental patterns to be described in this chapter, Blinder (1966) touched the underlying dynamic generating those negative attributions in noting that the mothers of hysterics were so conflicted about their own identity issues that they could be of little assistance to their daughters.

Maternal deprivation may also be differentiated from the mother's inadequacy as a role model. A cold, withholding mother, if accurately portrayed by the client, is a different matter from a mother who is inadequate and helpless in the face of the father's controlling and sexualized behavior toward the child. The latter pattern would be the dynamic fodder for developing passive, controlling, and manipulative traits, characteristics commonly attributed to the adult hysterical client.

The differing views concerning the developmental process suggest the need for further definition and interpretation. The issue is to reconcile the family patterns and their variations, as retrospectively reported by the adult hysteric, with the turns that hysteria takes in adulthood. Certain character traits may predominate in some cases and not in others. Conversion symptoms may vary or be absent. The ego style and functioning may reflect differences in cognition, and areas of conflict-free functioning may be more or less circumscribed. Sexual behavior may vary from promiscuity to anxieties, phobic reactions, inhibitions, and other evidences of externalization and overcontrol or undercontrol.

DEVELOPMENTAL THEMES

In working with the adult hysterical client, one is impressed by the similarity in the reports and perceptions of family interactions and the dynamics that those interactions reflect. Admittedly retrospective in analysis and based in the perceptual process of clients, those reports nonetheless are compelling in the commonality of emotional and interpersonal themes. In addition, the parallel patterns in the hysteric's reports of her ongoing relationships lend credence to the emotional strains from the past. The hysteric's own perceptions of the therapist and the transferences and countertransferences that develop provide added reliability to the assumed family dynamics.

Within the context of the general developmental theme being

proposed, differing familial patterns cause variations in the defensive style observed in the hysterical personality. Two patterns of family relationships can be used to illustrate the potential for varying hysterical styles. The first representative parental theme consists of a paternal figure who is manifestly dominating, self-centered, and self-sufficient. He is complemented by a weak, ineffectual, and inadequate mother. In the second theme, the father emerges as manifestly passive in relation to the mother and overtly responsive to and collusive with the daughter. The mother is perceived to be competitive, nagging, and controlling.

Those patterns, however, are variants on a general theme that affect defenses rather than personality structure. In many cases the manifest ineffectual, needy, and inadequate behavior of the mother emerges as the latent trend underlying the self-sufficient "macho" father. In turn, the dominance of the father emerges as a suppressed maternal trend.

It is the conflicting set of trends and the common inadequacy reflected in both parents that contribute to the conflicts and defenses of the hysteric. The underlying theme common to the two representative pictures is one of inadequacy in both parents to meet their respective parental roles and relate as such to the hysteric (Blinder 1966, Celani 1976). It is the similarity in the latent trends in the parents, despite their manifest behavioral differences, that sets the hysterical personality. Whether the mother is resigned to a weak, ineffectual role or is threatened by the child and reacts competitively, the basic issue remains one of not having achieved a mature mutuality as wife and the generativity of mothering. Similarly, whether the father's adequacy conflicts are expressed through a brittle, pseudomasculine exterior or directly in warm, sexual, or collusive ways with the daughter, he indicts himself and reveals his own immaturity. The common themes pervading each representative pattern shape the hysterical personality; the variations in manifest and latent characteristics shape the particular defensive patterns.

Central to the thesis of this chapter are the observations of Easser and Lesser (1965) and the work of Herman (1981) in her study of father–daughter incest. The familial patterns and supporting clinical data Herman provides in discussing seductive "but not overtly incestuous" (p. 109) fathers are strikingly similar to the dynamics undergirding the hysterical personality. In particular, Herman's observations about the dominant, seductive, and self-serving father whose behavior becomes rejecting at the daughter's adolescence parallel the observations of Easser and Lesser (1965) and can be considered invariant themes in development. In addition, Herman's reports of the subservient mother who sacrifices the daughter for her own security, and her observations about the daughter as "pawn in the marital struggle" (p. 115), are equally crucial intrafamilial dynamics that shape the hysterical personality.

In general, the environmental conditions favoring the development of the hysterical personality include a father whose portrait has been well drawn in the literature. He has been described as seductive and stimulating (Easser and Lesser 1965, Halleck 1967, Hollender 1971, Celani 1976) and is perceived to be "dominant, arbitrary, excitable, volatile, controlling and imaginative" (Easser and Lesser 1965, p. 395). From the perspective of the propositions to be advanced in this chapter, the crucial issue is embedded in Easser and Lesser's comment that father authored and orchestrated "the family comedies and tragedies" (p. 395). Therein rests the dynamic core of the hysteric's problems with her father—his narcissism. Despite variations in the manifest traits of the fathers, the common latent personality trends reflect a phallic–oedipal orientation. The fathers are self-centered and possessive, and view relationships as an extension of themselves.

From very early in her life, the child who is targeted to reflect the father becomes the depository of his inadequacies. The father develops a collusive—often seductive—relationship with the daughter, disparaging the mother and usurping her role. The child who develops a hysterical style is viewed by the father as an extension of himself and as the projective target of his inner conflicts. The child then becomes the vehicle for his self-gratifications, the object of his neurotic frustrations, and the tool for the father's hostile "affront to his wife" (Celani 1976, p. 1416) by "flaunting the special relationship" with the daughter (Herman 1981, p. 115).

During her prepubescence, the daughter may accept this role

and attempt to reflect the father in her undertakings, sacrificing a personal identity for the sake of the father. During this
period the mutual seduction noted in the literature (Halleck
1967, Hollender 1971) is evident, although the daughter may be
burdened by guilt about her position and attempt to mobilize
the mother. What becomes clear to the hysteric only in adolescence is that her power in the family is conditional on "fitting
in," catering to the father's ego, and asserting nothing that
threatens him.

The shift in paternal behavior at the daughter's pubescence
is crucial (Easser and Lesser 1965, Herman 1981). Easser and
Lesser's thesis about the motive force in this abrupt change in
paternal behavior and its consequences in interpersonal functioning will be examined later from several additional perspectives. In a general way, however, we propose that the latent personality trends in the father become manifest at the daughter's
puberty. In his shift from fostering an unhealthy alliance to taking a hostile, rejecting stance, the father seeds a number of
repetitive themes in the adult hysteric's interpersonal relationships. Themes of insubstantiality and lack of personal worth,
issues of power and betrayal, and negative attitudes about male
egocentricity and defensiveness have their roots in the unmasking of the father at puberty.

Whereas the literature is rather consistent in its portrayal of
the father of the hysteric, the mother, as noted earlier, is variously seen as withholding, cold, and remote or as consistent and
responsible. The propositions we put forth here are in accord
with the views of Blinder (1966): The mother is viewed as a
highly conflicted person whose preoccupation with her own insecurities precludes her providing an adequate role model for
the daughter. This view in no way exonerates the mother; it
simply explains her.

The mother is insecure and anxious, and her security operations in negotiating her position with the father take precedence
over the welfare of the child. Whether the mother actively competes with the child or takes a noninterference attitude in the
father–daughter relationship, she indicts herself as mother and
ally of the child. The mother may actively collude in binding the
child in the father–daughter relationship for the sake of her own

well-being. Or, following a rupture in the parents' own relationship, the mother may use the child to wield power in relation to the father or as a vehicle to express her resentment toward him.

The child is not only the "pawn in the marital struggle" (Herman 1981, p. 115), but also the depository of the parents' separate inadequacies and inner conflicts. In the face of two parents who hold conflicting views, express oppositional personality trends, and devalue each other, the hysteric must negotiate a separate alliance with each or abandon one for the sake of the other (see Herman 1981). To feel complete, the individual must integrate the emotional introjects of both parents. It is that ego function of attempting to integrate disparate emotional states that defines the life-long task of the hysteric.

This unique set of developmental circumstances provides part of the dynamic force for the many interpersonal conflicts that have been observed in the adult hysterical client. Issues of control and manipulation (Halleck 1967), themes of victimization, helplessness, and irresponsibility (Horowitz 1977), and distrust of maternal figures (Hollender 1971) seem natural outgrowths of such familial dynamics. The sense of being depleted that has been observed in the hysteroid personality (Easser and Lesser 1965) finds its counterpart in the hysteric's having been the depository of parental conflicts and irresponsibility. Having been the pawn in parental discord to be sacrificed for maternal security, as well as an extension of the father and the projective object of his inner conflicts, the hysteric is ripe to develop the feelings of insubstantiality that Shapiro (1965) reports.

Because of the separate alliances the adult hysteric was forced to negotiate with her parents, her relationships may have a dyadic cast, and the hysteric often experiences her relationships in that way. In the hysteric's search to integrate the disparate voices of disjunctive parents, the underlying triadic nature of those relationships may be screened from view. But, as Blinder (1966) noted, it is "the ego integrative capacity" of the hysteric as she sets about her task that places her "closer to the phallic than to the oral phase" of development (p. 235). And it is the underlying triadic nature of her pursuit that sets her apart from the borderline client. She is, as Zetzel (1968) proposed, someone who has "paid too heavy a price in the attempted resolution of the oedipal triangle" (p. 257).

CRITICAL STAGES IN DEVELOPMENT

The determinants of the hysterical personality can be recast as a series of six critical developmental stages: (1) unseating the mother, (2) the mother's resignation, (3) the father–daughter pact, (4) the unmasking of the father when the daughter reaches puberty, (5) the mother's collusion in rebinding the daughter, and (6) the daughter's attempts to renegotiate a relationship with her parents. The residue of conflict from these six stages leads to unique efforts at resolution, which will be discussed in the next chapter. Throughout this section, case material will be used to illustrate the stages and their effects on functioning and defense.

Stage One: Unseating the Mother

The hysterical client often has vivid memories of early scenes in which she played the role of confidante to the father, who revealed his difficulties with the mother and possibly even hinted at the eventual dissolution of that bond. Out of guilt and insecurity, the child who is caught between the parents may attempt to mobilize the mother to realize what is transpiring in the marriage. The mothers of hysterics, however, seem to be masters of denial, and the child's warnings fall on deaf ears.

Over time, the father often becomes openly disparaging of the mother in the presence of the child. Through sarcasm and ridicule, he renders the mother incompetent. Although he may invite her interventions in family affairs, he criticizes her decisions, withholds emotional support, and, in general, undercuts maternal authority. The father must be stage center in the family. In orchestrating his position, he usurps the mother's role, invades her territory, and redirects the center of attention to himself at the expense of the forfeited mother. In one such case, the father thoroughly decimated the mother's influence on the child, took over all family functions, carried out both roles, and, symbolic of the skewed power base in the family, signed his letters to the daughter as "Mother and Father."

It has often been observed that the hysteric who seeks an exclusive relationship with the father is fixated at the second positive stage of the oedipal conflict (Nagera 1975). In seeking exclusiveness with his daughter and in his self-aggrandizing behavior, the father reveals a phallic-oedipal orientation. Essentially, the daughter becomes the object of his own transference longings. He must be the only man in her life, and, as the hysteric learns at puberty, the father will trample anyone in his path in hostile, competitive ways to retain his position with the daughter.

The father's undercutting of the maternal role and targeting of the daughter for the enactment of his conflicts sets the stage for the schism between mother and daughter and the ensuing alliance with the father. Matters sometimes come to a head in rather dramatic scenes, as they did in the following case:

> The client, who was the depository of parental conflicts, had been the confidante of the father from an early age. The father freely discussed his marital problems with the daughter and predicted an eventual rupture in the parental relationship, making the daughter privy to information that was guilt inducing and left her feeling insecure. The client recalled an early scene in which the father told her he preferred her bed to that of the mother's. Amidst their hugging and holding in bed, the mother attempted to intervene, stomping her feet in rage at the bedroom door. The father simply dismissed her, and the mother was impotent to effect any change in his behavior. The client recalled feeling a sense of power in her favored position.

Aside from the seductive component, the major issue is the way in which the child is used as decoy in the father's assault on his wife. The daughter is the object of the father's self-absorbed needs. Competition is the issue. The father has set mother against daughter in competing over him. The competitive feelings aroused in the daughter and her sense of power set a wedge between mother and daughter. And the mother's impotent rage simply exacerbates the child's perceptions of the mother as incompetent, ineffectual, and without impact. The power base of the family is set.

The alliance with the father is not based in a nurturing attitude, however, nor is it set in the child's turning to the father for nurturance in lieu of a depriving mother, as suggested by Halleck (1967). Rather, it is set in fear and in identification with an aggressor. The alliance has been established with a male who is nonsupporting, self-centered, humiliating, and hostile. Commitments can be withdrawn and redirected for self-gratification.

When the breach in the father–daughter relationship occurs at puberty as the daughter stretches her ego and turns outward, those subliminal perceptions will crowd in on her. She will see how illusory and circumscribed (Celani 1976) her power is. The power tactics of the father in arousing competition over him are the tactics that the hysteric later uses in her own relations with the men in her life.

Stage Two: The Mother's Resignation

In light of the overpowering father figure, the mother may recede from view and refrain from interfering in the father–daughter relationship. As the father–daughter relationship escalates, the mother may become ill on vacations, leaving the daughter to fend for herself. Replacing the mother, the daughter may become the father's dance partner and his drinking companion.

The implicit collusion by the mother in the father–daughter relationship will be discussed later. At this point, we will note that passivity, denial, and externalization often emerge as the mother's favorite defensive modalities. Although there may be gains for the mother in her own passive-aggressive frustration of the father, the child is left vulnerable and without an ally. One can infer from the father's increasingly blatant assaults on the mother that her passive-aggressive defenses are effective in frustrating him. The mother's defenses are incorporated into the hysteric's repertoire, and later, when her own relationships with men go sour, she uses them to good advantage in discomfiting males and gaining redress.

In her reports during psychotherapy, the hysteric may attach parental conflicts to sexual matters. She often has substantial evidence to support her views that the mother uses her sexuality to frustrate the father. Unfortunately, the daughter may become the decoy in the father's frustrations with his wife, as seemed evident in the following case:

> The father was inappropriately and sexually intrusive into the life of his 12-year-old daughter, inquiring of her, in the presence of the mother, if she was aware of the mechanics of intercourse. The mother sat idly by, although the client sensed her anxiety. The client reported feeling humiliated, unable to understand her father's motives, and confused.

The issue here is that the child was the pawn in the parental conflicts and that the target of the father's hostility was likely the wife. But the daughter bore the brunt of the hostility, and it took its toll in the daughter's later sexual activities:

> In attempting to interpret the father's sex talks, which would also occur in a private, warm context, the client stated that she felt the father was trying to help her, to protect her. She offered an additional possibility: "I feel like a long time ago he must have seen that I was going to be somewhat promiscuous or something." As an adult, the client was promiscuous and used her sexuality in hostile ways, often being so aggressive that she confused and humiliated her male partners with her behavior.

In itself, the mother's resignation is binding, but the mother may bind the daughter further by identifying with her. If the mother were resigned but allied herself with the daughter's strivings, matters might be different. But one sometimes hears symbolic messages of pessimism relayed from mother to daughter, as occurred in the following case:

> The daughter, as a young adult, had displaced her conflicts from her father onto a relationship with a boyfriend. The boyfriend was a carbon copy of the volatile, possessive, and jealous father. The relationship was stormy and the daughter was becoming increasingly nervous. She discussed the relationship with her mother. Rather than helping the daughter to work through the conflicts and understand the emotional undercurrents that stirred anxiety, the mother suggested abandoning the relationship and reawakening a previous relationship with a meek male with whom the daughter had been associated.
>
> In her own relationship with the father, the mother was no match for his volatile outbursts. She was passive and subservient to his wishes and mediated his conflicts with the daughter. The maternal message seemed to be that the daughter should resign herself as the mother did. The mother identified her conflicts in the daughter, who became the projective target of her own solution. In discouraging the relationship, the mother essentially communicated the pessimistic message that the daughter should deafen her ears to her feelings—deny, suppress, and comply. In such instances, the daughter may feel depressed and not know why.

The message from mother to daughter to suppress and comply takes various forms that have been reported in the literature as instrumental in shaping the hysterical personality. Maternal messages to be sweet and feminine are two favorites (see Easser and Lesser 1965). The mother is communicating her own unconscious depression about self-actualization *in the context of an identification with and prediction about the daughter*. That is what is so immensely binding to the hysteric: in her unconscious identification with her mother, she seals her fate.

Stage Three: The Father–Daughter Relationship

The literature is replete with examples of the hysteric who has been the "good girl" and whose coyness and cuteness have been fostered by the father as a source of pleasure for himself. The child's seductive behavior is considered the condition for nurturance and sustenance, and a mutual seduction develops (Halleck 1967). The daughter's seductive behavior, however, stems not from her needs but from those of the father. And in that bartering process, the father indicts himself and reveals his immaturity.

The daughter barters for security, but the price she pays is high. The father of the hysteric demands a "possession," someone to reflect him, to be an extension of himself. As one client noted, she was her father's "little possession or something that he could protect and kind of shape." The conditions of the pact consist of the daughter's accepting this role in exchange for the security of being under the wing of the powerful figure in the family. But the security the child experiences is couched in insecurity, because it is based in a self-centered male whose own needs at any given moment may take precedence:

> One client reported feeling confused when the therapist addressed her by her given name in a session following a distressed phone call in which she experienced the therapist as distant. The client's own father would oscillate within the same week between warm responsiveness on one occasion and a distant, businesslike air on another.

The father of the hysteric seems internally conflicted about the daughter's dependence. He fosters an unhealthy dependent relationship but seems repelled by dependent women. He may speak favorably of assertive women, but he is easily threatened by assertiveness. Essentially, the father seems to demand docility but disdain dependence, a uniquely binding state of affairs. The daughter, who by this time has learned to read underlying attitudes, must walk a tightrope.

The daughter selected to reflect the father learns to center in him, not herself. As a reflection of the father, the hysteric fits in, feels no inner core, and develops no sense of her own substance. The adult hysteric's feelings of having no substance, of floating sensations, and of being unprepared for life, and her infantile fixations, stem in part from the compromises she made for the promise of security. And at puberty, when the daughter turns outward to establish an identity, the punitive, rejecting behavior of the father leaves her floundering, vulnerable, and helpless.

When the father turns to the daughter for fulfillment, he demands conformity. If the daughter complies, she fills the required role; yet in complying she seeds her own demise. The dilemma she faces is that she learns to conform to receive, yet the father's sarcasm and nonsupporting reactions to the compliant mother provide a living example of the untoward consequences of compliance. In adolescence, when she tests her will against that of the father, she is threatened with rejection. Either way she loses. But, as Farber (1966) has observed, the hysteric is a willful person, and in her willfulness she arrives at a creative solution: she complies, but she does not submit. Unfortunately, during her earlier development, the daughter may not have learned the fine art of dodging the horns of a dilemma until considerable damage has been done.

One of the unforeseen conditions of the pact for the child is that she is to be the projective target of the father's inner conflicts. Not only is she to reflect him, but she also is to be the outlet for his gratifications and frustrations. Those conflicts seem evident in the many invitation–rejection themes that pervade the father-daughter relationship. The father's projected conflicts about compliance–dependency, about sexuality, and about affection-competition contribute to the confused state of the adult hysteric:

> The father–daughter relationship was riddled with mixed invitational and rejecting messages. At an early age in the child's life, the father would lie on her bed, singing songs to her, or the child would enter the parents' bed and be held by the father. In the process this behavior stimulated

many blatantly sexual dreams in the child. This stimulating relationship came to a sudden halt without explanation, and the child who had accepted the invitation pushed for its continuance but was met with cold resistance.

Later the child withdrew into some rather elaborate romantic fantasies. Apparently anxious, the father encouraged her to spend more time with friends. When the daughter did so, the father objected to the time she spent away from home.

The child tried to reflect the father in whatever she did. She reported feeling that she was his "possession." She was sensitive and cried easily. The father apparently resented her being so sensitive and wanted her to toughen herself, ignoring some real injuries she suffered. He roughhoused with her, but when she reciprocated, he would reject her. She felt that she didn't know how to tease.

Near adolescence, being thoroughly confused about her role as mate, she made the error of jumping on the father's lap when he was entertaining a woman friend. His insensitive and caustic rejection of her left her feeling humiliated.

This particular client described herself to the therapist as a contradiction, saying that she didn't know whether she had been reared to be independent or dependent. As an adult, she had major difficulties in her love relationships, often selecting in serial order men who had very different dominant traits. In that way she isolated the components of conflict and attempted to work out an integration in more manageable packages. This unique defensive functioning is described more fully later.

Stage Four: Puberty: Unmasking of the Father

When the daughter reaches puberty, the father–mother–daughter triad often escalates and the hysterical style is solidified. Easser and Lesser (1965) and Herman (1981) have painted a compelling picture of the turmoil of the adolescent era. In particular, Easser and Lesser (1965) note the abrupt change in paternal behavior that occurs when the daughter begins to socialize. The seductiveness that has characterized the father–daughter relationship changes, and the father condemns the very behaviors that he has stimulated. Easser and Lesser cite dramatic instances of the extreme intrusiveness of the father into the activities of the daughter during that developmental period. They ascribe to the fathers the motive of wanting "to preserve their pleasure in their little girls" (p. 395). The outcomes are romanticized substitutions for sexuality and infantile fixations to the father.

The motive force they attribute to the fathers and the effects on functioning they propose need reexamination from several additional perspectives. Chodoff's observations (1978) are more to the point. *Control* is the dynamic underlying the father's reactions. A crucial issue in the abrupt change in paternal behavior is that the daughter asserts her will. She no longer centers in the father; she no longer bolsters his ego; he is no longer stage center. She has broken the pact. It is as though the father has suffered a narcissistic injury, arousing rage and competitiveness, with ensuing efforts at taming the daughter's spirit and thereby regaining control. Many hysterics can recount specific points at which their fathers stopped loving them, and those events are clearly associated with the hysteric's asserting her will over the will of the father.

Through her responses to two sequential cards of the Thematic Apperception Test (TAT) (Murray 1943), one client poignantly described her dilemma in the face of a possessive father who turned on her in adolescence:

The client, in dress, posturing, voice, and makeup, was sexually provocative. Her volatile father had been possessive and demanded attention from wife and daughter alike. When the daughter began to date seriously, the father had become increasingly controlling. The family had vacationed together or the father had sent the mother along with the daughter, presumably to guard the daughter's virtue. And when the father assumed that the daughter was sexually involved with a male friend, he had become furious.

The client's response on the TAT reflected her quandary. The stories were brief but transparent. On one card, the client projected the following theme: "She has been out on a date and came back and entered her home and found that a member of her family had died while she was away. And then, with all this anxiety built up inside of her, she just retreats to her room, very upset. And after she gets through the doorway, she probably just collapses on her bed and cries herself to sleep."

The client's dilemma became even more transparent in her response to the following card: "These two have been going out for a while. He really loves her, but he never knows where she worked. And finally, he finds out where she works, comes over to that place and sees that she works in a burlesque show or something, and he's very disappointed and tries to leave, and she's stopping him, telling him that he just doesn't understand, he's just a little upset. And he just storms out." (The examiner inquired about her inner feelings.) "He's upset, he's frustrated because he really loves this girl, but he doesn't agree with what she does. And she loves him, too, but she can't really face the reality of it. Her job is just to keep her alive, money-wise. She really doesn't like it, and now the threat of losing the man she loves has got her perplexed. She's going to watch him walk out the door, and then she's going to go over to his house afterward."

Of particular note is the thematic progression of the client's productions. From the history of this client, we know that the relationship with the father was threatened when she began dating; it was essentially "dead," and the client was left with her anxieties. In the response to the next sequential card, the client's quandary is elaborated. The relationship with the father had been a long-standing one, but he really didn't know her. What was confusing to the client was that the behavior that had been elicited, her "sexiness," was condemned.

In her story the client reveals her confusion and the defensive character of her sexiness. The job in the "burlesque show" is a survival technique "to keep her alive, money-wise," a job she "really doesn't like." She is left "perplexed." Her solution is to conform and return "to his house." The client actually spent much time trying to placate the father. What the client didn't realize was that she had threatened the father's self-absorbed needs through her socializing efforts.

When the daughter asserts her will and threatens the father's well-being, he often converts her socializing attempts into sexually motivated urges and actions. He does so in rageful, aggressive ways, assaulting her person. In one case the father accused his sexually naive daughter of being promiscuous. In another case the father became enraged at an otherwise dutiful and conservative daughter who had had a brief interlude with a boyfriend. He hurled insults at her, calling her a "slut," and threatened to disown her. In a third case a client reported being shocked and frightened by hearing the "hate" in her father's voice when he discussed what his reactions would be to any man who impregnated her (see Herman 1981).

Aggression in light of a bruised male ego is the issue, but the sexual content within an aggressive context weds the two emotional components. The father's hostility, coupled to the humiliation and fright the daughter experiences, makes the prospects of a satisfying sexual encounter a myth, relegated to the romantic—a retreat well known to the hysteric. Ironically, the earlier experience of the hysteric consists of the sexualization of affectional needs. Is it any wonder, then, that sex becomes the symbolic conveyer of the hysteric's needs, the medium for bartering (Hollender 1971), and the expression of her own aggression?

In linking aggression and sexuality, the father fuels the hysteric's later problems in both areas. Eichler (1976) has commented that the aggressive component in hysteria has been underrated. Certainly, in light of the overpowering father, his retaliatory behavior, and the daughter's vulnerable state, one might expect some reaction formations to avoid conflict. And the hysteric's hypernormal, "sweetness and light" behavior suggests an ego defense that provides an effective cover for the indirect expression of her own hostility.

Additional learnings accrue from these encounters with the father. Ruptures in later relationships can often be traced to the hysteric's panic reactions when she feels that the man is becoming too possessive or dependent. Possessiveness implies entrapment, circumscribed feelings, and self-depletion to fill up the male. Above all else, it implies the activation of male hostility if the hysteric "steps out of line." And, as will be noted later, the client's anxiety becomes intense when she takes even the slightest nonconforming stance during psychotherapy.

Other conflicts in the adult hysteric are based in this paternal reversal and threatened rupture of the father–daughter relationship. Having been the good girl, and having centered in the father, the hysteric is left unprepared for life. The pact with the father implied promises, and the rupture sets anger and distrust of men into motion. Any man who breaks promises or who retreats from the hysteric will certainly feel her anger. The rupture, involving such hostility, also leaves the hysteric feeling incomplete and may account in part for the "sentiments of incompleteness" that Janet (1929, p. 312) observed in hysterics. In later love relationships the hysteric constantly returns to unfinished business, attempting to end the relationship as friends. In such relationships the hysteric wonders why she was so blind and didn't "see" the eventualities, much as her mother was blind to the events in the parental relationship and she herself was blind to her own fate.

Crucial also is the issue of power. Celani (1976) noted that the hysteric learns that her power is limited to a particular behavioral repertoire. Not only is the hysteric's power limited to a particular repertoire—such as catering to the male ego by behaving provocatively—but the hysteric's power evaporates if the target of her provocative behavior is someone other than her father. The confusing thing to the child who develops a hysterical style is that the father condemns the behaviors that he encouraged. More generally, in adolescence the hysteric learns that her power is illusory and that she and her mother are truly alike, powerless to effect change in others or in their environments.

And, as will be observed, the hysteric makes some futile attempts at mobilizing her mother in order to counter that belief.

Stage Five: The Mother's Collusion in Rebinding the Daughter

In light of the father's rejecting behavior and efforts at controlling the daughter, the mother's role is critical. Unfortunately, the mother may ally herself with the father and attempt to control the child. At the daughter's puberty, the mother may become the instrument of the father in attempting to control the daughter's willfulness. Personal insecurity may fuel attempts to keep peace in the family and placate the irate father. But in a more damaging action, the mother may actively collude with the father in rebinding the father-daughter relationship. Several examples can illustrate the differential effects:

> One client, on returning home for a visit, was instructed by the father to perform some menial chore. The daughter resisted and the father became irate, with a minor physical altercation ensuing. After such outbursts, the father would turn to the mother and insist that she do something about the daughter's recalcitrance. The mother became enraged with the daughter, telling the daughter that she should look at what she had done: she had stirred up the father again.

This scene typifies the daughter's power to elicit intense reactions in the father. The sense of power is lost, however, in the daughter's sense of helplessness and fear of the potential danger of inciting the father. But the main point is that the mother's message to the daughter was to conform and submit as the mother had done. Rather than finding an ally in the mother, the client felt betrayed by her.

The instrumentality of the mother was evident in another

case, in which the daughter was contemplating marriage, albeit a potentially disastrous one, to a man her father's age:

> Increased tension, discord, and a potential separation characterized the parental marriage around that time. The client reported that the only "time [her mother] got really close to me and broke down was when they [the parents] were having trouble." When the parents were talking of divorce, the mother confided to the daughter that she "could never imagine life without [the father]," and the daughter felt that her mother was "scared to death to be alone." The daughter did not marry and returned to the family home. The parental marriage stabilized, and the client reported feeling strange hearing her parents having sexual intercourse.

The "distrust of maternal figures" (Halleck 1967, p. 752) reported by adult hysterics may have its origins in such dramatic examples as the following:

> There was a breach in the parental relationship during the daughter's adolescence. The parents separated and lived a considerable distance apart. The daughter, splitting her loyalties, attended a school located half-way between the parents. The father, who had been very possessive of the daughter, acting the role of suitor rather than father, wanted her to join him. The mother actively strove to restrict that alliance, and the daughter, out of loyalty to the mother, avoided the father and rejected his bids. When, however, the parents settled their differences and the mother precipitously joined the father, she changed her stance and encouraged the daughter to transfer schools and join them. In a telephone conversation, the mother pursued the idea, which the daughter rejected. The mother turned the telephone over to the father. In the ensuing therapy session in which the interaction was reported, the client's plaintive plea to the mother had been, "Why do you do this to me?" That plea encapsulated the entire emotional

experience for the client. The client felt angry, betrayed, manipulated, and confused.

The daughter had been the pawn in the parental security operations, with maternal collusion as a central feature. The mother's security took precedence over her concern about the vulnerable position in which she placed the daughter. The client's sense of having been deceived and exploited seems to explain in part the hysteric's feelings of being victimized, of being an object with no intrinsic worth, and may contribute to the manipulative and somewhat psychopathic behavior sometimes noticed in hysterical clients.

Stage Six: Attempts to Renegotiate with the Parents

The hysteric does not give up easily. The stakes are high. In general, the daughter attempts to negotiate a separate peace with each parent. In her negotiations the daughter seeks to have the parents take appropriate responsibility for their respective roles in the breach between the two of them. From the father she seeks mutuality, a nondefensive and open relationship in which she can feel fully and freely and in which she feels power and substance. The daughter tries, in turn, to mobilize the mother to accept responsibility for herself and to shoulder her fair share of responsibility for the developments between father and daughter.

The infantile fixations attributed to hysterics, and the sense of being incomplete, seem dynamically determined in part by the wish to complete the relationship with the father, without which the hysteric feels incomplete. Having bargained for security at the expense of self-fulfillment, the hysteric feels unprepared for life and still in need of a guiding father. Of crucial importance are the feelings remaining from the rupture at adolescence. The father's hostility is fixating, and it is the quest to reestablish love in that relationship—not in an infantile sense—that haunts the hysteric.

It is her sense of being incomplete and her experience of what

is amiss in her relationship with her father that sets the pattern
for later relationships. And it is the pattern of later relationships
that leads to a misdiagnosis of the hysteric's points of major fixation. The hysteric's later relationships often have the cast of
an orally fixated person in that she creates relationships in which
platonic love, affection, caring, and nonsexual encounters are
sought. But it is her wish to convert the father's hostility into
the loving relationship it once was that energizes her behavior
and undergirds her preoccupations.

The hysterical client is often deeply upset that, despite
repeated efforts, she cannot break the barrier between her and
her father or turn his rejection into love. She experiences the
problem as a deficit in her character; she feels that she just is
not worth the trouble. This is a partial fixation of the hysteric.
She seeks and feels deeply that she needs her father's approval.
Without his imprimatur, she feels incomplete and valueless, because she is not considered worth the time and effort to work
matters through and finish the relationship on a loving note.
This recurrent, poignant theme is illustrated in the following
excerpt:

> The client's parents divorced when she was 8 years old.
> She continued to pursue a relationship with her father,
> who remarried when she was in early adolescence. The
> father's family of his second marriage took precedence, but
> the client continued to seek ways of negotiating a relation-
> ship with the father. In doing so, she catered to the father's
> needs, inflated his ego, and abided by his wishes at the ex-
> pense of her own needs. In midadolescence the client re-
> belled against the self-serving father. When the client as-
> serted her will against that of the father, he severed all
> emotional ties with her.
>
> For years after the rupture, the client tried fruitlessly to
> overcome his resistance. The slightest signal from the fa-
> ther that there was hope of repairing the relationship
> stimulated an unrealistic euphoria, which was followed by
> suicidal feelings when the rebonding failed. The client's

depression centered around her increasing realization that "I can never bring him around, and... I better start dealing with it now, or I'm going to be carrying this for years and years and years. [Crying.] That's not fair to me." The client attributed her lack of confidence in herself to having missed the guiding hand of a father. Those needs were displaced onto an ongoing relationship with a man similar in personality to her father. The client wanted someone who "would give me the love I needed, so I would have that confidence."

During one session, the dilemma was summed up in a particularly anguished plea of the client: "It's, well, when he [the father] constantly says that it's my fault, and I try to show him that it's not, or that I care—what I can't say is that I don't care anymore. He is forcing me to accept the fact that he doesn't care, and I can't. I do care, and I think that if he accepts me and deals with me on a mature basis, then I would feel a lot better. I guess that really is what it is. I just realized that—just now—that I would feel a lot better as a person. That I really, I don't feel whole."

Similarly, the hysteric struggles to make a mother of her mother. The hysteric is often heard attempting to mobilize the mother to accept personal responsibility, to be open with her feelings, and to admit personal conflicts. If a divorce has occurred, the daughter may want the mother to admit partial responsibility for it. Inducing the mother to "admit" anything of consequence, however, seems to be a losing battle, as indicated in the following case:

The daughter, as the father's confidante, was aware at a very early age of his feelings about an eventual divorce. The daughter made repeated attempts in later years to force her mother to remove the "blinders" and note what was transpiring in the marital relationship. Following the inevitable divorce, the daughter's strident efforts turned to attempting to convince her mother that the mother had some responsibility for the parental discord and divorce. The mother, however, denied any part in the parental problems and blamed the father for her plight.

The client's persistence was motivated in part by guilt about her favored position in the family and her collusion with her father. But the client did not feel her guilt. In dramatic ways and with exaggerated affect during sessions, she contended that she had such feelings; dynamically, however, she could not experience the guilt so long as the mother did not accept her share of responsibility. Without such a maternal admission, the client was burdened with total responsibility for her mother's distraught state. On one occasion during therapy, the client was ecstatic because her mother had admitted some minor flaw in her behavior.

The client's relief had other determinants as well. In her hypersensitivity, the daughter often perceives the mother's anger toward her, although it is generally expressed in subtle, indirect ways. Some material thing may become the symbolic representation of anger, resentment, withholding, and lack of forgiveness. Mother and daughter may battle over ownership of some possession, screening the underlying maternal resentment about the daughter's violation of the mother's territorial rights with the father. In admitting some flaw in her character, the mother may imply forgiveness and potential reconciliation.

Above all else, the hysteric tries to activate her mother because she needs a mother. The hysteric realizes that she must identify with strength in a woman to break her bonds, and often a therapist can hear the hysteric go through a series of relationships with women in which she seems to be searching for a strong mother. In fact, hysterics often enter triadic relationships to be the child rather than to separate the partners. An adult status does not lend itself to the child role, however, and the effects may be other than those intended, particularly if the hysteric attends to the male partner.

When the hysteric's efforts to negotiate a mutual relationship with her parents seem futile, she turns outward and displaces her conflicts onto ongoing relationships, attempting to rework the past under more favorable conditions. To facilitate ego mastery, she isolates the emotional components of conflictual experiences, packages them separately, and plays them out in multiple or serial relationships. But her isolating mechanism precludes integration. The client enters psychotherapy, trailing her emotional disarray behind her, fights the alliance, and resists transferring. These rather complex interpersonal patterns will be discussed in the next chapter.

Chapter Three

The Expression of Conflict: Residue of the Past

The effects of the parents' manifest and latent personality trends are evident in the daughter's adult relationships and in the conflicts, feeling states, and defensive maneuvering that characterize them. The hysteric's history makes her stormy relationships meaningful if not rational. The insecurities of the mother and her character defenses find their counterpart in the hysteric's own ways of coping with conflict. Whether the mother resigned herself to a subservient role or was competitive with the daughter, she revealed her inadequacy as mother. The self-indulgence of the father and his illusory strength, whether expressed through a brittle, counterdependent attitude or through passive, collusive behavior, share a psychogenic base in adequacy problems.

Those developmental experiences take their toll in the hysteric's constant struggles with issues of control and mastery, concerns about dominance, and her self-imposed passivity. They are reflected in the hysteric's continual and disappointing search for a strong mate (Halleck 1967) whose strength does not evaporate, or in her nurturing of the weak male whose hidden strength the hysteric works to activate. The struggle for the hysteric is always a two-edged sword, because she fears finding what she is searching for. Her history of an insecure mother and a self-centered father with shaky controls makes the oedipal arena fraught with unrest and anxiety.

Without the protection of a mothering one, the hysteric constantly tests those waters but withdraws in fright. But the oedipal arena is enticing, and that enticement keeps the hysteric balanced between searching for a father and mother and having lovers and jealous female companions. That intricate interlocking and oscillation between neurotic gratification and attempted resolution keeps the hysteric safe but thwarts integration and growth. It binds her anxiety momentarily but sets her frustrations into motion. The conflict between activity and growth and the enticements of the neurosis is visible in the hysteric's reports of her interactions and the themes permeating them.

THEMES IN ONGOING RELATIONSHIPS: THERAPEUTIC GUIDELINES

Neurotic conflicts in the hysterical personality are often evident in the patterning of interpersonal relationships (Horowitz 1977, Krohn 1978). The hysterical personality is often involved in relationships that are perceived to hold promise of romantic, idealized fulfillment (Shapiro 1965). The patterning of those relationships can be characterized as "repetitive, impulsive, stereotyped" (Horowitz 1977, p. 5), with variations on victimized, helpless themes. Depressive reactions (Krohn 1978), mood swings, bodily complaints, and hysterical phenomena seem associated with the conflicts and repetitive ruptures in interpersonal relationships, particularly in heterosexual relationships.

Given the character traits accorded the hysterical personality

(Alarcon 1973, Chodoff and Lyons 1958), such neurotic interpersonal themes are predictable patterns and reflect the residue of unresolved past conflicts burdening the hysterical client's relationships. Often it is a ruptured or disturbed heterosexual relationship with associated reactions that consciously motivates the adult hysterical client to enter psychotherapy.

Recurrent themes in the hysterical client's ongoing relationships guide the therapist in understanding the dynamics of conflict for the client. Those themes provide the pathways to the past. In addition, the client's movement into and out of specific relationships during psychotherapy, along with the changing themes characterizing those relationships, provides the therapist with a vivid running account of the *processes* of conflict. Often those dynamic processes within the client parallel the client's movement in psychotherapy (Kell and Mueller 1966).

Themes in Displacements as Guides to the Dynamics of Conflict

By classical definition, one of the hallmarks of the hysterical client is her facility in transferring her developmental conflicts onto her ongoing relationships and attempting to rework the past in the present. Displacements block emotional insights into genetic sources of conflict and work against recovery of affectively charged memories. Those investments, and the "acting out" that characterizes them, discharge affect without reflection. As such, the resistances to emotional experiencing counter therapeutic efforts. But those powerfully charged displacements, betrayed by their intense, driven, repetitive, and unsatisfying quality, provide the therapist with a fully orchestrated production and a running account of the nature and dimensions of conflict.

Of particular importance to the therapist is a clear understanding of the emotional residue of previous interpersonal experiences as they are reflected in those investments. Themes from development are echoed in the hysteric's current relationships, and the dynamics of conflict are vividly played out. From the recurrent emotional themes and behavior that permeate client reports of her male and female relationships, the therapist gains insight into the client's neurotic conflicts, character defenses, coping strategies, and points of fixation. One may hear the male invited and then rejected, strength revered yet feared. The hysteric may complain that men are self-centered and weak, that they seek only their own pleasure, and that she is not taken seriously. Mixed anger and frustration may predominate. Yet when the hysteric is taken seriously and is shown respect, she tends to retreat, perhaps terminating a relationship or creating such havoc that the man is driven away or dismisses her as a "hysterical" woman.

The hysteric may pursue a desirable male with unyielding tenacity. If he seems cold and distant, she may be driven to wear him down, to bring him out of his shell, to draw out an emotional response. She "feels" that the man's rough exterior shields a warm, sensitive person. She strives to attain an unattainable object. Yet if she wins, she loses. For if she wins the object, the hysteric feels that the man must be weak or lack self-esteem. An underlying dependency in the man may emerge from the seemingly independent self-sufficiency, and the hysteric panics. She may then feel that she has rendered the male impotent. So she becomes nurturant, perhaps playing the docile, helpless role in efforts to restructure the situation, partially out of her own images of masculinity.

Alternatively, her winning may mean that she has become the dominant partner. She may feel that the man has been trapped and that she has circumscribed his freedom. She doesn't want to dominate a male and is careful not to do so. But she feels that the male is weak and easily swayed by other females. Not wanting to hold the male against his will, she wants to offer him his freedom but fears that if she does so, he will leave. So she is caught in her own net.

The hysteric finds it difficult to lay to rest a disturbed relationship, particularly one that has been sexual. She may return to it time and again despite her conscious will not to do so. In the relationship, she fears being possessed and treated like "property." She wants to love but feels it is binding, and so she runs from possessive, jealous men. Yet she returns to the relationship and attempts to negotiate her independence within the relationship. She seeks mutual independence. Yet if the man becomes independent and she feels unneeded, she fights her own independent strivings and becomes the dependent one.

The dependent, docile, helpless role is a coping strategy that is "out of character" for the hysteric, simply intensifying her frustration. And the hysteric finds herself on a familiar treadmill, feeling angry, complaining, and confused. Having recycled through another unsatisfying relationship without experiencing mutuality, the hysteric is left feeling more depressed, terrified that she is destined to be alone and needy.

Displacements and the Isolation of
Affect: Companion Defenses

The displacements in the service of repression characterizing the hysteric's relationships are readily apparent. But displacement in itself seems insufficient to explain the hysteric's defensive maneuvering in relationships. Less apparent is the extensive use and interesting twists that the hysteric gives to the companion defenses of isolation of affect and displacement as a way of resolving her underlying ambivalence toward objects and attempting to achieve ego mastery.

Although the defensive use of isolation of affect is often identified with the compulsion neuroses, some forms of the mechanism appear to describe the ways that the hysteric attempts to manage her ambivalence toward objects and integrate disjunctive emotional experiences. Certainly, the conjunctive use of isolation and displacement to interpret such maneuvers is more parsimonious than the more complex construct of "splitting," which Pruyser (1975) has pointed out can confuse rather than clarify. In another context, Glazer (1979) observed that displacement and the isolation of affect are sufficient mechanisms to explain certain defensive functioning. In hysteria these companion defenses serve at least two complementary functions: the resolution of ambivalent feelings and the attempt to achieve ego mastery.

Krohn (1978) noted that in hysteria, "in contrast to the borderline personality, objects are ambivalently regarded" (p. 221). Underlying ambivalence toward objects does appear to be a dynamic motivating force in the use of these mechanisms. Mueller and Kell (1972) defined ambivalence as the experience of feelings and thoughts about an object that are incompatible. Because ambivalent feelings arouse anxiety, those authors suggested, the opposing sides of the ambivalence may be isolated by experiencing the incompatible feelings alternately in relation to an object.

Rather than using a time frame to avoid incompatible feelings toward an object, the hysterical client uses relationships. Essentially, the hysteric isolates the opposing emotional components of the conflict and displaces them onto separate ongoing relationships. With the sides of ambivalence thus well insulated, the hysteric then works feverishly but fruitlessly to settle her conflicts.

Two general forms of this defensive maneuvering are manifest in the hysteric's relationships. In the first and more obvious case, the emotional components of a conflict situation are isolated and the isolated components are displaced onto two or more ongoing relationships. Fenichel (1945) cited this use of isolation in cases in which the "sensual and tender components of sexuality" (p. 156) are isolated and played out in separate relationships—a confusion, incidentally, that is shared by a good many hysterics. Because the hysteric is masterful at peopling her environment with the counterparts of her various conflicts, finding suitable subjects to meet her displacement criterion of sustaining the isolation is no problem.

The problem arises in relationships when the hysteric's isolating mechanism no longer functions effectively. If the isolating mechanism becomes faulty because of events in a relationship and the hysteric begins to experience ambivalence toward the same object, perhaps feeling warm *and* sensuous, anxiety is aroused, and she may tend to rupture the relationship or displace one or the other emotional feeling onto a new relationship to settle the ambivalence and maintain distinctions.

This same dynamic seems to operate in psychotherapy with hysterical clients. Krohn (1978) sensitized the therapist to the defensive power of displacements and to the potential "splitting of the transference feelings onto current life objects'' (p. 322). It is the hysteric's adroitness at isolating the emotional components of conflict and displacing the part-equivalents of conflict onto numerous object relationships that makes splitting or the transference predictable, even inevitable. During psychotherapy, Mueller and Kell (1972) suggested, impasse may occur when conflict is generated by the merging of oppositional feelings about ambivalently regarded objects. One or another side of conflict may be displaced outward when the sides begin to merge. For example, if warmth and strength are disjunctive constructs, the therapist's warm response within the context of therapist strength stimulates anxiety, and the warmth may be displaced onto a safer object, whom the hysteric is creative enough to embody suddenly in her environment. Following such a displacement, the client may contend that the therapist is too cold or distant, thereby keeping anxiety at bay.

The second form in which the companion defenses of isolation and displacement are used is less readily apparent and more intriguing. It emerges when one studies the many relationships of the hysteric from a developmental perspective. In this case, the unresolved conflicts of different developmental periods are isolated from one another and acted out separately in ongoing relationships, with each relationship representing the conflicts that Sullivan (1953b) described as characteristic of specific developmental periods. One can often hear the conflicts of childhood, preadolescence, and adolescence encapsulated and enacted in separate relationships, without awareness and without integration. An ego-integrative function seems to be at work, that is, the mechanisms are employed for purposes of ego mastery of disjunctive developmental experiences. And, as will be noted later, mastery of her environment is the nemesis of the hysteric.

Thus, one may find a hysterical client embroiled in a number of seemingly incompatible relationships. In one relationship the hysteric may talk of platonic, idyllic love. In another, impulsive, sexually gratifying behavior may permeate the relationship. A triangular relationship may appear on the horizon. Another may be fraught with moralizing, interactions of a parent–child type, reactivity, and rebelliousness. Yet another relationship may include a man who is a free spirit, disorganized and undemanding, feeling oriented and nonthreatening in any sense. The various relationships taken together provide a personality synthesis.

Whether those relationships occur simultaneously or serially, they reflect the hysteric's struggle to rework and correct past problems. In Blinder's study of a cross-cultural sample of hysterical women (1966), he found the first marriages to be to abusive men and the second husbands often to be passive and nondemanding. The issue is the same: Through isolation and displacement, the hysteric attempts to overcome her neurosis, but her efforts are unsuccessful because her anxiety interferes and her problem-solving methods preclude integration. The hysteric polarizes to master, creating a "good" father and playing him off against the "bad" father. She fails because she is just not a good borderline personality. She differs in that she has a self-consciousness of her own fears and feelings in relation to the object. She differs in that she senses the latent personality trends in the object despite her efforts to maintain distinctions; then, in her anxiety, she flees the relationship.

Displacements as Guides to Dynamic "Processes"

From the client's movement into and out of specific relationships as certain emotional themes reach ascendance during psychotherapy, the therapist can reconstruct the dynamic processes within the hysterical personality. As Kell and Mueller (1966) observed, as conflict unfolds in the therapeutic relationship, it recapitulates the developmental course of conflict and provides an index of the "temporal, shifting, and changing quality of the client's conflicts" (p. 43). With the hysteric, the therapist extends this view to a study of the complex of ongoing relationships. The client's shifting into and out of different relationships as material emerges during psychotherapy provides a most useful index of the processes of conflict within the hysteric.

The recurrent themes in such relationships provide the therapist with a sense of whether the client is at the heart of the oedipal conflict, whether and how she retreats, whether she has yet to enter the arena, or whether she is in stages of resolution. From the regressive and progressive features of simultaneous or sequential relationships, the therapist gains insight into how much the need for neurotic gratification is outweighed by frustration and healthy strivings, how much the need for redress overrides the wish for closeness, and how strongly the client needs to protect her vulnerability through passive means. Those relationships, and the emotional charges projected into them, are crucial not only because they are the pathways to the past, but because they are the client's predictions for therapy and are the emotional foundations of transference.

For example, as the heat of conflict is fanned by her feelings in one or the other of her male relationships, the hysteric may retreat and settle for something less or attempt to re-create the idyllic spirit of her past. There is often a man involved in the life of the hysteric who is kind, sympathetic, and not sexually demanding. The hysteric may turn to him for advice and consolation, and as a touchstone when matters go awry in other relationships. In such a man, the hysteric has created the "good" father in fantasy. Problems often develop in such a relationship when the hysteric begins fearing that she will become dependent. Even in mental images, the hysteric cannot tolerate the awakened anxiety of becoming dependent on a man because of her history with a possessive, self-indulgent father.

A second relationship may find the hysteric involved with a man who, she contends, is critical and close-minded. He may not listen. She may struggle to be open and clear in the relationship. She may want him to "see" her. Often this is a relationship that the hysteric continually reopens and in which she strives again and again to be heard and accepted as an independent, thinking person. The man unknowingly represents the "bad" father and symbolizes some of her negative feelings about males.

In a very real sense, this relationship often is a replay of the client's reports of her encounters with her father during her developmental years. She has re-created the scene in the present and strives to convince the father to behave differently. Anger and issues of dominance, independence, value differences, and her own sexual activity reflect the interpersonal battles of the preadolescent and adolescent years. Through such a relationship, the therapist may learn much about the characteristic style of the client and see more clearly why she found it necessary to use passivity and superficiality to ward off feeling deeply and caring.

The client's entrance into psychotherapy may parallel her venture into a triadic relationship. It is as though she has decided to reenter the oedipal arena as a last-ditch effort at reworking the past, and her healthy side needs a strong ally to support her efforts. In the triadic relationship, the therapist can perceive the neurotic side and the healthy side in some kind of internal struggle. The client may talk of the other woman in the triad as someone who denies conflict over the common man. The client may feel powerful and gratified at the attention she receives.

To attribute the client's motives in such a triadic relationship solely to oedipal fantasies and infantile objects is to miss the intentionality and growth potential that the relationship reveals. She may see the man as strong, responsible, liberated, and able to relate to a woman without domination. And therein lies the conflict: the hysteric hasn't found such a man, and she wonders how such a state of affairs could occur in a relationship. That curiosity runs counter to the neurotic gratifications that bind the hysteric.

Although here we are anticipating later chapters about the processes of psychotherapy, we will note that the therapist keeps an ear tuned to the client's movement into and out of relationships for another, more crucial reason. Through her reports of the emotional conditions in those changing relationships, the therapist receives a picture, often replayed outside the therapy hour, that is very much a reflection of the client's experience with the therapist (Doehrman 1976, Kell and Mueller 1966). The therapist thereby derives a set of ongoing guidelines as to how and why conflict is aroused and mediated in the client. It is in that sense that one speaks of an ongoing, changing conceptualization of one's client as conflicts are reawakened and replayed, with the therapist as the stimulating figure in the reenactment.

The introduction into therapy of one or another of the emotional themes of an ongoing relationship is often dynamically determined by the emotional climate of the therapeutic relationship itself. When such a theme is introduced, its significance for the current client–therapist experience must be given priority (Mueller 1973). The therapist's response, therefore, must be conditioned by such a potential symbolic representation of the therapeutic relationship. In addition, in touching on the triggering events in the relationship, the therapist will gain an enriched understanding of the conflict-engendering dynamics in the client in ways not otherwise possible.

REPETITIVE THEMES IN THE HYSTERIC'S ONGOING RELATIONSHIPS

A number of interlocking interpersonal themes recur with regularity in the many disturbed relationships of the hysterical client. Issues of substance, power, control, mastery, responsibility, performance, sexuality, victimization, and commitment are some such themes. Recognition and analysis of those themes, their psychogenic bases, and their dynamic functions is important for an adequate assessment of the hysterical personality, providing an organizational framework for integrating levels of personality functioning. Such themes contribute to a functional diagnosis of the hysterical personality and anticipate some of the transferential and countertransferential themes that characterize work with the hysterical client. Leary (1956, 1957) suggested a multilevel analysis of interpersonal functioning, and his influence is evident in the analysis we propose.

A thematic category can be analyzed according to its contents, structure, form, behavioral manifestations, dynamic functions, and psychogenic base; we will consider each aspect in turn. The contents of one such theme consist of variations on the issue of reponsibility. The theme is structurally represented as a set of polarities: being totally responsible or irresponsible. The form that the theme takes reflects a unique cognitive style and set of defenses and character traits. Irresponsibility is expressed through a vague, global, and impressionistic cognitive style (Shapiro 1965). Corollary character traits of superficiality, emotionality, and flightiness are coupled to such defenses as passivity, externalization, and compliant behavior. Those defenses serve multiple purposes. They reinforce repression of the submerged pole, that is, experience of the self as responsible. In turn, the consciously experienced feeling states of being victimized and helpless, with no sense of inner control or mastery of circumstances, serve a similar reinforcing function.

Manifestly, the hysteric acts helpless, is swept along by environmental demands, and is given to uncontrolled emotional reactions. Multiple dynamic functions are embedded in the hysteric's behavior. In part, the ego-integrative intentionality of the behaviors is to elicit responsible, caring behavior from others. The motives, however, are a mixture of neurotic gains, defense, and healthy strivings.

Dynamically, the consciously experienced helplessness and inability to cope forces responsibility on the significant other, incites anxiety in the other, and activates controlling behaviors. The controlling behaviors then provide the hysteric with justification for the expression of otherwise inhibited anger. When the significant other feels impotent to help, anxious, and exploited, the hysteric has successfully communicated her own inner state. Finally, when the significant other becomes angry and rejecting, the punishment alleviates guilt, makes the fantasied retaliation real, and confirms the hysteric's hypotheses about others. The cycle can continue on its interminable course.

The psychogenic bases of the hysteric's issues with responsibility are manifold. In general, the developmental experiences of the hysteric, discussed in the last chapter, can be seen to be fertile ground for her issues here. To cite just one example, the polarized structure of the hysteric's stance about responsibility is a function in part of her preferred status in the family as her father's confidante. Dynamically, the hysteric cannot consciously experience herself as a responsible person. During her development, collusion with the father is in itself guilt inducing. But when that collusion is coupled with the mother's denial of any maternal responsibility for parental discord or marital problems, the daughter is left as sole perpetrator of parental discord. The hysteric is "stuck" with all the blame, so she feigns irresponsibility to avoid overwhelming guilt.

A thematic analysis lets us integrate a number of features of the hysterical personality. The interlocking of character traits, defenses, cognitive style, and concomitant feeling states, and their mutually reinforcing character, are evident. The dynamic functions served in anxiety reduction, discharge of inhibited affects, and ego integration are brought into bold relief. Not only is such an analysis effective in elaborating the multifaceted dimensions of conflict, but, of more importance, it provides the therapist with guidelines for understanding the complexities of the therapeutic transactions in work with hysterical clients.

The Theme of Insubstantiality

As noted earlier, the hysterical client frequently enters psychotherapy when she is in the throes of a conflicted and unsatisfying relationship with a man, or shortly after such a relationship has ruptured. Her distress is often a recapitulation of past interpersonal experiences that have left her feeling unworthy, empty, depressed, and out of control. Correspondingly, during the initial therapy hours she shows feelings of helplessness, fragility, and an inability to cope.

Those feelings are the manifest expression of corollary character defenses and traits. The hysteric's passive, submissive, and compliant defenses, coupled with her emotionality, flightiness, superficiality, and dramatic traits, contribute to her being experienced, by herself and others, as insubstantial. The hysteric's behaving in interpersonal relationships as if she were insubstantial has led to a characterization of her interpersonal style as superficial, dependent, and affectively shallow (Chodoff and Lyons 1958). A vague, diffuse, and impressionistic cognitive style (Shapiro 1965) reinforces the picture of an insubstantial child in a woman's body.

The hysteric's "self-image" has been described as one of "inauthenticity rather than integrity" (Chodoff 1982, p. 278). She is hypersensitive to the feelings and motivation of others, and she is particularly adept at complying with the perceived expectations of her interpersonal environment. Celani (1976) contended that hysterics' perceptions of themselves as lacking substance are the "logical result of playing a complementary interpersonal role to others" (p. 1416). The hysteric's chameleonlike ability to blend in and adapt to perceived interpersonal demands may serve to initiate relationships, but her apparent lack of success in maintaining relationships only reaffirms her personal insubstantiality—thus, she is continually anxious about her ability to sustain a relationship.

To the extent that a significant male responds to the hysteric's compliance and submissiveness with an attitude of dominance, protection, and control, her maladaptive interpersonal style is reinforced, her insubstantiality is confirmed, and her needs for recognition and genuine relatedness go unrealized. Patronization is implicit in the role of the male savior, and adult interpersonal mutuality is sacrificed to a collusion with the hysteric's insubstantiality. Because she is so adept at eliciting responses in others that confirm her insubstantiality and are ultimately unsatisfying, it is not surprising that the hysteric has been described as overly dependent and demanding in relationships.

Although the interpersonal context in which insubstantiality is expressed varies, the trait is especially evident in the hysteric's sexual relationships. The hysteric has learned that her sexuality is a means of attracting and holding men (Hollender 1971). Hysterics may present an exaggerated sexual orientation to life, but they alternately may feel that "sex gets in the way of relationships." The hysteric may feel that she is treated like a "sex object," yet she has little recourse to other ways of negotiating a relationship. Therefore, other interpersonal conflicts involving dependency or anger may be expressed through the medium of sex. For example, when the hysteric's needs for trust and intimacy have not been met, she may withhold sex.

A variation on this theme is found in psychotherapy, when a frank and open discussion of sexual issues follows a resolution of more basic issues of trust and commitment in the psychotherapeutic relationship. Until other matters are addressed and resolved, the therapist simply takes note of, but does not become preoccupied with, the hysteric's manifest sexuality and seductiveness. If the therapist instead becomes prematurely preoccupied with the hysteric's sexuality, he aligns himself with other males who are "only interested in sex," and he inadvertently reinforces character defenses that confirm insubstantiality. Furthermore, he has colluded with the unfolding of compliant, albeit conflicted, transference, because the hysteric's supposition of what men find interesting and attractive about her has been confirmed.

The theme of insubstantiality is a central and continuing theme in the psychotherapy of the hysterical personality. It is experienced by the hysteric as a feeling of helplessness and emptiness with nothing to give, as an absence of mastery over the environment and of personal identity. Those feelings are reinforced by superficial, flighty, highly emotional, and irresponsible behavior. It is manifested in a cognitive vagueness and may be accompanied by hysterical "bouts," floating sensations, and a sense of depersonalization. In a later chapter, therapeutic guidelines for countering the hysteric's insubstantial self-concept are addressed.

The family patterns described earlier are fertile ground for the development of a sense of insubstantiality. Having learned to center in the father, the daughter lost a sense of her own substance. And, as she learned in adolescence, the stakes for asserting herself were too high. Rejection in light of feeling unprepared for life was too anxiety provoking. Of deeper significance to her feelings of being an object with no intrinsic worth was her role as pawn in the marital conflict. Sacrificed by the mother for the mother's security and treated as a possession by the father, she was left feeling empty and victimized.

A case excerpt may illustrate the psychogenic base, defenses, and multiple dynamic functions that are encapsulated in the theme of insubstantiality. The case material also provides the opportunity to note the way in which the conflicts of different developmental periods are displaced onto a series of sequential relationships.

The client was the daughter of two successful professional people. Neither parent, however, felt fulfilled, and both were bitter about their lots in life. The mother was an addictive personality; the father was moody. Their life together was unhappy, and they were divorced during the daughter's adolescence.

The client entered psychotherapy because of discord in an ongoing male relationship. The client felt rudderless, with no sense of herself, of what was important to her, of what she valued, or of what her future held. She was given to emotional outbursts; she felt controlled by others, yet helpless to effect any changes in her ongoing relationships or in her parents. Although the client fantasized being assertive, she was passive and compliant. In situations in which she felt that she had "stepped out of line" or aroused the enmity of another, she would experience intense anxiety.

During her life she had experienced a series of disastrous and unhappy male relationships. In serial order, she had been involved with a rather unusual assortment of men, ranging from extremely narcissistic personalities to "macho" types to passive, weak males. When she entered therapy, her current relationship was with a man who was perceived to be dominating but caring. The client was both attracted to the caring aspects and repelled by the jealous, possessive, and controlling features of the relationship.

The client felt that she had no substance. She felt that she was treated as an "object" and that so long as she behaved herself and didn't "make waves," her relationship would continue on course. In particular, she felt as though her lover thought of her as a possession with no mind of her own and as someone who needed constant guarding, else she be swept away by a more desirable suitor. Such remarks infuriated the client, but she felt helpless and too anxiety ridden at the thought of being independent to confront the issues. Her only means of expressing her anger were through the rather circuitous routes of becoming highly emotional or so irresponsible that the man would encourage more independence.

In her early childhood, the client had been treated like a doll. She had been dressed in party attire, paraded in front of guests, and then dismissed to her room. Although this behavior contributed to her sense of being treated as an "object" with no intrinsic worth, the full meaning of her deep-seated feelings of having no substance or personal worth, so characteristic of hysterical clients, emerges only when the intrafamilial dynamics are scrutinized.

During childhood, the client's principal value had been catering to her self-absorbed parents. The client had intervened in their battles, negotiated their truces, and truly mothered her mother and father alike. In his better moods, the father would "show off" what he knew, rather than work to increase the daughter's understanding of matters that troubled her. In his self-absorbed state, the father had disregarded the daughter's day-to-day developmental anxieties. In his worse moods, the daughter would spend time shoring him up and encouraging his ventures.

Throughout childhood, the daughter had worked equally feverishly, but unsuccessfully, to alleviate her mother's repeated depressions. Her sense of impotence to effect any changes in the mother, to bring out the hidden substance in her, or to mobilize the mother to act maternally had left her feeling empty and meaningless. She centered in both parents and developed a hypersensitivity to their moods, losing a sense of herself in the process. Her development had been sacrificed to becoming and extension of the parents. After the inevitable divorce, the client had been bounced around, splitting her loyalties in efforts to continue to meet the parents' respective needs and problems in living.

The turbulence of childhood and preadolescence had been tempered somewhat by surrogates who provided the client with some guidelines. As a result, in adolescence she had turned outward and attempted to socialize. The panic reaction of the father had been apparent. His controlling behavior and intrusiveness into her relationships were a source of deep embarrassment to the daughter and to the friends with whom she related. So she had backed away from the anxiety-laden taste of independence and continued to cater to the father.

As an adult, she displaced the residue of the developmental conflicts onto a series of relationships in which she attempted to rework the past, indirectly express her anger at her parents for leaving her unprepared for life, and "act out" the polarity of the role in which she had been cast as a child. In her relationships the client was passive, compliant, and hypersensitive to the nuances of reactions to her remarks or behavior. When she tested any independent move, she accompanied her test with such "hysterical" behavior that the significant other was forced into the role of protector and assumed responsibility for her errors. Through her highly emotional reactions, she continually reinforced her self-image and projected image of insubstantiality.

Her displacements were replete with the conflicts of the past, and different sequential relationships reflected the hurdles of different developmental periods. In serial order, she lived out her narcissistic wishes with one man, attached herself to a "macho" lover, and then related to a passive man. In that way she isolated sides of the emotional conflicts with the father. Finally, she entered a relationship with a man in whom the dominance, possessiveness, and jealousy were coupled with a caring, nurturant side. And, in her sensitivity to the latent characteristics of the man, she sensed that his dominant behavior was a veneer that covered his dependence on her.

In a real sense, the last relationship represented the unresolved conflicts and turmoil of the client's adolescence. The client was frustrated with the passive role that her beau reinforced, yet his dominant, protective, and possessive attitude permitted externalization of her own conflicts about behaving more independently. Periodically, she would test the limits of the relationship in her bids for a personal identity, yet she would retreat in panic when a potential breach in that relationship became real. In her anxiety, she would reestablish the "good" girl role and deny her strivings. Those behaviors, reactions, and feelings paralleled her own adolescent conflicts in relation to the father and provided the foundations for transference and countertransference themes in psychotherapy.

INTERLOCKING THEMES IN
THE HYSTERICAL PERSONALITY

The theme of insubstantiality is closely allied to the themes of lack of preparation for life, exploitation, irresponsibility, absence of control, and powerlessness. The sense of having no substance is behaviorally reinforced in irresponsible actions. In the face of two parents who behaved in irresponsible and exploitive ways toward her, one can sense the function that the hysteric's lack of responsibility serves in discomfitting others. Having been thrust into the role of the one who must be responsible for tending the parents' needs, who must be submissive and compliant, and who was left helpless and vulnerable in the face of the needs of others, the hysteric adroitly turns the tables and uses helplessness, irresponsibility, compliance, and passivity as ways of expressing her anger and as vehicles to engender anxiety in significant others.

The theme of control interlocks with insubstantiality and irresponsibility. Feeling that she has no personal substance leaves the hysteric susceptible to control by others. Although she may invite such control because she feels dependent and unprepared to master her environment, the flip side—being controlled—stirs the anxiety. She is truly trapped between her wishes and her fears. Accordingly, control becomes of paramount importance, and the hysteric enters her relationships, including psychotherapy, armed to battle against being controlled.

Those interlocking themes are evident in the hysteric's conflicts in her ongoing relationships. As noted earlier, the hysteric can often be seen attempting to relate to a strong man, only to be disillusioned (Halleck 1967). She may seek the challenge of a man who appears strong from afar, only to lose interest up close. She changes course when a man becomes too interested or accommodating. From her reports of the conflicts generated in her ongoing interactions with male partners, we learn that a paramount issue is the concept of responsible responsiveness.

In her relationships, a hysteric is often angered by men who do not take responsibility for themselves or for their roles in relationship conflicts. She becomes incensed when a male partner is arbitrary, blames her for his problems, or becomes defensive when she points out his inconsistencies. She seeks a man who is responsive but whose responsiveness is modulated by some inner sense of self-respect, who does not become overreactive, possessive, or too dependent. And when a partner who seems outwardly strong changes and becomes the dependent one, the hysteric flees the relationship.

The dynamics of those interactions reveal much of hysterical conflicts. The hysteric fights being dependent because it is overlaid with being controlled and engulfed. In a relationship with a man, she is constantly caught between her dependent needs and her anxieties about being controlled. If the beau becomes dependent, the hysteric feels that his possessiveness will restrain her autonomy and that his neediness will be depleting. Essentially, she is again trapped as she was in childhood in her relationship with her father, and she tends to back away.

If, however, the man shows signs of strength and independence, she becomes anxious and dependent. The reasons are many. She can then relate to the man and rework the past—that is, the unconscious fantasy is that of regressing to the role of the dependent child in relation to the strong father and progressively overcoming her developmental deficits. Her anxiety is also stirred because of her collusive relationship with the father, which took precedence over his relationship with his wife: The hysteric lives with the anxiety that any woman can turn a man's head, and she has no guarantees that her lot will not be that of her mother's.

Outcomes in Adult Functioning

The hysteric often says that she fears feeling too much. As Allen (1977) noted, the hysteric doesn't feel enough. Allen pointed out the defensive use of "acting" to avoid "fully feeling what seems to be felt" and suggested that the therapist must teach "the hysteric to *feel more*" (p. 318). Paradoxically, as others (Siegman 1954, Allen 1977, Chodoff 1982) have observed, the hysteric also defends against feeling too much by feeling too much. Ironic as it may seem, the hysteric needs to learn to be less sensitive and to feel less so that she can feel more.

That fear of feeling too much is a complex phenomenon in hysteria. It is rooted in part in having felt too much, in having been too involved, and in having sacrificed self-indulgence for the self-indulgent. The hysteric's efforts at relating to her father exemplify that struggle and its meager and unwarranted dividends.

The hysteric fights feeling too much because she is vulnerable to becoming dependent in a relationship. She feels that she is easily swayed, that she is suggestible, and that she must harden herself against her feelings. She does so because her own dependency needs have gone unmet and remain active. But the consequences of becoming dependent are anxiety provoking. The stakes in her own family for being dependent were too high. Dependency meant docility, self-effacement, and sacrificing independence, as the mother did for the sake of a relationship.

And even then, docility was rewarded but dependency was disdained. To depend in order to become independent is outside the understanding of the hysteric. The father of the hysteric was too self-absorbed and erratic for the daughter to risk the dependence that was necessary for self-understanding. And because such dependence is what the therapeutic alliance is all about, we can see why hysterics have trouble forming that alliance.

The hysteric avoids being dependent by "acting" helpless and demanding care. If her demands are met, she never knows whether she "got" because something was freely given. She feels that she has been manipulative, which leaves her feeling empty (Celani 1976). She does the same thing with her basic sense of vulnerability. She feigns fragility and is responded to at that level, and the basic vulnerability goes unnoticed.

The hysteric fights feeling too much because intense, subjective feeling is equated with the emotionality of the weak, unstable mother. She disavows feeling intensely, suppresses her feelings, and attempts to deal with matters rationally. But she has been taught that rationality is the man's world, teachings that have been supported by the aroused male defensiveness that confronted her when she entered the arena of rationality and attempted to argue with her father. Thus, she feels that she doesn't have the tools to fight on those grounds, and she loses before she begins. In her fight to deny her emotional side, she is vulnerable to the emotional outbursts that occur. Her fate, then, is that of the mother's.

The hysteric fears feeling because she experiences her feelings as too powerful. She avoids feeling too much through superficiality. She moves from one relationship to another, avoiding deep feelings, commitments, and being taken seriously. Her superficiality seems governed by fears about the intensity of her feelings. Based on the father's turning to her for gratification, and in the context of an inadequate mother, the hysteric is left with the feeling that she has too much power over the feelings of others.

The controls, then, must be hers. She must hold back. If she lets go, she can act, so she acts to avoid feeling too powerful but disowns the actions. In relationship after relationship, she feels that she has the power. She is the one who holds the other person's feelings in her hands. She will try to deny it; she will attribute power to the man. She wants to relate to a strong male but feels that men have an "ego" that precludes mutual sharing of power. Basically, she believes that men are weak despite their manifest traits.

These feelings seem to be the reason for the hysteric's concern if a man becomes too responsive to her. In this response she reads possessiveness and being bound, as she was in her own family. Every child is entitled to fantasies of power and wishes to supplant one or the other parent, but the hysteric cannot tolerate such fantasies because of an overly responsive father and an insecure mother. That fact may contribute in part to the dearth of conscious fantasy that has been noted in hysterics. Shapiro (1965) observed that hysterics don't have romantic fantasies, they live romanticized lives. Fantasy is an internal process, one of "letting go." For the hysteric to fantasize is to make herself vulnerable to having the fantasies realized. Fantasy and action don't make good bedfellows. The hysteric acts to rid herself of her conflicted feelings somewhat in the style of individuals with certain eating disorders. By acting, she avoids the conflicted feelings before they reach overwhelming proportions and achieves some sense of mastery, in a kind of convoluted way.

Mastery, a less pejorative word than control, is the nemesis of the hysteric. The hysteric's efforts at mastery reflect the developmentally determined, intricate network of conflict and defense. The hysteric may construe the resolution of her conflicts in relationships as mastering the male's feelings toward her. She may seek out a paternal-appearing man. This father figure is to remain solid and impervious to her advances, yet she wants responsiveness. So, in driven ways, she struggles in the relationship to bring to the surface the warmth that she assumes his exterior covers. She strives to avert masculine defensiveness; she wants the man to know her and be personal with her. To effect a relationship, she feels she must be the submissive one. Thus, she may be seductive and compliant, subjugating her own feelings in favor of male demands.

Many of those defenses against affects, power, and dominance are mediated through the hysteric's prime safeguard against activity—passivity. The passive stance taken by the hysteric has appropriately been called the "myth of passivity" (Krohn 1978, p. 225). According to Krohn, the hysterical ego "actively strives to sustain the illusion of its own passivity" (p. 159). Such a construction retains passivity as a primary defense but defines it as an active ego function.

A passive stance allows the expression of anger, shifts responsibility, and incites frustration in the partner. Passivity appears compliant and docile—the hysteric's assumptions about the needs of the male ego—but it leaves the man with a burden of responsibility that he has not bargained for. Through passivity, the hysteric's anger is made palpable. From the safety of her passivity, the hysteric can observe the man's discomfort as he jumps through the hoops that she hurdled for the benefit of the father. Through her passivity, the hysteric induces anxiety and obtains redress for her own discomfort in the face of a discomfitting father. If the male partner feels helpless and anxious, then he is feeling what she has felt.

The hysteric's passive stance, however, restricts her free, spontaneous expression. It keeps her from feeling fully because of anxiety about affects. If she attaches her conflicts about affects to performance and expression, the hysteric may not perform well in the creative arts. Her teachers may inform her that she holds back. She herself will feel the frustration of not allowing herself to flow freely. She is aware of her strangulated affects and sees comments about her expressiveness as critical and unhelpful.

Through her passive stance, the hysteric defeats herself. Passivity finds its allies in and is reinforced by such character traits as superficiality, but it fuels the emotional outbursts of the hysteric. The hysteric's self-imposed passivity counters her active strivings and the vestiges of oedipal intrusiveness that she must experience. She holds back to avoid the responsiveness that she feels she will elicit if she feels fully. That seems to be why hysterics are so reactive to overreactivity. They want to be sensuous and test their sexuality, they want to be angry and test their impact, without those feelings affecting the other party's sexual or angry response. Until she can experience those feelings, the hysteric cannot attend to herself; in short, she cannot become *aware*. To become aware, the hysteric must experience a relationship in which the other person responds responsibly and with self-awareness. Despite her ambivalence, that is the hysteric's hope when she enters psychotherapy—and that is the continuing psychotherapeutic task.

Part Two

Psychotherapy: Guidelines for Intervention

Chapter Four

The Conditions of the
Therapeutic Relationship

The hysteric is interpersonally hypersensitive and reactive. The interpersonal orientation and sensitivity of the hysteric are both a source of strength in psychotherapy and, paradoxically, its greatest roadblock. The hysteric's reflexive behavior is immediate and compelling. Her defenses and coping strategies are well established and effective. Reflection and feeling give way to action. She reverts to displacing and acting out her conflicts in ongoing relationships, and the therapeutic relationship is no exception.

The hysterical client will immediately respond to the therapist as a significant other in the construction of her world (Allen 1977). Conflicts are readily activated and replayed in therapy, but the hysteric is adroit at using her sensitivity to avoid anxious moments. And her sensitivity to a therapist's weakness is impressive, as is her ability to turn the tables on the therapist to minimize her anxiety, induce anxiety in the therapist, confirm her hypotheses about significant others, and confuse the issue.

THE COMPLEX COMMUNICATION OF THE
HYSTERICAL CLIENT

The emotional conditions the hysterical client reports in the content of her productions—the nature of interactions, her reactions, her perceptions, and the outcome—are the expectations she holds for the course and outcome of therapy. Of greater significance is the fact that even in the first moments of contact, while reporting those interactions, the emotional conditions embedded in those interactions and the dynamics undergirding them are already activated and being played out simultaneously in relation to the therapist. It is as though every utterance is triply charged: it relates to an ongoing relationship, it is a replication of a historical interaction and it reflects the dynamics of the therapeutic interaction. In working with any client, regardless of the form of the neurosis, one expects to find an interlocking of the past, present, and therapeutic hour in client productions. But the hysterical client is unique in the immediacy, pervasiveness, and intricacy of this dynamic interplay.

The therapist who attends to the content of a client's productions as though it itself were the major issue misses the real point of the content: to elicit from and to repeat with the therapist what is dynamically central to the productions. The therapist may perceive some dynamic issues in the contentual matter of a client's reports, but it is only in the client's reactions to the therapist's responses that the emotional and dynamic themes that are undercurrents of psychotherapeutic sessions become clear. Often attention to an elaboration of the emotional tones underlying sessions must take precedence over any further attendance to the themes in historical content (Mueller 1973).

Perhaps of more importance is the fact that the content often reflects what has already occurred in the relationship in the moments before its introduction (Kell and Mueller 1966). What the hysterical client introduces, remembers, and reports is likely to be a symbolic representation of the therapeutic interchange or is intended to stimulate a dynamically equivalent response pattern. Therapists in working with hysterics should use caution in early interpretations (Allen 1977); if interpretations are advanced without reflection as to the possible parallelism in the relationship (Doehrman 1976, Kell and Mueller 1966, Mueller and Kell 1972), the therapist misses the most crucial avenue to change: the therapist's own significance in triggering the production.

With the hysterical client, the therapist must constantly check his participating behavior. At the outset of therapy with a male therapist, the client may seem overloaded with undischarged affect, emotionally distraught, and helpless. She may talk of men as sexually aggressive and exploitive. Content about being victimized may be reinforced through reports of nightmares and phobic reactions with rich associational material. The client's productions may invite interpretation. As the momentum of the session increases, the therapist may push for insights or interpret material.

Following such interpretations, the client's responses and reactions may be baffling to the therapist. He may find himself withdrawing, feeling guilty and confused. Symbolically, the therapist has dramatically reenacted—that is, simultaneously, in a nonsexual context, he has acted out with and confirmed—his client's hypotheses about the assaultive, self-centered men she has described. The phallic-aggressive potential of such interpretations (Krohn 1978) or their self-enhancing motives (Sullivan 1953a) trigger the client's reactions.

The therapist, however, may be confused enough to miss noticing that he was encouraged to act as he did. And when he withdraws or feels deflated, the client may introduce content about men who behave impotently with her. That content must also be construed as dynamically determined by the therapist's reactions, perhaps the flash of anxiety or guilt he experienced or the subliminal blow to his ego that triggered his withdrawal.

The immediacy with which the hysterical client introduces material that is symbolic of the emotional tone of therapeutic interactions is truly astonishing. At any given moment in a session, the client may introduce a story or a fragment of an interpersonal event that may seem disjointed. On the surface, such superficially unrelated material may have the flavor of "loose" associations. If a therapist interprets the many affective-laden stories of the hysteric as so much defensive chatter to avoid issues, not only does he miss a most crucial avenue to understanding the client, but he also communicates disrespect for the client's inner process and for her primary means of communicating her inner turmoil. As Chodoff (1978) observed, the hysteric will sense this lack of respect and react in highly emotional ways. Such a therapist attitude not only activates intense anger in the client, but also suggests that the therapist's chances of working effectively with hysterical clients are limited.

If the therapist attends carefully to those seemingly disjointed stories, however, he may note that the client's reactions represent a heightened sensitivity to what has just occurred in sessions that triggered the association. As such, those stories reflect an impressive unconscious associational process and are worthy of genuine respect. If, for example, the therapist becomes defensive for some reason, the hysteric will produce some material from her repertoire that will reflect what defensive men have signified for her. But her content also will be a living TAT (Murray 1943) of the conditions and outcomes of those interactions in her emotional experience, thus providing the therapist with an excellent opportunity to understand the dynamic processes of conflict in the client.

INTERLOCKING THERAPIST–CLIENT ATTITUDINAL SETS

In work with a hysterical client, a psychotherapist is sensitized to such character issues and defenses as control, manipulation, irresponsibility, and histrionics. Despite some of the more comprehensive efforts at understanding the interpersonal meaning of hysterical behavior and complementary intrapsychic dynamics (Baumbacher and Amini 1980, Krohn 1978, Horowitz 1977, Blacker and Tupin 1977, Celani 1976), those less-than-appealing character traits still take their toll in therapist attitudes about working with hysterical clients. In a rather refreshing way, Chodoff (1982) observed that some of the basic issues in successful work with hysterical clients are attitudinal. In outlining the unseemly history of negative attitudes about the hysterical personality, Chodoff described the many deleterious effects that accrue from a therapist's own preconceived negative feelings.

The therapist who ponders issues of appropriate therapeutic distance and is preoccupied with whether the client is controlling and manipulative is likely to be guarded, defensive, and of little help to the client. One might hazard the guess that such distancing behavior reflects the therapist's own inner concerns about control and involvement, suggestibility, and dependency. Essentially, such concerns may be the manifest representations of the anxiety-reducing operations of the therapist. Because of aroused anxiety, the therapist may retreat from involvement and personal anxiety under cover of a reassessment of the client as manifesting a borderline condition (see Glazer 1979). Levenson (1972) noted that "it is an old saw that the more anxious the patient makes the therapist, the more likely he is to label or call names" (p. 201). Such a retreat from encounter will most assuredly lead to an escalation of the very behaviors the therapist is attempting to circumscribe.

In contrast, the therapist who holds a basic respect for and genuine interest in the client (Chodoff 1982), who has a sense of comfort in working with the client, and who is honest (Halleck 1967), open, and responsible in relating may be helpful. If the therapist takes considerable personal risks in efforts to understand, reach out, and offer strength, the hysteric may become genuinely anxious and dependent and allow the alliance through which she can begin to attach words to feelings and gain some inner control over an otherwise chaotic, powerless existence.

The therapist's attitudes about the client extend to the content and associated affects of the client's productions. The therapist assumes substance in the client and validity to the communications. For example, rather than being preoccupied with the defensive function of exaggerated affects, the therapist searches for the experience that is communicated through such an elaborate modality. Under such conditions the hysteric's submerged strength and substance can emerge.

Halleck (1967) noted, in the context of characterological issues in client behaviors, that the therapist must be "rigidly honest" (p. 756) in dismissing nothing that occurs in the therapeutic transactions. That attitude must be coupled with a personal openness in the therapist to his part in the emotional conditions of the relationship. In this vein, Krohn (1978) has suggested that the countertransference potential in pejorative attributions must be assessed.

Negative therapist attitudes about the hysterical client find their complement in the attitudes of the female hysterical client about men and male therapists. Both parties may enter the therapeutic relationship with preconceived notions about the other. Whereas the therapist may hold the belief that the hysterical client is irresponsible, manipulative, and controlling, the hysteric holds the counterbelief that men are controlling, self-centered, unreliable, and irresponsible. And when the hysteric enters psychotherapy, she has more evidence from her developmental experiences to support her convictions than the therapist has for his attitudes. The attributions of the hysteric interlock with those of the therapist and set a series of complex dynamic interactions into motion.

The power struggles during initial encounters with a male therapist reflect the attitudes and preconceived notions of both parties. The therapist may have entered the relationship girded for battle because of general attitudes about hysterical disorders and control issues. Those attitudes are likely to be reinforced early in therapy, because hysterical clients do have control issues, although they have been overemphasized at the expense of their motivating force.

The therapist may see his role as championing the cause that this client will not control his destiny, and his concerns may extend to many matters, including setting limits, keeping a therapeutic distance, and maintaining rigidity in the usual negotiations that occur at the outset of therapy. What the therapist may not realize is that, in his internal set that this client will not control him, he has already locked horns with the willfulness (Farber 1966) of the hysteric. Under conditions of such an interlocking willful attitude in both parties, very little of benefit will be accomplished. Further, in his concerns about control, the therapist reveals his own needs to control and his susceptibility to being controlled. Along this dimension, it seems that he and his client have some personality issues in common.

The hysteric, however, has her own issues with power. The hysteric's power struggles reflect her attitudes about male self-centeredness and her need for redress. Those struggles reveal her feelings that males are basically inadequate and irresponsible. They reflect her underlying dependency conflicts. And above all else, they reflect her basic vulnerability.

The entrance of a hysterical client into psychotherapy is often heralded by a barrage of material about abusive males. Subtle remarks may suggest a vengeful spirit because of her victimized state. She may suggest that she wants a powerful, intense, and complete relationship and point to other professionals who failed to provide her with what she needed.

The client's entrance may also consist of behaviors, attitudes, and reactions that suggest that the client is unable to care for herself. She may provide information about her behaviors that indicates lack of impulse control and minimal ego strength, and sends subtle messages of suicidal ideation. She may suggest that she will be around for a long time, dependent and needy. She may anticipate her problems needing immediate attention and the therapy hours as being unsuited to her times of stress. She may support such feelings with reports of contacts with men in which she became demanding at unusual times, and their frustration, anxiety, and urging may have been a motivating force in her seeking professional help.

The two stances are simply polarities that reflect similar underlying personality conflicts. One dynamic generating such reactions is the hysteric's sensitivity to male chauvinism. The client's entrée into therapy and her initial "shock waves" often relate directly to her feelings about male dominance, self-centeredness, and chauvinistic attitudes. The hysterical client's need for redress is one of the first things that the male therapist encounters. How badly the hysteric has been bruised, how much she has given for what she has gotten in significant relationships, and how much she has been exploited are initial conditions that may set the course of psychotherapy on a rapid or slow course.

The client will have learned to use passive means to gain her goals. The extent to which she needs to make the therapist feel what she has felt, to be as anxious as she has been, to feel as helpless as she has felt, are all diagnostic indicators of the amount of emotional turmoil and reactivity in the personality. And they will take their toll unless the therapist manages to attend to his client's conflicts at the expense of his own discomfort and anxiety. The hysterical client's intense reaction to therapist anxiety is a central and continuing theme in psychotherapeutic work with hysterics.

The Therapist's Anxiety

Comfort in working with a hysterical client despite the onslaught of labile, unmediated behaviors is one of the harbingers of successful psychotherapy. The hysteric is quite willing to have the therapist be anxious so long as she experiences his anxiety as related to her conflicts and the difficulties she is experiencing. Thus, if the therapist responds with anxiety to the apparent helpless or uncontrolled state of his client because of his concerns about her welfare, the hysteric's antenna will accurately interpret his concerns for her and she may temporarily settle down to becoming genuinely anxious.

If the client notes that the therapist is anxious because of his own discomfort in working with her, however, or because his competence is threatened, the hysteric will react strongly. If the therapist attempts to control the client for his personal comfort reasons, if he becomes anxious about the potential demands of the relationship, or if he attempts to set limits prematurely on the client, the hysteric will intensify her acting out because of anger at the therapist's self-centered concerns.

If the therapist, in other words, attends to his personal anxiety, he will activate his client's passive expression of anger, and she will most assuredly give him more discomfort than he can fantasize. It is self-centeredness that the hysteric despises in males, the therapist no exception. If the therapist construes the opening sessions as primarily evidencing transference reactions, he may miss a very crucial dynamic. The client is reacting to what in reality is transpiring in her current relationship with the therapist. The hysteric has lived a lifetime of protecting herself and is very alert to self-protection in others. And because she has had to protect herself from self-serving males, her sensitivity picks up such reactions accurately and sets her responses in motion.

Although the client's anger is aroused if the therapist attends to his own needs, the neurotic side wants the therapist to become anxious—so that she can act out her anger and satisfy her need for redress. A strong part of the client is tremendously angry at males and wants her revenge for previous transgressions. That side of the client hopes the therapist will fail—that he will attempt to control her—for then therapy can be played on the hysteric's home court, with control issues as paramount features of the interaction.

Not only is the hysteric immediately reactive to the therapist's attending to his own comfort, but she would like to see him anxious for other reasons as well. In her own development, the hysteric was anxious in situations over which she had no control. She felt controlled, overwhelmed, and anxious in the presence of others, and often that anxiety was induced by a self-absorbed and irresponsible father. In addition, she was offered little protection, comfort, or help in how to cope with her anxiety. The hysteric's anger about her discomfort and her helpless state is experienced in relation to the therapist. If the therapist becomes anxious in her presence, then he is feeling what she felt. Not only might the therapist become anxious, but he might also feel helpless. The therapist then knows experientially what his client has felt (Mueller 1973).

That condition of having been helpless and controlled with no protection from a mothering one during development seems to contribute to several turns that hysteria takes in adulthood and explains some of its effects in psychotherapy. Being anxious in relation to an overwhelming male figure certainly contributes to the hysteric's anger toward male figures. It also contributes to the way the anger is expressed–through a passive stance that frustrates without danger of counterassault. It explains the client's interest in having the therapist feel helpless and anxious in her presence, a neat role reversal. It also explains the client's hypersensitivity to any nuances of therapist anxiety—she knows what anxiety is all about.

Although the hysterical client is neurotically motivated to "drag" the therapist through her anxieties with her because parenting ones left her in an anxious state, that motive provides only a partial explanation for her reactions. Of crucial importance in work with the hysterical client is an understanding of the interpersonal link that this communication of anxiety intends. Although the hysteric wants to keep the therapist off balance because of her underlying vulnerability, she also uses her anxiety to test the therapist's mettle.

Those concerns about therapist strength, reflected in the elaborate character defense, learned traits, and ways of coping, suggest the underlying belief and fear that men are basically unreliable and irresponsible. To understand the depth of those experiences, it is necessary only to follow a client's reactions to a therapist who does not become anxious initially but whose anxiety emerges under pressure of his client's defenses. If in initial sessions the therapist attempts to "come on strong," as though he will protect or rescue the client, she will react as intensely but in a seemingly complementary way. She will be what she assumes the therapist wants her to be—docile, childlike, and with reactions that seem to be oedipal in character. The client may, for example, break off other male relationships and seem regressed and petulant in her contention that she has been promised help and remains distraught.

The hysteric will, in other words, seem helpless. At such times the therapist may have second thoughts about continuing with the client. In such a case the therapist may attempt to circumscribe the relationship, back off, interpret, blame, or in some other way distance the relationship—for reasons of his own anxiety, anger, and frustration. When he does so, the client will most assuredly "pull out all the stops," and her vengeful spirit will be enacted with the therapist as a principal. At such times, the therapist will have a much clearer picture of what is meant by the "myth of passivity" (Krohn 1978, P. 225). Through the hysteric's passive stance, the therapist will effectively feel the punishment that Sullivan (1956) noted the hysteric can mete out through her own self-absorbed concerns about her sanity.

When the anxiety in the therapist shows through the seemingly strong exterior, the hysteric will have confirmed—in the therapeutic hour—one of her basic beliefs and fears: that underlying the male exterior is inadequacy and irresponsibility. That belief partially explains the anger, but the anger also reflects the anxiety. And it is the anxiety that sets into motion some counterhysterical behaviors that are efforts at restoring the therapist. Those mixed feelings of anger and fright that she will never be able to relate and depend explain in part the hysteric's ensuing reactions to the therapist.

The Belief that Males Are Inadequate

In opening sessions the hysterical client will often "set up" a therapist and "knock him down." The client may, for example, encourage the therapist's diagnostic powers and invite his strength by appearing weak, helpless, and needy. If the therapist accepts this role, he may find himself confused by his own ineffectiveness. Then when he feels helpless, he may find the client bolstering his ego again. The dynamics of that interchange are complex and revealing. Others have pointed out that attributing conscious intentionality to the hysteric in such an interchange is erroneous (Krohn 1978). The motives are mixed and unconscious, the generating sources of anxiety outside awareness, the feelings displaced, and their conscious representation distorted.

The hysteric realizes some gains from the dominant-submissive power plays of such an interaction. Because of her history, the hysteric's reactions are partially motivated by counterwishes to identify with and retaliate against dominating males. Dominance is associated with power, and the hysteric's lack of mastery over her environment makes the prospect of interpersonal power attractive. At the conscious level, the hysteric feels that males have the power.

Although attracted to such a male, the hysteric despises the self-indulgence and controlling features that in her experience are equated with power. She equates power with exploitation. Power means "power over," and its complement is a submissive, docile partner. Submissiveness counters the dominant drive and is construed as a necessary corollary to being dependent. The hysteric wants to be dependent, but dependence means being vulnerable, and vulnerability means being exposed to a potentially exploitive and self-indulgent male.

In the "set-up" the hysteric passively attacks because she feels vulnerable, belittled, and frustrated. Although frustrated with her submissive state, the hysteric is bound by anxieties about the consequences of her anger and assertiveness. Therefore, she converts those anxiety-evoking motives into conscious feelings of helplessness. She then passively frustrates the therapist, who struggles helplessly to help.

The hysteric may then bolster the therapist's ego. On the surface, such a move may be construed as "setting the therapist up" again for another passive assault on his ego. That interpretation, however, short-circuits some dynamics and completely misses the most crucial and central dynamic of the interaction: It bypasses the client's intervening anxiety about being "castrating" and her fears of retribution. If the therapist is taken aback and confused by her attack, the client, because she is partially motivated to retaliate for past injustices, sees this as a function of her "castrating" attack.

Because of her angry feelings, the hysteric often holds the misperception that she is basically an angry, cutting woman. Eichler (1976) has observed that the hysteric experiences extensive difficulties with her aggressive drives, which need careful attention in psychotherapeutic work. Surely because of mixed motives, but mainly from anxiety and confusion about her own aggressiveness, the hysteric experiences any angry feelings as suspect, unjustified, aggressively motivated, and destructive.

Because of her enforced passivity in the face of uncontrolled others, the hysteric has not had the opportunity to learn much about herself in many areas, aggressive behavior included. Such matters need clarification during therapy, but the hysteric's anger is often reactive, expressed in strident, pleading tones. Her anger is experienced toward males who are defensive and self-centered. That has been her history, and that is what she attempts to rectify. The hysteric wants to relate to a male who responds to her responsibly and whose reactions to her are guided by her needs and by a nondefensive "listening" and interaction with her.

Partly motivated by fears of retribution for her angry feelings, the client may make efforts at restoring the therapist. Retreating to a submissive, helpless, nurturing, or seductive role in order to appease the male ego are some of the learned modes. There is, however, a more crucial dynamic operating, which touches on the hysteric's basic belief about males. When the therapist becomes confused, feels ineffective, and responds defensively, the client fears that she is now in a relationship with a defensive, weak male.

The impotence of the male—whether therapist or another—activates the other side of the conflict. Accompanying her submissive, nurturing response to restore the therapist is the arousal of depressed feelings, in that the hysteric senses that she is again "stuck" emotionally. For if the male is impotent, her neurosis is reinforced, her dependent needs will go unmet, and another relationship has taken its toll. Such would seem to be a partial dynamic basis for the depression so often seen in hysteria following ruptured relationships. And with each rupture, the hysteric's depression deepens.

The central dynamic issue in the interchange becomes clearer. At the conscious level, the hysteric attributes power to the male, but at a deeper level, the hysteric feels that *she* has the power. The hysteric does not really believe that males are strong. She believes she sees through a strong masculine exterior to the inadequacy that the brittle exterior represents. Such has been her history: she feels that the power—the therapist's potency—is in her hands (Kell and Mueller 1966). She projects onto the therapist what her experience has taught her—that what seems to be strength is a veneer, that the dominant male "doth protest too much," and that an inadequate person huddles inside and will emerge in times of crisis.

If during the early stages of therapy, the therapist oscillates between signs of strength and of defensiveness, he confirms his client's hypotheses. In particular, if he becomes angry, openly or by withholding, for reasons of his inadequacy to cope with his own feelings in the relationship, he will exacerbate his client's anxieties and depression. The hysteric will be reinforced in her feeling that what she wants in a relationship she can get only by demanding it. If she "gets" she feels she has manipulated it. She equates her assertive bids with being castrating, her anger is felt as devastating, and her nurturance she senses is provoked by guilt. So nothing is real, and she feels she has no substance. There is little wonder she has "floating" sensations.

But the hysteric's need to relate is strong, so the client may continue for a while to feign fragility and nurture the therapist's ego in the hope of strengthening him so that she can respond to him dependently. The fear is that the damage has been done. The reason is apparent. In the therapeutic session itself, the therapist has reacted to her in ways that parallel her previous problematic interactions with significant males. She has again discovered that the therapist's feelings about himself are a function of her reactions to him. The consequence is that the hysteric is left feeling angry, guilty that she is a "castrator," anxious about retribution, and fearful of revealing herself and relying on the therapist.

Fortunately, the hysteric is a contentious woman who will have her way (Farber 1966), as any therapist who has tried to curb that "will" knows. So the hysteric will cycle through the same relationship issues time and again in her efforts to relate, providing the therapist, as Allen (1977) noted, with many opportunities to help. Perhaps the interlocking of three feeling states in the hysteric—fragility, contentiousness, and anger— and their expression in "hysterical episodes" can provide a further example of the hysteric's beliefs about males, the effects in the therapist, and the subtleties of therapeutic interactions.

The "Hysterical Episode" as a
Reflection of the Relationship

In his insightful and humorous style of describing hysteria, Sullivan (1956) noted what he called the "happy idea" that occurs to the hysteric one day—the idea that "this thing is driving me crazy" (p. 205). Reversing roles for a moment, a therapist who thinks that "this woman is driving me crazy" after a particularly stormy session with a hysteric has touched on a central dynamic. Converted into a more professional tone, the therapist may muse that "this woman is someone to contend with." That thought embodies many critical issues in the psychotherapy of hysteria.

The fact of the matter is that the hysteric has not been contended with; rather, she has been the one to contend with a set of parents whose own needs were paramount. Within that developmental picture, the hysteric sacrificed her feelings, suppressed her strivings, and overcontrolled in the face of parental irresponsibility. In short, she shouldered the responsibility of attending to parental demands and needs at the expense of her own. She was an adult before her time, and as an adult she sheds the responsibility of adulthood. Her developmental task was to reflect the father and center in him. Accordingly, the hysteric does not feel ready for life because she hasn't been prepared for it. She feels fragile, unprotected, used, and angry.

Thus, the adult hysteric often reports that she feels she lacks the tools to fight, that she must toughen herself, that she feels no substance, and that she isn't treated as though she were a person or taken seriously. The accompanying feelings of being fragile, too feeling oriented, and unable to master reflect the genuine lack of defenses that the hysteric feels in relationships. Those feeling states serve defensive purposes as well. They run counter to and are intended to counter the hysteric's contentious spirit and her anger, areas of considerable conflict for her. In a sense, the hysteric uses a defenseless posture as a defense against experiencing and encountering anger and as a vehicle for its expression.

Variations on the theme of wanting to be contended with, anger about having had to contend with others rather than be the contentious one, and feeling defenseless interlock and provide some insight into certain hysterical behaviors during psychotherapy. The hysteric is extremely angry about her defenseless state and about having taken responsibility for those who should have taken responsibility for themselves and who left her defenseless. It is that sense of being angry but defenseless that leads to intense anxiety about even feeling angry, much less expressing it. The net result is that the hysteric is impressively ingenious and imaginative in finding routes to achieve redress without danger.

The "hysterical episode," in which the client calls the therapist because she is experiencing a crisis, provides a good example of the interplay of defense, anxiety, secondary gain, and the hysterical style of communicating. The hysteric's intense reactions at such times convey multiple messages to the therapist. The hysteric often had been the good girl, of little trouble to anyone. In her emergency she lets the therapist know that she is someone to contend with. If the therapist becomes anxious, she has effectively communicated the depth of her anxiety. But the hysteric also uses her hysterical reactions to punctuate her anger at the therapist.

In her call, the client may sound as though she is "falling apart." If the client is convincing enough, the therapist may reconsider whether she is, in fact, a hysterical client or more severely disturbed. The comments of Glazer (1979) and Levenson (1972) about the countertransference aspects of increasing the severity of the diagnosis under anxiety seem applicable here. In any case, because of his own anxiety, the therapist may then become inappropriately supportive, essentially changing horses in midstream. When he does so, the hysterical client has a vivid example of the inconsistent, vacillating man she thought he was in the first place. His exterior has exploded, and she sees the insufficient, weak, and self-centered man that her father was. At that point in psychotherapy, the hysteric may become immensely anxious.

That anxiety is mobilized, however, and the hysterical client may appear at the next session with some rather interesting and well-thought-through emotional insights into herself. The therapist may be impressed, relieved, and ready to move ahead. But dynamically what has happened is a replay of her history. The client has found the male inconsistent and has needed to demonstrate to him that she is safe to work with. In essence, she has shored up the therapist as she does other males. Her needing to covey symbolically her being "safe to work with" dynamically makes him unsafe. She has needed to take responsibility for the therapist, and that is an accurate reproduction of her history. She is again being the good girl. At such times the hysterical client's depression may increase.

The issue is that the therapist, through his inconsistency, has activated anxiety, and the hysteric must retreat to overcontrol and be the responsible one. She must then measure what she says and does because of her perception of the therapist's inability to confront his own anxieties, much less hers. Trust again becomes an issue. Taking responsibility for males is not the core issue; the hysteric is well versed in that area. The problem is that the therapist's oscillation has reawakened the emotional approach–avoidance conditions of her childhood and adolescence in relation to paternal behavior and to the push–pull in ongoing male relationships.

Whenever a hysteric becomes hysterical, it is surely a sign that something in the therapeutic relationship needs attention. It may well be that the therapist retreated from engaging the client or somehow did not take appropriate responsibility, no matter how briefly. Or the hysteric may simply have perceived some response as inconsistent, distancing, or erratic. Chodoff (1982) suggested that the hysterical episode results from a hysterical client's perception of her therapist's negative attitudes about her, which serve to increase her feelings of desperateness and helplessness. The point is that the countertransference elements—and the reality conditions in the relationship (French 1946)—must be examined before relegating the reaction to evidence of a character disorder, thereby exonerating the therapist of responsibility.

The hysteric's intense reactions are overdetermined and provide the opportunity to ferret out the genetic sources of conflict. If the past is attended to at those times before the air is cleared in the therapeutic relationship, however, the hysteric will continue to feel that the therapist is denying his role as the stimulus in their relationship. Accordingly, the hysterical bouts will intensify until those matters are addressed.

The therapist must first attend to the rumblings of anger as they relate to the events of the therapeutic sessions and to the anxieties about feeling angry that necessitate such a dramatic and circuitous route for expression. The triggering events in the relationship can then be recast in terms of the stimulating conditions in the past. The therapist and client can then get on with attending to the generating sources of anger in the past—which by that time have relatively limited therapeutic value, because the affect has been discharged in the present in relation to a significant other (see Alexander 1946a, pp. 18–23; 1952, pp. 29–34).

In a sense, what seems to happen is that the hysteric has a brush with anger during a therapeutic hour. The feeling of anger is so overlaid with anxieties that it is felt only after the session, and then only as a hysterical outburst with accompanying affects related to past figures. After a session, for example, a hysteric may suddenly have an insight into some injustice in the past, perhaps some irresponsible behavior on the part of her parents. The feelings associated with the emotional insight may be intense. And the hysteric may sound as though she is losing her grasp on reality because of the flooding of emotionally laden memories.

Although the contents of the outburst relate to past figures and are felt in relation to past injustices, the hysterical outburst itself is the crucial factor. If the therapist attends to the affects in the context of the verbalized historical contents, he misses the hysteric's intentionality, and the affect is drained off rather than integrated, only to be reexperienced later. That is another way of saying that when the hysteric becomes hysterical, she is expressing her anger at the therapist, and the contents of her memories, dramatic and traumatic as they may sound, reflect the intensity of her feelings in the present and in relation to the therapist. At such times, if the therapist acknowledges the client's suffering and nondefensively explores the emotional conditions in the therapeutic relationship that may have gone awry, the hysteric's fears of retribution may dissipate somewhat and she may experience some anger at the therapist and confront him.

Such matters are, however, not easily settled. The hysteric's fear of retribution is strong. Her development has often been such that the volatile father was permitted his anger, but she was not. Even in families in which the father was manifestly warm and collusive, the hysteric has had the experience of seeing the explosive side of the father when she stepped out of her docile role and brushed against his brittle ego. Her anticipation with the therapist is that he, too, will have his retribution for her confrontation and chipping away at his "male ego."

In the sessions following a hysterical episode, the client may produce significant material about some of the problems that she experienced in coping as a child. Although the contents will vary with individual cases, the impact is that of parenting gone wrong and of the client's vulnerability. In her accounts, the client may seem very vulnerable, and indeed she is. The dynamics of such a session are particularly complex. The client is recalling material that elicits sensitivity on the part of the therapist. But the question is how the therapist should attend to that material, because it is dynamically determined in part by the client's fear of retribution for having "stepped out of line."

In discussions of hysteria, the literature is replete with examples of the transference compliance. In some respects, the foregoing behavior represents such compliance. In working on the past and producing vivid memories of being mistreated, the client is both being docile in relation to the therapist and symbolically representing her fears of what will happen to her for her misdemeanor with the therapist. If the therapist attends to the affect-laden historical contents as though they are the entire issue, he will have missed an opportunity to help the client know *why* she feels that vulnerable. At the same time, he will reinforce the primary character defense of passivity—that is, through his sensitive behavior when the client is complying and seeming vulnerable, he may inadvertently convey to her that he will be helpful when she is weak, the traditional male–female stereotype that the hysteric holds.

The client *is* feeling vulnerable, however, and if the therapist attends only to the fact that she is being docile and interprets the defensive character of her behavior, he will heighten the hysteric's defensiveness, because his reaction will most assuredly be construed as critical. The hysteric is aware of her strangulated affects, and pointing them out to her is appropriately experienced as pejorative. But the time would certainly appear to be ripe for the therapist to help the client to learn how her inner processes work.

The central dynamic seems to be that the hysteric's docility is a function of her feeling vulnerable to assault for having been motivated out of anger to bruise the male ego. If the therapist informs the client about how the content of her memories helped him to see the conflict in her, then she will learn something of how she defends. At the same time she can attach the affects to the appropriate ideational material. Eventually, she may be able to catch herself converting her affects. Such a therapist response lends validity to the affects that are appropriately attached to the reported contents; the client can then experience her genuine needs without their being confounded by compliance.

But a hysterical client's compliance can be a therapist's nemesis. In early psychotherapeutic work with the hysterical client, the character defenses and resistances must be a continuing focus (Halleck 1967, Krohn 1978, Reich 1949). Reich (1949) observed that such resistances are "present from the very first moment in a fully developed, but typically *hidden* form" (p. 86). In his analysis of such resistances with a hysterical personality, Reich clearly indicated the pitfalls of interpreting deep material: the effect of such interpretations is to reinforce defenses. Reich further noted that interpretations are not beneficial when they are offered in the context of a complying client until the compliance is addressed.

During psychotherapy, compliance can be a major roadblock to change. It is a powerful defense, because it is a particularly slippery one. At times a therapist may feel that progress is being made—insights seem to occur, memories seem charged with affects—only to find after a while that behaviors aren't changing, attitudes remain fixed, and affects are neither neutralized nor discharged nor sublimated. Displacements retain their driven quality. The client has effectively preserved her neurosis. Chodoff (1978) referred to the rapidly evaporating insights of the hysteric as "pseudo-insights" (p. 505), which are mul-tidetermined phenomena. According to Chodoff, one motivat-ing force for such seeming insights is to please the therapist so that the therapist will gratify the hysteric's desires.

In this regard, Masterson (1976) advanced several propositions about compliance and the approval-seeking behavior of the bor-derline personality that are equally applicable to the hysteric. According to Masterson, borderline personalities are highly "sensitive to and compliant with the therapist's unconscious wishes" and may provide the therapist with the oedipal con-tent "they think he wants" (p. 127). Consequently, therapeu-tic sessions may seem progressive, whereas in fact an under-lying "therapeutic stalemate" (p. 127) exists since the focus has been distracted from core preoedipal conflicts. Leaving aside the oedipal-preoedipal issues, Masterson's observations about the borderline personality are just as relevant to the hysteric who uses her sensitivity and compliance in similar ways to distract the therapist and ward off anxiety.

As a keen observer of others' reactions to her and in her sen-sitivity to what is pleasing and rewarded, the hysteric is partic-ularly adroit at complying without getting caught at it. In her sen-sitivity, the hysteric will accurately assess a therapist's orientation to problems such as hers and in short order will be able to pro-duce material that fits the therapist's theory of human develop-ment and its disorders. As such, she will have a good sense of what she is supposed to feel about such matters as sexual feel-ings toward fathers and anger toward mothers. Those appraisals of what would please the therapist can stand the hysteric in good stead when the going gets rough and she experiences emotional reactions to a therapist that may get her into trouble.

Whenever a therapist feels that his hysterical client is having some real insights into the effects of the past on her current life conflicts, he needs to search carefully for evidence of compli-ance. At times when the client is complying, attending to the content of historical issues is useful only insofar as it elaborates the emotional themes and undercurrents of sessions that may have activated the compliant attitude at that time. To state the case more generally, Mueller (1973) suggests that an appropriate therapeutic response to any client communication is conditioned by a multilevel assessment of its meaning. In that assessment the therapist must consider the motivational factors in any themes that are introduced, including the *"defensive functions"* and *"symbolic meaning"* (p. 100) of the communications as they relate to the client's experience in the therapeutic relationship.

When the thematic productions of the hysterical client are viewed from the perspective of what motivated their introduction, those productions can sometimes be seen to serve at least two functions: The dominant theme in the material may serve the defensive function, and the submerged theme may symbolize the client's experience and conflicts in the therapeutic relationship. We can elaborate this concept by returning to the session in which the client had a hysterical outburst because of a brush with anger toward the therapist. In a succeeding session, the therapist can count on some compliance, because the hysteric's anger about compliance is countered by anxiety about noncompliance.

In her compliance, as Masterson (1976) proposed, the client may introduce themes that seem to fit the therapist's notions about her problems. The client may, for example, recall events or recover memories of her relationship to her mother and father that seem highly charged emotional experiences. Those memories produced under pressure to comply will, however, carry a submerged theme, often related to the hysteric's reactions to those who historically controlled her or enforced compliance and to her anxieties about the consequences of her defiant behaviors. The submerged themes may be in the form of "tag ends" to stories in which the client felt victimized and angry, and in which retaliation and rejection occurred, leaving her helpless.

The dominant theme often represents the hysteric's defensive solution: to comply. The submerged theme is a reconstruction of the conflict situation that generated anxiety. As noted earlier, the hysteric's stories are strikingly like a living TAT in which a conflict situation, a precipitating set of events, and a solution are elicited. The conflict situation in this case is the arousal of anger and accompanying anxiety about retaliation. The precipitant was the therapist's "backing off" because of his own anxiety. The solution is to comply as a way of warding off anxiety about angry feelings. As noted earlier, any work on the historical issues without a prior consideration of the dynamics of the compliant solution will provide mythical insights. Furthermore, such therapist behavior simply confirms the client's hypothesis that men like compliant women, which intensifies the client's anger. The anger finds indirect expression. Compliance is invoked as a defense against anxiety about anger and as an expression of the anger. The character defenses are still in place.

To attend to the compliance in straightforward language, however, will probably do no more than intensify the client's compliance; it is akin to telling a complying client that she is complying. The choices open to the client are limited. She can contend that she is not complying, in which case she is resisting. The more likely response in a compliant client is to respond compliantly, "Yes, I see that."

The therapist must help the client to note the events precipitating the feelings of anger during the therapeutic session, the arousal of conflict, and the solution. In helping the client to see how her anxiety is converted into compliance, the therapist uses the client's productions as his guide. But the therapist needs to go beyond his own insights. He must help the client to see how he learned what he did from the themes in the client's productions and her associations to symbolic material. In that way, the client senses her own inner processes, learns to listen to herself, and can turn to advantage what may have seemed chaotic and overwhelming.

A productive therapist goal is to constantly help the client to monitor her inner life and develop her resources. Such a therapist attitude may find expression in keeping the client involved in the process every step of the way. For example: "In what you have told me, do you see how that works in you? You experience a flash of anger and anticipate rebuff, so you pull back, which just frustrates you." The dynamic core—the experience at the felt level, the prediction, and the solution—must be addressed simultaneously, or the glimmerings of emotional insight are lost until the frustration intensifies again.

This is not to say that the compliance will evaporate. But the seed is planted, and the client may over time note her compliance before the therapist does. If the client simply notes her compliance, her observation may still be a defensive, compliant maneuver. But if she notes her compliance, reintroduces the conflict situation, and works on it, that may be an index of progress and of genuine emotional insight.

Compliance and Willfulness

Compliance also has strong self-preservation aspects. Chodoff (1982) noted that the hysteric's submissiveness may actually belie her willfulness. Or, as Farber (1966) observed, the hysteric's apparent compliance is in fact a willful noncompliance that precludes subjugating herself to parents and teachers. Despite the negative effects that such willfulness may have on the hysteric's learning, that opposition of wills is to some extent what saves the hysteric. The hysteric must resist, for to do otherwise is to lose her individuality. The phenomenon of resisting the will of another is generally evident in psychotherapeutic work with clients whose behavior is sometimes construed as "self-defeating."

One often sees students who continue to fail in their academic work despite what seems to be an intact and high-level intelligence. To construe such behavior as "self-defeating" misses a core issue. The behavior should properly be called self-enhancing, because dynamically the student cannot afford to succeed. In studying such cases, one can often uncover a central dynamic issue and an inner equation: to succeed is to fail, or success equals castration. Often the student's parents have pushed the student to succeed, and conflicts over resistance, resentment, self-assertion, and individuation become attached to academic performance. Succeeding means submitting, "giving in," and is the dynamic equivalent of self-effacement. Admittedly, the student is waging autonomy wars in the wrong arena and with undesirable outcomes, but until those matters are rectified in psychotherapy, the fight itself is emotionally healthier than the dynamic implications of submitting.

This same dynamic—performance being equated with submission—is a central issue in work with the hysterical client. A variation of this same resistance is evident in the hysteric's reports of her sexual activities, her inability to reach orgasm, or her frigidity. If the male partner pushes for sexual activity, he directly confronts the hysteric's willfulness. In a similar way, the client's resistance to accepting the therapist's theories and interpretations is dynamically determined by what acceptance means, that is, submission. As such, it is healthy resistance. The hysteric must resist; else she is the castrate. The developmental picture clearly indicates that the mother of the hysteric submitted to the demands of the father, only to find herself faceless and, ironically, the object of his disdain. That is what the hysteric foresees for herself and what contributes in part to her disaffiliation with the mother. But she sees herself as having limited alternatives. If she resists submitting, she arouses male defensiveness and anger. If she submits, she loses herself and risks rejection for her trouble.

Within the confines of the alternatives she sees available to her, the hysteric often attempts to work out a compromise solution. She may symbolically offer to comply if the therapist will bend a bit in return. Because of her intense interest in achieving mutuality in relationships, the hysteric will attend closely to the therapist's needs and may "go along with" the therapist in the hope of negotiating something reciprocal. Compliance is construed as holding promise of such mutuality, despite its risks. In complying, the hysteric hopes that the therapist will comply in return—admittedly something less than ideal mutuality, but then the hysteric has not had much practice with solid relationships.

Because she lacks practice in how to achieve a mutually satisfying relationship, the hysteric may attempt to achieve mutuality in ways that confuse the therapist. She may interpret the desired therapist response as one of accepting her neurosis or hysterical behaviors, of changing his therapeutic stance, or of helping her avoid her anxieties. If the therapist misses the motive and responds to the inappropriateness of its expression, he may consider the client's demands as resistance to change or

attempted manipulation. In contrast, if the therapist understands the client's demands as dynamically determined resistance to being the one who must always submit, then he may
approach his client with a more respectiful attitude and "mutually" work with her on how to achieve a more mature
mutuality.

FURTHER CONDITIONS OF THE RELATIONSHIP

Eventually, the hysterical client will touch on some oedipal issues. In some hysterical clients those issues are encapsulated
and surface only after some character defenses are addressed
and anger is spent. In others, however, the rumblings of oedipal fantasies emerge early in sessions. Such fantasies are sometimes evident in the client's obsessive complaints about the
mother, in competitive attitudes toward female associates, or in
a supercilious attitude about women in general.

In early sessions, intermixed with her expression of anger at
males, the hysteric may report much material about a disastrous
relationship with her mother. In her reports, the mother may
be variously perceived as inadequate, cowering, a seemingly resigned woman who is the "doormat" of the family and servant
to the father. Alternately, the client may allude to the mother's
apparent threatened position in the family, describing vividly
her nagging, "hysterical" behaviors and controlling attitudes.
The mother invariably emerges as a woman who was inadequate and insubstantial.

As noted in Chapter Two, these perceptions have considerable validity because of the insufficiency of the mother to counter
the dominant, overbearing paternal figure and protect the
daughter. More damaging was the mother's collusion with the
father to rebind the daughter for the sake of the mother's security. Those conditions partially explain the client's anger at the
mother. But the client's motives are mixed. Her collusion with
the father was not without its pleasurable side, and that neurotic wish for exclusiveness with the father colors the client's
disparaging attitude toward the mother.

As Blinder (1966) noted, the mothers of hysterics have been too busy with their own conflicts to attend to the needs of the daughters. But the attribution of cold, remote, and depriving does not characterize their underlying trends. The mothers' neuroses interfered, but often the submerged substance in those mothers surfaces later in therapy. In fact, it is often the mother's ''push–pull'' in relation to the daughter that seems to lead to the daughter's mixed feelings of anger, guilt, disdain, and concern for the mother's welfare.

It was observed earlier that the therapist should be cautious in interpreting the meaning of the maternal picture in hysterical development. If the therapist accepts the client's compelling picture of the mothering one as depriving when in fact the client's motivations are oedipally determined, the course of psychotherapy may be delayed. A number of dynamic consequences accrue from a mistaken assessment of this crucial issue. Krohn's observation (1978) that the misdiagnosis of oral fantasies reinforces hysterical defenses is applicable. In addition, the potential symbolic collusion in such a misconstruction, briefly mentioned, is worthy of expansion.

In symbolically colluding as the father did in ''up-ending'' the mother, the therapist perpetuates and exacerbates the client's oedipal conflicts, inducing guilt, reinforcing passive defenses, and delaying movement during therapy (see Kell and Mueller 1966, pp. 50–53). One can sometimes hear a therapist wondering why the client seems more depressed, angry, or resistant. Unwittingly, the therapist has re-created the oedipal scene and contributed to the very reasons why the client is emotionally fixated at that stage, because identification with the mother is a critical factor in resolution.

If the hysterical client has elicited collusion in a male therapist, she has symbolically gained an excluding and exclusive relationship with the father, and her second state is worse than the first. Dynamically, the client cannot experience her feelings toward the male therapist because she is without the safeguard of a female figure in fantasy. The male therapist has come to represent the oedipal father, and although she sought exclusiveness, what should have remained at the wish-fulfilling, fantasy level has become ''real.''

The dynamic effect of such a collusion is to inhibit the resolution of conflict, because client and therapist have ridded themselves of any safeguard to the ensuing erotic feelings that are aroused by the collusion. Without a mother figure in fantasy, the biological mother or a surrogate, the hysteric is unable to experience sexual feelings without anxiety. Dynamically, her passive defenses must intensify. As a corollary to the arousal of sexual anxiety, the collusion is bound to generate oedipal guilt, because the hysteric has been partially motivated in her intrusive fantasies to supplant the mother. So she may be compelled to leave therapy or to displace those feelings and act out. At best, she may develop angry feelings toward the therapist for his role in binding her and stimulating guilt.

Besides the collusive aspects, the hysteric's motivation for introducing material about the mother's insufficiencies is to set herself apart from the mother, whom the father may have openly disdained. Essentially, the hysterical client carries with her the belief that was instilled in childhood: to receive the attention of the father, she must disavow any allegiance to the mother. If the therapist works to help the client to separate from the mother under conditions in which she equates winning male favor with disaffiliating with the mother, the therapist binds her strongly. To ally herself with the male, she must contend that "she isn't like other women." In so doing, the hysteric sacrifices the prospects of achieving a solid identity. The maze she finds herself in has no escape. It is not surprising that the female client becomes depressed at her prospects of achieving mutually satisfying relationships with men.

Developmentally, an identification with the mothering one allows the father–daughter relationship to run its course and eventually to generalize to other male relationships. In general, the male therapist has an advantage if the client holds a maternal figure in fantasy during his work with her. Otherwise, the male therapist is attempting the dynamic feat of settling oedipal issues without a supporting internal representative to assist the hysteric in traversing the stresses of that period. Initially, the male therapist is better advised to leave the client to her own devices with regard to her problems with her mother and attend to understanding the client's relationship to the father. Through it he may learn why the client found it necessary to divide her loyalties to win the heart of the father.

Hysterics, however, despite fuzziness in some areas, are rather clear-headed thinkers, and one often hears the hysterical client search for a strong maternal figure in her environment. That person may be unaware of the hysteric's intention of making a mother of her. When such a female appears on the hysteric's horizon during psychotherapy, the therapist must attend closely to the dynamic issues in that relationship. The hysteric, in her ambivalence, may introduce the relationship in ways that suggest that she is being exploited, that the woman is destructive, or the like. That relationship, however, often is one in which the hysterical client attempts to bridge the chasm in her relationship to her mother so that she can get on with settling matters with her father. The therapist must search through her ambivalences with her and interpret her conflicts in that relationship. He must, in short, help her to bond with a woman and interpret her resistance to doing so.

Often the hysteric produces material—dreams, stories, reports of ongoing relationships—that reflects mixed feelings about the women in her life. If the therapist interprets the distortions, inconsistencies, and projections in those reports, he may elicit anger, but he will put the hysteric at ease. Only when the hysterical client feels that the therapist does not want to possess her and that he has an appreciation for her female relationships can she experience her feelings of wanting exclusiveness with him, of feeling attracted to him, and perhaps wondering what he feels about her. The safeguards are in place, so both can proceed to help the client resolve her conflicts.

In an ongoing relationship with a female friend, the client will often set up a "maternal" counterpart to the "paternal" therapist. The client may report that she discusses "everything that happens" in therapy with her female friend. If the therapist construes this as a defensive maneuver, a diffusion of affect, a splitting of the transference perhaps, he misses the point. The client is not acting out or displacing emotional components of conflict outward; rather, she is reworking the conditions within development wherein she had to divide her allegiance. In accepting the client's need for such a confidante and in taking a nondefensive stance, the therapist has already countered the emotional conditions of the past. He has provided the "corrective emotional experience" (Alexander 1946b, p. 66) and therapy is on a solid course.

A BRIEF ENCOUNTER
WITH COUNTERTRANSFERENCE ISSUES

In the same way that the hysterical client may attempt to elicit collusion in dismissing her mother and female relationships, she may attempt to arouse competitive, intrusive attitudes in the therapist about her male relationships. Often such a client's reports will include interactions in which she felt victimized by self-serving males. Alternately, she may describe interactions in which the male was impotent, weak, or overly dependent. The competition-arousing aspects of those reports seem to be a central dynamic. How the therapist responds to such seemingly insensitive men may be a crucial factor in the hysteric's progress.

If the therapist becomes angry at the client's victimized state or attempts to help her break the ties of one or another of those apparently destructive relationships, all is lost. The therapist in essence sets himself up as the client's savior, and hysterics don't really want to be rescued; in fact, it is the male notion that he can rescue the hysteric that sets off her anger. Such a notion says much about the savior's sense of his own omnipotence— a characteristic that the hysteric has encountered in many settings during development.

It has been observed by Allen (1977) and Chodoff (1982) that the hysteric may unsuccessfully seek complete gratification in a series of relationships with men. In the present case, however, the therapist has set himself up as the one to gratify the client by becoming inappropriately intrusive into the client's relationships. Instead of helping the client to explore the meaning of those relationships in relation to her own dynamics, the therapist has taken over her ego functions. More than likely, his own unconscious fantasies—for example, that he is the better man—have motivated his behavior.

The hysteric will most assuredly lean on the therapist who thinks he can rescue her, and in short order the therapist will wish that he had never taken such a role. The hysteric may proceed to break off her male relationships, both for reasons of the exclusiveness that the therapist's protective mantle implies and as an expression of anger at the "ego" of the therapist in his setting himself up as savior. The refrain of "do something" that characterized early sessions will be replaced by the lament of "broken promises." The hysteric will report that her situation has worsened and that she feels alone and withdrawn socially. Demands will increase, and the therapist's own countertransference will have caught him on the horns of the hysteric's "omnipotence and helplessness" dilemma (Allen 1977, p. 297).

At such times, interpretations of the hysteric's reactions in terms of past "broken promises" are meaningless and defensive. Construing the hysteric's reactions as transference phenomena will simply help to spiral the therapeutic relationship into a deeper morass, because the issue is one of countertransference. The only hope for the hysteric is the self-awareness of the therapist. If the therapist retrospectively sees what he got himself into, he has hope and so does his client. Not out of guilt or shame, but rather out of a sense of realization, can he extricate himself.

As noted earlier, Halleck (1967) observed that in work with a hysterical client, the therapist must be "rigidly honest" and that through his honesty the client learns "that she, too, can be honest" (p. 756). In this case, through self-awareness, the therapist can honestly approach matters from the perspective of using what transpired in sessions as a guide to the way in which conflict is aroused in his client. Such honesty the hysterical client can respect. Among other things, it doesn't place blame; it simply states that through their interactions, certain dynamics have become clearer. It is nondefensive and centered in the client's conflicts, it does not deny the therapist's personality or his brushes with omnipotence, and it is respectful of the client.

By assessing the sequence of events in the relationship, the therapist arrives at a vivid picture of the factors generating conflict in the client as well as an insight into the dynamic processes of conflict (Kell and Mueller 1966), because they have been replayed with himself as a principal. Using what happened productively to help the client discard a central belief about male relationships is the therapeutic goal. "Using what happened productively" means that the therapist must be open to admitting his own suggestibility without guilt or defensiveness, and different therapists may attend to those matters in varying ways with clients.

Clearly perceiving the events of sessions and recognizing his own stimulus value is itself freeing to the therapist, because he is not trapped within the confines of his own countertransference. Once free, the therapist can approach matters within his own style. His hysterical client will be relieved, because she generally sees things more easily than others anyway and will probably readily forgive and attempt to renegotiate the relationship on firmer ground.

When the therapist decides to confront the issue of what transpired during therapeutic sessions, in whatever way he deems most suitable, he has regained the therapist's chair. Through his confrontation of the issues, the therapist communicates his regard for wanting to assist the client, he takes appropriate responsibility for himself, he acknowledges the client as a person who can cope with her anxieties, and he credits his client with having an impact on him. The net result is that the client feels more substance and recognizes the therapist's strength in his self-awareness. And only in the presence of someone with self-awareness can the hysterical client afford the risks of becoming self-aware.

The hysteric, after all, does want a therapist. And she is likely to forgive mistakes if she feels the concern is with her health. She may even learn something about human relationships and how errors can be turned to her advantage. Among other things, she will learn that she does have an impact in relationships and that what she says and does is considered worthy of exploration. Under such conditions she may even attempt another male relationship on healthier, more mutual grounds, because she has learned that she has certain rights in relationships and that her anger may be justified. She will have received some affirmation of herself as a thinking, feeling person—teachings that unfortunately did not grace her development.

Chapter Five

The Thematic Productions

RECURRENT THEMES IN PSYCHOTHERAPY

In Chapter Three, some of the recurrent themes and displacements that characterize the disturbed relationships of the adult hysteric were introduced. In this chapter we reintroduce those themes. The focus is on the guidelines those themes provide for appropriate psychotherapeutic interventions. Similarly, the displaced character of the hysteric's relationships guides the therapist in understanding the dynamics of conflict as they are replayed in those relationships. Further, in following the client's movement into and out of specific relationships during psychotherapy and the changing themes of those relationships, the therapist is guided in understanding the processes of conflict in the client. Of particular significance, the emotional conditions that the client reports in those relationships often reflect the client's reactions to therapy and the therapist.

In psychotherapeutic work with the hysterical client, themes of responsibility and control, insubstantiality, sexuality, and mutuality recur with regularity. Embedded in those themes are issues of trust, commitment, honesty, intensity, and feelings of being unprepared for life. Those themes have their bases in the developmental conflicts that were described earlier. They find their expression in the many disturbed relationships of the client. And they find their way into the psychotherapeutic relationship with unerring certainty.

The themes are multifaceted. They simultaneously represent the conflict, the defense, and the efforts to integrate what has been overwhelming. Taken at face value, the themes contribute to the pejorative attitudes about the hysterical personality. The hysteric may act irresponsibly, reflect an insubstantiality, and behave in sexually provocative ways. She may seek immediate gratification, thus confirming her insubstantiality. The defensive aspects and indirection of the hysteric's intentionality are often the stimulus for the disparaging attitudes about hysterics.

But a therapist is committed to understanding rather than simply reacting. At a deeper level, the themes subsume the hysterical style of communicating, that is, creating an empathic link with another. Through such thematic productions, the hysteric intends that the significant other feel what she feels, accept and understand the depth of her experience, and nondefensively accept appropriate responsibility for problems in a relationship. The task of the therapist is to counter the defensive aspects of the client's presentation of herself, search for the substance, and nondefensively acknowledge problems that occur in the therapeutic relationship.

RESPONSIBILITY AND CONTROL

No theme has been as overworked in therapy with hysterical clients as has the theme of control and responsibility. There certainly are issues of control in working with hysterical clients, and such clients can test a therapist's patience with their manifest irresponsible behavior. Halleck (1967) has appropriately pointed out some of the control issues that characterize initial sessions with a hysterical client, but often it is the therapist's own issues with control that perpetuate the theme beyond the initial hurdles with a hysterical client.

The hysterical client does have issues with control because of her developmental experiences. Often, however, the client's issues interlock with those of the therapist, and the two battle for control of the therapist's chair. If the therapist feels comfortable with the chair, many of those battles may be short-lived, because a hysterical client has more pressing issues about dependency, trust, and commitment. Those more crucial issues may be short-circuited by a preoccupation with "who is in control." In a general way, if the therapist simply sits back and assumes that the client has had severe problems in being controlled, and uses that understanding instead of reacting against the controlling behavior of the client, therapy may be set on a more productive course.

Essentially, the countertransference issues embedded in battles over control must be evaluated. In a later chapter describing the interlocking of transference and countertransference during psychotherapy, the deleterious effects of the preoccupation with control issues become evident. The issue of irresponsibility has the same overtones. If the therapist assumes that the client is irresponsible, the client will in all likelihood confirm the therapist's hypothesis and give him a good dose of irresponsible behavior. It is the hysterical client's immense sensitivity to a therapist's underlying attitudes about her (see Chodoff 1982) that triggers continued and escalating irresponsible behavior.

When the hysterical client enters psychotherapy, she brings with her a list of demands. She demands an intense, personal, and "real" relationship, one in which honesty and openness are emphasized. Her demands are supported by evidence of males who were capricious, self-centered, possessive, and rejecting. The hysteric's demands are often couched in "either-or" propositions. The therapist may be put off by the demands or attempt the impossible task of meeting them. In either case, the therapist has completely missed the hysteric's intentionality.

Several features of the histories of hysterics guide the therapist in intervening. The father of the hysteric invited a close relationship with the daughter, but it was contaminated by collusion and negotiated at the expense of any identification with the mother. The daughter was eventually threatened with rejection for her trouble, leaving her "hanging" with her feelings, feeling unprepared and left to try to mend walls with the mother. The family context was one in which communication was minimal. The mother was passive and used denial to avoid reading the impending disaster. The daughter read the signs clearly but was helpless in the face of the mother's denial and a pawn in the parents' indirection with each other.

Such irresponsible parental behavior underlies the client's search for an honest, open relationship—a relationship in which communication is highly valued. The wish for an intense relationship is countered by fears that history will repeat itself. The hysteric tries to mute her intensity; she tries not to be possessive or demanding in relationships. She treads lightly on the male ego. But the wish to relate outweighs the fear. And, because the hysteric feels that others do not freely give and that she is helpless to effect change in others, she demands. The hysteric wants a solid relationship but does not quite know how to define it. She has no guidelines. It becomes the therapist's responsibility to help her in that definition by being responsive to her in responsible ways.

Therapist behavior that is appropriate, without loss of compassion and humanness, is very relieving to a hysterical client. If a client asks to be seen twice weekly and the therapist explains to the client the reasons for maintaining weekly sessions, the client can accept the explanation if she feels that it is presented in a noncondescending way. If a client asks for an immediate solution to her problem and the therapist honestly informs her that her problems are complex and not to be treated superficially, the client will be encouraged by this respect for her.

These issues become very important if the client is seeing a male therapist because of her previous problematic encounters with men. In those relationships, matters were often settled on the male's terms. So when the therapist sets time limits on the relationship, it both is relieving to the client to know that the therapist is in control of himself, and also activates anger that this relationship, like the others, is determined by a male authority. Such matters, however, can be settled if the therapist is willing to explain to the client why those limits are essential to their work together.

Communication is one of the keys to successful work with a hysterical client. With any client it is important to monitor the relationship continually for evidence of communication breakdown, aroused resistance, and transference reactions. But with the hysterical client, communication takes on added meaning, particularly when the untoward effects of minimal communication in the home are considered. Clarity about the emotional conditions within the therapeutic relationship is an important, continuing concern. Such clarity does not entail the therapist's inquiring of the client how she is feeling toward him or their work unless the therapist senses some undercurrents that impede their work together.

A key factor in the communication process consists of the therapist's constant work to be clear with the client about why he took a particular direction, raised certain questions, or believed certain matters needed attention. The therapist makes clear that he is guided by the client's productions. The therapist does not condone a client's attributing mystical qualities to the interpretations that he makes, else they tend to empower the therapist and disenfranchise the client, increasing the client's sense of powerlessness and reinforcing externalization. Rather, the therapist lets the client know how he arrived at his interpretations based on her productions.

Through such measures the therapist tends to counter the client's external frame of reference and invites her participation in the process. Thus, the alliance is formed and some effective work can be done. Despite some initial resistance to the cooperative struggle, such an endeavor speaks to the healthy side of the client. Issues in communication are critical, as evident in the following case.

The client's parents had divorced when she was a preadolescent. The children were unaware of the extent of the parental discord, and the client was left with her fantasies about the problems. In loyalty to the mother, the client blamed the father for the divorce and ensuing problems. There had been a complete breakdown in communication with her father, and in an ongoing relationship to a male friend, there simply was no communication. When the client entered psychotherapy, honest, open, and reciprocal communication was her most prized ideal.

Because of content and associated affects of the first session, the therapist was sensitive to the need for honest communication if therapy was to be effective. When the client entered the second session, she wanted an immediate solution to her problems. The client asked to increase the number of weekly sessions. When the therapist suggested that they continue on a weekly basis, the client responded, "You're the therapist," which is a variant of "You're the boss." At the end of the session, the therapist had another opportunity to create a working alliance when the client asked for some advice on a decision she had made. The therapist told her that he felt that her problems were complex and that it would take time to work on them. In this case, the client felt that "was a good answer."

This particular client had a strong need to communicate and worked assiduously to facilitate the alliance. In a later session, when she was very distraught, the client commented that "I'm just trying to picture the way I look to you, right now. All you see is a tear-stained face, and I can't really give you any more insight because this is the way it is inside." The therapist responded, "I know that."

The intense need to communicate and to bond with someone became even clearer later. The client was an artist, and in describing an art form, she pointed to the therapist's telephone and noted the way that light and shadow fell on the two sides of the telephone. The client said that she would "work to death, I would just work and work until that phone looks great." The telephone symbolized the one-sided conversations that the client had had with her father and male friend and her hope for a two-way communication. Later, the client again expressed her anxiety about communicating. She commented that "If I cry, immediately afterwards, I tell you. If I'm laughing, I immediately tell you. It's sometimes hard when people don't do that, isn't it?''

At a later point in the same session, the client gained some insight into the emotional–cognitive split in herself. When the therapist commented that her insight was ''really good,'' the client responded, ''I mean, you helped me with that. I didn't do it on my own.'' And therein rests an issue in hysteria. The hysterical client needs someone to internalize, and she searches for guidelines.

The hysteric has not had guidelines, and she needs them. The therapist helps her to develop inner guidelines. In initial sessions the need for guidelines is often expressed through such externals as ''Can I smoke in here?'' or ''Can I put my feet up?'' Only later does the client begin to distinguish between feeling something and expressing the feeling appropriately without necessarily acting on it. In one case, a client whose relationship with her father had ruptured on a discordant note constantly asked what the rules were. In a later session, she brought an award she had received to show the therapist. While the therapist was reading the award, the client informed him that she had felt like coming around behind him and putting her arms around him to show it to him. The therapist thanked her for the very nice thought. The client had verbalized what she felt, had acted within the rules, and had received confirmation that her feelings were accepted and valued.

As therapy proceeds and the relationship deepens, the therapist maintains a steady course in facilitating the client's expanding self-awareness. If the client introduces a dream, for example, the therapist works intently with the client in discovering its meaning in relation to her problems. In helping the client to gain mastery over her inner processes, the therapist counters the client's previous experience of males who want to possess her or inhibit her expansive, assertive strivings. Such therapist behavior reduces the client's fears about becoming dependent, because dependency is redefined as a necessary condition for independence. If the client feels that the therapist is not preparing her to be his possession she will take the risk of regressing and reintegrating what has been poorly learned.

INSUBSTANTIALITY: A DISABLING CONCEPT

A client's irresponsible behavior reinforces her basic belief about herself—that she lacks substance. This belief has many developmental roots, which we have described. This self-image of insubstantiality is reinforced not only through irresponsible behavior, but also through acting out, immediate self-gratification, and a vague, global cognitive style (Shapiro 1965). Those defensive tactics ward off anxiety about being substantial and being the responsible one.

The issue here is that the client, on entrance into psychotherapy, conducts herself as though she were insubstantial, and an initial issue in psychotherapy is to counter that belief. The therapist who accedes to a client's wishes for extra or extended sessions or whose anxiety dictates an overly supportive attitude without supporting clinical data simply reinforces the client's feelings of insubstantiality. Under such circumstances, therapy is set on a tortuous course. In contrast, the therapist who "sits on" aroused anxiety, maintains a course based on a solid diagnosis, and resists the client's bids for an immediate anxiety-reducing panacea may profit in the long run from such consistent behavior.

From the very outset of psychotherapy, the therapist's general interpersonal stance is one of countering the hysteric's insubstantiality. Behavioral manifestations of the hysteric's feelings of insubstantiality are evident early in the development of the psychotherapeutic relationship. Although she may pay particular attention to the superficialities of dress and appearance, the hysteric may present her concerns in a vague, flighty, and disconnected manner. The denial of intentionality and responsibility is frequently expressed through such fatalistic statements as "I don't know. . .these things just happen to me." Despite the manifest press for an immediate solution, which counters feelings of substantiality, the hysteric wants to be treated like a real person in a genuine encounter; but she is conflicted about it.

The hysteric wants to be treated as a complex, thinking adult, but when responded to on that level, she acts like a little girl, wanting answers and resisting further exploration. Yet if the therapist accepts the invitation to treat her fragilely, she may show her disappointment and resentment by missing sessions. Following a progressive session in which the therapeutic relationship has intensified and her substantiality has been acknowledged, the hysteric may retreat to an indecisive, submissive, and docile posture. If the therapist retreats, however, the hysteric may introduce themes suggesting that she lacks challenges in her life.

The hysteric's tendency to act out behaviorally rather than express her feelings verbally not only reflects but also intensifies her conflicts regarding substantiality. For example, acting out through missing therapy sessions is viewed as irresponsible behavior and confirms character traits of insubstantiality. A psychodynamic treatment approach is aimed at helping the client express verbally those feelings she may act out, thus bringing into awareness the motivating factors underlying her behaviors and making them available for conscious control. The hysteric then learns the connections between feelings and behaviors, and this lays the groundwork for responsible action. Achieving this link counters externalization and the hysteric's belief that "these things just happen to me."

Through her acting out behavior and subsequent responses to the therapist's interpretations, the hysteric also presents a complex of interpersonal dynamics that reveal her core conflicts about substantiality. If the client misses a session on impulse with no "substantial" reason and the therapist excuses that behavior without a careful evaluation of its motivating forces in the client and its meaning for the psychotherapeutic relationship, he has colluded in the client's irresponsibility and confirmed her insubstantial character traits.

Such therapist behavior encourages continued acting out. Escalated acting out reflects the client's disappointment and anger with the therapist and fuels the belief that the therapist is weak and inconsistent. In her acting-out behaviors, the client attempts to mobilize the therapist to treat her seriously and to take appropriate responsibility for himself in relation to her. Halleck (1967) suggested that the therapist must be alert to a hysteric's dishonesty and repeatedly confront it. Indeed, the hysteric must learn to take responsibility for her thoughts and actions, but within an interpersonal framework her apparent irresponsibility also comunicates her feelings about the responsibility or lack thereof in the therapist. If therapy is to be successful, the therapist's interpersonal behavior must be consistent with his honest confrontations.

The theme of insubstantiality is often manifest in the hysteric's vague, global, and impressionistic cognitive style (Shapiro 1965). Her language in therapy may be replete with incomplete thoughts and expressions of "I don't know," which invite the therapist to complete her thoughts and sentences for her. But the therapist must resist the invitation to demonstrate that he presumes to know what has been left unsaid. Such a presumption reinforces the hysteric's insubstantial position in the relationship. In addition, although the therapist's presumptive behavior may be motivated by the wish to be empathic, he may in fact be allying himself with the client's unconscious neurotic wishes—an unspoken communion of the minds. And a collusion may be in the offing. A more therapeutic stance is to acknowledge the client's struggles and facilitate continued self-exploration.

One of Shapiro's contentions about the cognitive style of the hysteric (1965) is that the vague, global, and diffuse style functions as a repressive mechanism. The hysteric's incomplete thoughts represent only one small facet of the hysteric's problems with completing things. Often, the hysterical client reports that she was unable to finish a given task. She has the same difficulty with following through, and she tends to hold back. Often that difficulty is experienced in competitive situations. In a similar fashion, the hysteric does not allow herself to experience fully. Her feelings are truncated (Allen 1977). The hysteric likewise feels incomplete (Janet 1929), and she will return time and again to a former relationship because something in the relationship is unfinished.

The interlocking complex of dynamics that undergird and energize those various behavioral expressions and feeling states have their bases in the developmental patterns that have been described earlier. The point being made here is that subsumed under the theme of insubstantiality are issues that touch the very core of the hysterical personality. Intense anxiety and guilt are avoided through a self-perception of being an insubstantial person.

The extensive measures taken to avoid anxiety suggest compassion and patience be used by the therapist in the work to counter insubstantiality. The therapist's sensitivity to the interpersonal dynamics as they unfold within and across sessions is a precondition for working through a relationship that counters feelings of insubstantiality. The many ruptures in the hysteric's relationships contribute to her feelings. Her relationships frequently have ended on a disrupted note, and she is left with the feelings of incompleteness and of not being worth the time to work through a relationship. She experiences people as seeing only one side of her, often the smiling, easy-going, nurturant and cooperative. Eventually, the submerged, depressed, anruptive and are associated with ruptures in relationships. Ultimately, she cannot feel fully with one person.

During psychotherapy, the hysteric may initially be compliant and cooperative. Eventually, the submerged depressed, angry side may emerge and *she* may want to rupture the therapeutic relationship. The emergence of such feelings is a critical point in therapy, for old patterns can be reinforced or new patterns substituted, as shown in the following case.

The client was the daughter of a successful businessman. In her early childhood their relationship had been a solid one. It was based, however, in the daughter's loving attitude toward the father. The parents divorced when the daughter reached preadolescence. Following the divorce, her relationship with her father remained important to both of them. But when the daughter reached adolescence and became more rebellious, the father withdrew and remained distant. The conditions for a reunion were that the daughter acknowledge the importance of the father and cater to him and his new wife. The daughter resisted.

The rupture seemed irreparable. Despite many efforts on the

client's part to reawaken the relationship, work through their differences, and end it on a friendly note, the father was immovable. The client displaced her sense of incompleteness onto a relationship with a boyfriend. When the client wanted to intensify that relationship, the boyfriend told her that he wasn't ready for an intense relationship. The client remained in the relationship and tried to work out their differences. The male friend withdrew and informed the client that he didn't want to take the time to work things through.

In therapy the client interchanged her experience with the father and boyfriend frequently without insight into the parallelism between the two relationships. Often the therapist assumed that the client was discussing one of the significant figures only to discover under inquiry that she was describing an interaction with the other.

Often during sessions, when a particular issue was being discussed about some conflict the client was experiencing, the client would ask the therapist to go over a particular point a few more times, thus communicating her need for someone to be patient with her, show an interest in her, and take the time to work things through to completion.

The therapist felt that matters were proceeding well and that a solid relationship had been established. He was surprised when the client called before a session and said that therapy wasn't working and that she didn't feel she was being helped. A critical point in therapy had been reached.

Up to that time, the client had been "well-behaved." She had introduced relevant matters, had been intent on making progress, and seemed to be experiencing some emotional insights. Essentially, she had been the preadolescent who centered in the father and his needs. In her call, the client acted the role of the adolescent who had her own ideas about what she needed and wanted in relationships.

In his response to her, the therapist attempted to communicate respect for her wishes, acknowledge her feeling of not having made the progress she wanted, and also express his feeling that if therapy terminated before the client felt satisfied, she might feel the old sense of incompleteness. He suggested that they meet and try to hammer out their differences. The client appeared for the next session, and therapy proceeded on a better course.

In a general way, the immediate reactions of the hysterical client to many life situations reinforce her own and others' perception of her as insubstantial. Her immediate reactions are multidetermined, however, and they have various behavioral manifestations. One variation of the theme is evident in the formative stages of a relationship. As Allen (1977) noted, the hysterical client immediately includes the therapist as a significant other in her life. When the hysteric enters a relationship, she puts blinders on. Because of the series of disastrous relationships she has engaged in, the hysteric blinds herself to the possibility that this relationship may repeat that pattern. Her immediate reaction inhibits foresight, because foresight based on past experience would be depressing and disabling. But the hysteric's denial mechanism is faulty, for when a relationship ruptures, she can often point to specific conditions in the relationship that portended rupture.

When she enters psychotherapy, this same immediacy is evident. One client described herself as tired of being optimistic, stating that she had been foolishly optimistic in former relationships. Yet before the first session ended, she was buoyant about the prospects of therapy. Another client, within the opening moments of the first session, informed the therapist that she had been searching for a strong male all of her life and that she had now "found him." In those cases, it was as though the clients put all their doubts aside and plunged into the relationship to avoid the arousal of anxiety about the potential reality of disappointment.

Paradoxically, the hysterical client is immensely aware of the conditions in the relationship, despite her attempts at denying the reality conditions at the outset. As readily as the client's hopes are kindled, they can be extinguished. As one client noted, relationships start out "pretty good" and then fizzle. The therapist who is pleased by the client's buoyancy and anticipates an easy course is apt to be disappointed.

In a sense, the therapist's buoyancy is as mythical as is the client's sense of what constitutes a solid relationship. Such therapist anticipations about an easy, good client also set transference reactions into motion, because the client's history has been that of being the good girl. To some extent, the therapeutic task is to help the client modify her polarized views through sensitivity to her changing feelings toward the therapist and therapy. As those feelings change, and they inevitably must, the therapist takes responsibility to address them and searches with the client for the conditions of the relationship that triggered them. Such action provides the opportunity to trace them to their sources. In the process, the client begins to gather a more realistic sense of how the stresses in a relationship, and open communication, can be beneficial.

If the immediately responsive client becomes dissatisfied, the therapist's reactions are crucial determinants of the potential for progress. Whether the therapist feels disappointed or hurt is, in itself, not the telling issue. It is through the awareness of those feelings and by seeing how the events in the relationship paralleled the client's history that the therapist becomes free to use those feelings appropriately for the client's benefit. It is through being hurt and disappointed but unaware of the stimulating circumstances that the therapist's countertransference becomes an open book. In such circumstances, the client is burdened with responsibility for the therapist's feelings, and history has repeated itself.

The issue of immediacy takes other forms as well. It seems that often after an initial session in which the client has painfully reviewed her history, the therapist receives an urgent call. In her call, the client may suggest that her anxiety is intense, that she feels immobilized, helpless, and unable to cope. In one respect, such behavior reinforces the insubstantial view of the hysteric. The defensive function of such behavior is partially that of derailing the therapist from the task ahead. If the therapist's anxiety dictates a precipitous response, therapy may be set on a course of continual crises.

In fact, the urgent call may reflect the therapist's first brush with anger in the client. In the initial session a client is often expected to reveal her history, recite the many failures that she has experienced, and in other ways expose herself to a stranger who is perhaps relatively silent. When the client leaves the session, she may have some afterthoughts about the performance that she went through without any guarantees that matters would be better for her trouble.

Many hysterical clients begin the following session with some curiosities about the therapist, what was discovered about her, and what can be done for her. In a sense, her reactions suggest a kind of parallel play. The client performed in the first session, and the time has come for the therapist to perform. The therapist's performance will be a poor one, indeed, if the client's reactions are experienced as demands and efforts to control therapy. The client's concerns are understandable, and a therapist who is sensitive to the underlying motives may be able to respond in a way that addresses those anxieties.

No theme more clearly reflects the outcomes of the developmental conflicts and intrafamilial dynamics than does the theme of being unprepared. The hysteric may report that she lacks experience in practical matters, that she can't "make things work," and that others have expectations of her that are beyond her sense of readiness. She may feel that she is only good in, for example, art. She may have panic reactions when she has lost the safety of a dependent role. Behaviorally, such developmental milestones as college graduation or a job promotion may be delayed because the client feels that she is not ready to make decisions or compete successfully. Those reactions are accompanied by such feelings as defenselessness, vulnerability, and inadequacy.

During development, the hysteric centered in others and catered to their needs. Her own development was sacrificed. Neither parent was adequate to help her with her day-to-day developmental anxieties, nor did they treat her as though she were a person of intrinsic worth. Promises of security for the self-sacrifices the daughter made were often illusory. One father promised his daughter that if she gave up her outside interests and played the piano, he would take care of her. She did so. He later divorced the mother and remarried, and the promised support was redirected from the daughter to the second wife.

In another case, when the daughter brought some practical problem to the father, he would take over and complete the task. In itself, such behavior is not noteworthy. But the father was a self-aggrandizing man and his possessiveness became manifest at the daughter's adolescence. In his taking over the task instead of helping the daughter to develop her own skills, he fostered an unhealthy dependence on him. And whenever the daughter made a bid for independence, he would draw her back into the net. But when the time came, the father satisfied his needs, divorcing the mother and remarrying. As for the daughter, despite her drives for assertiveness and independence, she would become panic stricken at the thought of being on her own.

The father of the hysteric is not a man to be argued with, nor is he a man who likes his territory invaded. He often makes clear distinctions between the male and female roles and is volatile enough to override opposition. Within that context, the hysteric learns that she had better not tamper with his brittle, masculine exterior. Repeatedly, hysterical clients attach their sense of powerlessness to such phenomena as the father holding "all the marbles," having the "money," or, as one client put it who had a sexual orientation toward most things in life, the man's "ego is in his penis."

The father of the hysteric teaches her that rationality is a man's world. When she attempts to argue with him on rational grounds, she arouses his anger. When she becomes emotional, she is the object of his disdain. She can't win and, at a conscious level, may experience herself as irrational and may reinforce the belief by having difficulty in such disciplines as mathematics. But there is an interesting dynamic at play in such outcomes. Blacker and Tupin (1977), in describing a pseudofeminine adaptation, noted that the expression of aggression includes "subtle, indirect manipulation" and includes among other characteristics being "competitive with males" and provoking "guilt in others" (p. 125). In one case, the daughter of a man who stereotyped roles would take her mathematics problems to the father and incense him with her ineptitude. Eventually, the daughter far outdistanced the father in the field.

Earlier in this chapter, it was observed that the hysterical client feels incomplete. Such feelings are rooted in part in the stereotypical way in which the cognitive and affective components were divided within the family. It is often observed that hysterics perform poorly in the sciences. Such poor performances are not a function of a disability; those parts were not only negatively reinforced, but, in view of the paternal attitude, were also sources of considerable anxiety.

The therapeutic stance follows from the developmental experience. In his work with a hysterical client, the therapist avoids taking over, whether in completing the client's sentences or in being the one who has the insights. The therapist gains his satisfaction from observing the client's insights, and struggles with the client in her increasing awareness of her inner processes. The therapist allows the client to experience anxiety, but then he helps her to discover its sources and disabling manifestations in relationships. The therapist responds to the client's feelings of confusion, her "ups and downs," in a consistent way. He does not demand that she be pleasant and unconfused; he assumes that she will be confused and that that is part of the growth process. But he also recognizes that he must counter the developmental picture of letting her do the job herself.

In the therapeutic process, the therapist accepts the client's many mood swings and works with her to integrate the experiences that trigger them. But he also works to facilitate the integration of the cognitive–affective division. In a sense, to achieve a sense of being complete, the hysteric must find both components in the therapist. If the therapist is cognitive and the client affective, he complements her but does not provide the means for integration. If the therapist is affective and predominantly elicits and responds to the feeling side of the client, he reflects her, and the client's thirst for cognitive mastery remains untouched. In either case the client is left feeling incomplete. If, however, the therapist accepts himself as a thinking and feeling person, then he can provide the client with an integration of the bifurcated parental introjects.

THE THEME OF SEXUALITY:
ROADBLOCK TO THERAPY

The theme of sexuality is probably one of the most prominent features in the literature about hysteria. Its manifestations in dress, body language, and provocative behavior are well known, as are the substitutive functions it serves. The hysteric may use sex to express her hostility, confirm attitudes about males, and hold a man and negotiate relationships (see, e.g., Halleck 1967, Hollender 1971). From the family patterns described earlier, it can be seen that the hysteric's preoccupation with sexuality and her attitudes about it have been deeply ingrained.

In a very real way, the father's preoccupation with sexuality, coupled with his self-centeredness, sets the stage for the hysteric's own preoccupation with sexuality. Her sensitivity to his motives in marital discord, his seductiveness, his aggressively possessive stance when she turned to other males, and his sexualization of the hysteric's motives in those relationships were features of her development. Those factors combine to make sensuous, seductive behavior a survival technique for the hysteric. The issue remains the same in cases in which the client is promiscuous and uses sexuality as a medium for expressing her hostility and resentment or as a way of negotiating relationships.

The client has attached her conflicts to an external representative of those conflicts and attempts to achieve need satisfaction and neurotic gratification through the external representation. Sexuality happens to be the modality. But it is the externalization of conflict, and not the contents, that represents the roadblock to therapy. Most therapists do not directly attack symptoms, because this nets little return. So why should a therapist call attention to the hysteric's sensuous, provocative behavior? It is akin to telling an obsessive client that the client is obsessing. Both therapist and client can obsess about the client's obsessiveness with markedly little gain.

There is a decided difference between a therapist's communicating concern about the hysterical client's promiscuity because of concerns about her welfare, and the therapist who points out to a client that she is behaving provocatively. The former response registers as an honest concern about her; the latter response is received as an unhelpful condemnation unless the relationship is on solid ground and the therapist's observations are coupled with a discussion of the way in which her basic needs are thwarted through such behavior.

Because the hysterical client's many conflicts are externalized and attached to the body, the therapist might better spend his time attending to those underlying conflicts. Halleck (1967) observed that, despite the literature reports to the contrary, most hysterics do convert. The hysteric's preoccupation with sexuality can be viewed as a conversion of her needs to a bodily representation of those needs. Following from such a construction, the therapeutic stance is one of attending to the hysteric's sexual conflicts as symptomatic of the distortion of needs for affection and power. In putting sexuality into perspective, the therapeutic guidelines become clearer.

In early sessions, attendance to sexual cues is relegated to a minor position. Countering insubstantiality is primary. Only after the hysterical client has a sense of her own substance, feels some power in the therapeutic relationship, and experiences the therapist as responsibly responsive will sexual matters reappear, and their reemergence will have genital overtones. In a case to be discussed in a later chapter, this sequence of events seems to occur naturally, as it would in development.

THE THERAPIST'S ATTITUDE OF MUTUALITY AND RESPECT

The working through of a therapy relationship with a hysterical client is guided by the theme of mutuality. Interpersonal mutuality provides the experiential context in which the hysteric can discover her own substance. Mutuality does not mean that the therapist capriciously reveals his inner feelings or details his personal life. Such pseudomutuality is at best an expression of the therapist's own countertransference issues. Therapeutic mutuality means that the thoughts and feelings of the client and therapist are equally valid and important (Fromm-Reichmann 1950), that the hysterical client has something to give to the relationship, and that she is capable of insight. In this sense, mutuality counters the client's feelings of inner emptiness.

That the therapist respects her may be a new concept for the hysteric. When the client learns through her interaction with a significant other that the difficulties in relationships are not always her problem, and furthermore that her sensitivity may open the path toward resolution, she then can begin to experience her inner substance. Within a mutual therapeutic relationship, the client's personal development is the primary goal, but the therapist works with the awareness that he too grows through his contacts with her (see Kell and Mueller 1966).

The following report may illustrate the way in which a therapist's respect for the client and the validity of her feelings provided the client with the opportunity to experience herself differently. The report also reflects the subtleties of the therapeutic relationship and the highly perceptive sensors of the hysterical client.

The client was a very intelligent woman who had fought a losing battle to assert herself with the man she married. The marriage had been something of a disaster for the client. She perceived her husband as a strong but self-centered man who had abandoned her rather capriciously and without warning for another woman. One of the poignant issues in the marriage was that the client was left with the feeling that the husband didn't care enough to fight with her. When she entered psychotherapy, the client was still searching for a strong man but held the opinion that she had to submerge her own awareness to survive such a relationship, or settle for something less. Accordingly, she swore off commitments and became anxious when a relationship intensified.

After a considerable time in therapy, the client began to experience herself as ready to commit herself to a relationship with a strong, competent man. In attending to the client's discussion of her readiness to do so, the therapist lit a cigarette and pushed his chair back. Shortly thereafter, the client became increasingly vague and confused, and left the session with a feeling of being "disconnected." Prior to her next scheduled appointment, the client called for an emergency session, during which she appeared depressed and angry. She complained of feeling disconnected, out of control, and helpless. The therapist pursued her feelings of anger, exhorting her to be clear about what she was feeling toward him. The session ended with the client being frustrated.

In reviewing the sessions to discover what might have precipitated the client's hopeless and disconnected feeling, the therapist recognized that by reaching for a cigarette and pushing his chair back at the very time that the client was talking about commitments, he might have communicated his anxiety about being the strong and competent man in their relationship. Essentially, the therapist backed off at the time when the client needed his strength if she was to deepen the relationship and pursue conflictual material.

In the following session, the therapist acknowledged that the client might have recognized feelings that he was experiencing but unaware of. The client responded positively and made the connection between her hopeless and disconnected feeling and the therapist's pulling away from her. After the validity of the client's perception was acknowledged, she discovered the connection between her distraught feelings and the therapist's behavior, and in doing so experienced her own substantiality. Furthermore, through his interaction with the client, the therapist learned something about his own psychological processes, and the therapy relationship moved to a deeper level of exploration.

DISPLACEMENT AS A GUIDE
TO THE DYNAMICS OF CONFLICT

Many of the themes that have been discussed so far find their expression in the conflicted relationships of the hysterical client.

Those relationships serve as carrier waves for the residual conflicts from development. The emotional themes and the interactions in those relationships provide a clear dynamic reproduction of the client's history, the serial order of those relationships often reflects the developmental process itself, and the introduction of conflict in relationships and their changing nature reflect the processes of psychotherapy and the therapeutic relationship. In this section, each of these aspects will be considered from the perspective of their value in assessment and their potential for guiding therapeutic interventions. The nature of the hysterical client's displacements has been described in Chapter Three; this section will address applications of those ideas to case material, with running commentaries.

The client began the first session as many hysterical clients do. For the first few minutes, she attempted to be rational and present some demographic material about herself and her family. The orderly, rational approach was quickly overcome by the emotional press of the moment, and her cognitive style seemed typically hysterical. She had an artistic temperament but lacked cognitive skills. Her style was evident in an interesting variant of the repressive mechanism. She commented that "I didn't really remember that I wanted to study" some field of former interest. Her decision to change fields was impulsive—"I didn't think twice about it"—and that decision was based on impressions rather than facts. The client felt that she was too emotional, that she had difficulty in "carrying through" with things, and that she "wasted time" because of her scattered behavior and lack of control.

Almost immediately, the client moved to her problems in relationships with men. Several years prior, she had experienced a highly romanticized relationship—one that was a considerable contrast to the ongoing, stressful relationship that contributed to her seeking therapy. When she felt insecure, the client would reminisce about that romance. She felt that the current relationship was destructive to her and her rational side argued to terminate it, but she found herself continually returning to the relationship after ruptures. Her goal was to change the man so that he would "act the certain way that I want" and treat her with "respect."

In the relationship the client felt that she gave a great deal but received little in return. She perceived sex to be the primary bond that held the male's interest. Her beau disdained her emotionality and was critical of her intellect, yet he wanted her to perform with unbridled freedom when they engaged in sexual activities. But when the client wanted to set some ground rules and define their relationship, he resisted. After they spent a weekend together, which the client construed as an invitation to intensify the relationship, the man voiced his fears that the relationship might get too intense. The client mimicked his response: "Let's not get too intense."

Despite the apparent manifest behavior to the contrary, the client felt that there was an emotional bond between them. But she couldn't explain why she continually returned to the relationship—or why the man did. She felt that because of her vulnerability in relation to him, he didn't "have to put that much emotion" into the relationship. When she attempted to communicate her feelings and clear the air, he would become angry and convert her wishes into demands and possessiveness. The client lived in the fear that if she was clear about what she needed, he would vanish because he was "dead set in his ways" and she was "not worth it to him to work on my own grounds."

She felt that her lover was sensitive only to himself and his needs and that whenever she wanted to work on the relationship, it was "asking too much. . .demanding too much of him." The client didn't want to be demanding or attempt to "force him to love me. And at the same time, by not forcing him, I'm not happy. I'm dissatisfied." Everything the client attempted was construed as pressuring the man, and the client desperately wanted to know that "I fulfill certain needs for him. I know I fulfill his sexual needs. That's all I think I do." And the client then questioned her ability to communicate and her personal worth.

The client admitted to becoming possessive when she became insecure, which she felt led to her downfall. Another, more experienced woman, with better communication skills, entered the scene. The threat the client experienced was that the male friend did not "respect me like he respects her, and that's threatening. That's upsetting. I feel worthless." She then went on to note that the boyfriend was "critical of aspects of her personality" which left her feeling "tormented," and the relationship remained an open wound. Contrary to his view of the other woman, the boyfriend would tell the client that she was "pretty," which upset the client. She didn't "want to hear that." She wanted to know that she was intelligent, a good conversationalist, and that she could be fun. She felt the man didn't "know the real me."

Earlier, the relationship had been a more loving one. The client attributed the changing character of the relationship to a particular time when she decided to pursue her education at a university that would put distance between them. The decision was partly a function of pressure from her mother, who didn't like the boyfriend. The male friend "felt very rejected" because she "couldn't change her life around" to be with him. The client said that she "felt bad. . .that he felt rejected, but I wasn't rejecting him." She attributed to loneliness his turning to another woman who was "everything to him," whereas she couldn't "offer him everything."

At a later point in the session, the therapist inquired about her family relationships. The parents had divorced during her latency period. Her father had "turned off" to her completely. She saw him as an immature man who couldn't "handle a relationship. . .an emotional relationship" with her, and he wanted to "cut off emotional ties." As a consequence of his hardened attitude, the client was "becoming hardened, too, in many ways." She described the father as being a "very, very sensitive guy. And at the same time, he seems to be sensitive only to himself." The client commented that her mother was a "very emotional" person who was becoming "increasingly anxious" and whose life was in disorder. Since the parents had divorced, the mother had turned to the children as her only outlet, and the client felt this put intense pressure on her.

The client was responsive to the therapist's inquiries into the conditions within the family, but her anxieties, anger, and general distraught state about her involvement in the ongoing relationship were her foremost concerns. After a brief interlude in which she cooperated in providing the therapist with a sketch of the family situation, the client returned to her preoccupation with her ongoing relationship.

In some respects, this interview typifies an initial interview with a hysterical client. If the therapist becomes preoccupied with gathering historical information, he is apt to be disappointed. The hysteric doesn't operate that way; rather, she provides the therapist with a full accounting of her emotional history through her reports of the transactions, feelings, wishes, fears, projections, and intentionality in ongoing relationships. In the displaced conditions of those relationships, the therapist has a blueprint of the client's history and a prelude to what will be enacted in therapy.

In this particular case, it rapidly became clear that the client had massively reinvested her problematic relationship with her father in the person of her lover. Her brief comments about her father turned out to be the tip of the iceberg. The client's early relationship with the father had been a loving one; conflicts had arisen when the client stretched her ego and attempted self-definition. The father wanted her to retain her loving attitude toward him, but she resisted and wanted to test her own powers. She was rejected, and the father invested himself in his second marriage. The client felt that she wasn't as loving toward him as he would have liked and felt that her assertiveness led to the end of the relationship. The father was unshakable in his insistence that she submit to his demands. The client wanted to negotiate a relationship with him, but she wanted him to recognize her, to know her, and to respect her for her accomplishments and not simply as a reflection of him.

The mother played a significant role in the developmental conflicts. The mother denied her role in the divorces and became preoccupied with being nurtured by the children. The client split her loyalties and gave up her visitation rights for the sake of the mother. In the process, the client mothered the mother and tried to mobilize her to make something of her life so the client could free herself from her bondage to the mother. The client was left without a mother to identify with, or a father to relate to on a more mature level. Communication became her obsession. As in other cases, communication in the family was nonexistent, and blame-placing and critical attitudes were prominent.

In this case the client has clearly revealed the therapeutic conditions necessary for her to develop a relationship and change. The client assumes that sexuality is her salable commodity. What she seeks is an emotional investment in her, respect for her, and a regard for her as a multifaceted person. Her "prettiness" is responded to, but that increases her frustration and sense of being insubstantial. She wants to be seen as a thinking, feeling person with an intellect. She wants someone to take the time with her to work matters out so that she can feel that she is worth the effort. She feels insecure about herself in relationships and may become possessive and demanding because of her inner sense of worthlessness. She feels that she is not given to freely and may revert to demanding, but her demands are reasonable in that they voice her inner wish for communication. She wants honesty. She isn't threatened by another woman's sexuality; she knows that area well. She is, however, threatened by the feeling that she isn't respected. The hysterical client symbolically represents exactly what needs to be done. She defines the therapeutic task beautifully.

Not only does the therapist have guidelines to the corrective procedures, but if the sequence of events in the session is scrutinized, it reveals the developmental layers of conflict. In the case under consideration, the client noted that the ongoing relationship with her male companion had started on a loving note and that the breach had occurred when she made plans to move ahead with her career. A breach at such a time is an accurate replay of the histories of hysterics and their fathers. In adolescence, when the daughter turns from the father to expand her awareness, she is summarily rejected. That is precisely how the client described the crisis with her boyfriend.

The mother, however, had a role in that split by pressuring

the client to distance herself from the boyfriend. Although the issue was played out in relation to the male friend, symbolically the mother forced the client into a decision about whether she loved the mother or father, a historical fact in the development of many hysterical clients—and an issue that needs to be countered in psychotherapy.

In Chapter Four we noted that a male therapist might well consider the significance of the client's holding a mother figure in fantasy during therapy. With such a safeguard, the client can reenter the oedipal arena and experience any unresolved sexual feelings toward the therapist. In this case the mother was perceived to be inadequate in many respects. Later in therapy this client developed a strong attachment to a woman friend who seemed to be independent and assertive. During sessions the client often discussed the many things she had learned from the woman. Through that relationship the client essentially reworked her poor identification with her own mother. Had the therapist been threatened by her strong attachment to the woman friend and construed her behavior as "splitting the transference," much useful therapeutic work would have been lost. In his responding favorably to the learnings that accrued from that relationship, the therapist countered a major conflict in the client that precluded integration: her need to split her loyalties between a man and woman.

If we consider the client's conflicts in the displaced relationship with her male companion as a symbolic representation of those with the rejecting father, her compulsion to rectify that relationship and end it on a friendly note is understandable. Her search for recognition as a thinking, feeling adult is equally understandable. And her sense of wanting to be respected carries a poignant note when one considers the daughter's needs to feel loved and positively regarded by the father. From such a perspective, a therapist can gather the patience and compassion to listen to a hysterical client's driven, emotional, and repetitive anguish about an ongoing relationship that a lay person might dismiss as overly dramatic or reflecting narcissism.

For a therapist to attempt to interpret the parallelism in an ongoing relationship and its genetic sources is an exercise in futility. The determinants of behavior and accompanying affects are unconscious, their anxiety-arousing character forces the displacement, and interpretation is viewed by the client as so much psychological mish-mash. But the displacements provide the therapist with a very revealing preview of what will be enacted with the therapist as principal.

In the initial session just described, the therapist inquired into the client's family background. The client, however, was experiencing her anxiety in relation to conflicts with her male friend. She perceived herself as needing most of all a resolution of her conflicts in the ongoing problematic relationship. She had little investment in discussing her family history. At such times, if a therapist persists in pursuing her history, the client may begin to experience the therapist as having some theory or another into which he is trying to fit her. Such a client reaction sets into motion some transference reactions; she may comply as a ''good girl'' should, or she may rebel. In either case, the therapist can plan on some interesting times ahead. Some such consequences are inevitable, and can be worked through, unless the therapist is unaware of what his behavior has elicited and interprets the client's recalcitrance as resistant, controlling behavior.

Many hysterical clients are uncannily adept at displacing, and the displacement of transference feelings seems inevitable. The therapeutic task is one of being sensitive to the likelihood of displaced feelings (Krohn 1978) and listening intently to the emotional conditions of the client's ongoing relationships for evidence of displaced feeling.

During the course of therapy, the client we have just described developed in serial order a number of significant relationships that reflected the processes of conflict within her. Those relationships provided the therapist with an understanding of what activated conflict in the psychotherapeutic relationship, the meaning of the aroused anxiety, and the client's efforts at resolution. The precipitants of conflict-arousing reactions, the intentionality of the client, and the outcome in such relationships indicate to the therapist the course of action that must be taken in therapy.

As we observed earlier, noting parallelisms or interpreting behavior as reflective of therapy is of little help, because those conditions are outside awareness. In fact, a therapist's motives for noting such parallelism may be self-serving and reflect some kind of "ego trip" for the therapist, a behavior to which hysterics do not react well. But in being aware of the conflict-arousing situation that triggered the displacement, the therapist can focus on the conflicted experience without necessarily attending to its precipitants in therapy. In doing so, the therapist simultaneously clears the client's relationship of the displaced components and clears the air in the therapeutic relationship.

There are dangers in suggesting to a client that her conflicted feelings and reactions in an ongoing relationship reflect her feelings about the therapist. The client may assume that all her feelings are simply reflections of therapy, she may abandon an otherwise healthy relationship, and she may begin to feel that the therapist wants to "be everything" to her.

The client in this case was particularly adroit at displacing her feelings onto ongoing relationships. She also had that unusual talent of hysterics for being able to recall an incident, a fragment of a story, or an aspect of a conflicted relationship that characterized her feelings about the therapist or her reactions to events in the therapeutic relationship. Often she would introduce a recent anxiety-arousing conflict or features of a relationship that were transparent statements of residual aroused conflicts from a preceding session. Despite their apparent transparency, efforts to evoke insight into their connectedness were fruitless. Such efforts were really only intellectual exercises, because it is in the experiencing of different emotional responses that the corrective experience rests (Alexander 1946b).

In one session the client had been struggling with her feelings about her father and was beginning to relate them to her strong desire for open communication with her boyfriend. The glimmers of insight were in her discovery that some of the emotional conditions in the two relationships evoked similar disabling reactions in her. In attempting to discriminate between the

father and the boyfriend, she commented that they were two separate people, from different backgrounds and different gener-
ations, yet their behavior and her reactions were the same. Perhaps, she said, "it's because he's a man," and laughed. The
male therapist laughingly commented that he thought that "we
can find another reason." The session had been a difficult one
for the client; she had been repeatedly upset while discussing
her male relationships and felt "kind of drained," but she added that "I'm feeling very well."

During the session the therapist had felt close to the client as
she struggled with some relatively deep material. The client's
comments at the end of the session suggested that she was feeling grateful for the work they did during the hour. The following session began with the client's reporting that she had begun to form a new relationship but that it created considerable
concerns for her. The man was pursuing her with considerable
zest, but he was not her idea of an ideal male, and she didn't
want to get romantically involved with him. In relating the
story, the client began to cry, and the therapist asked her what
she was experiencing. The client responded that she was
"scared to have him fall in love with me and like me. I'm
afraid." At the same time the client felt that she was easy to get
to know and like and that she could be warm and fun.

The therapist considered the possibility that the client's conflicts were a displacement of some feelings that had been
aroused in the prior session. The therapist had felt close to the
client, he had been supportive in her struggles, and the session
had ended on a reciprocally warm, light note. The therapist
knew that the client felt that the primary interest men had in
her was sexual, that her relationship to her father had been
based on gratifying his needs, and that she felt emotionally very
vulnerable to kindness and regard for her. He also wondered
whether the client was concerned that the therapist, in being
responsive to her, might lose his objectivity or become overly
involved.

The therapist asked the client how the new suitor's feelings
for her would create a problem for her. The client felt that he
"would get caught up in my problems." Further, she was afraid

to "let him in to me, to my emotions, to open up and to be vulnerable to him." The client felt that she didn't know if she was in control and reiterated her concern that she and the boyfriend could become romantically involved. She felt that "a kiss could come between us."

During the remainder of the session, it became clear that any responsiveness the client experienced from another or toward another set up the expectation for a romantic encounter. Repeatedly, the client stated that she really needed affection but didn't want a romantic relationship. Her own vulnerability to becoming romantically involved contributed to her feelings. But the issue of the moment was to reduce the client's concern about the therapist's sense of his own responsibility without attenuating any of the emerging transference feelings or creating distance in the relationship. After making clear to the client that he understood her concerns about needing affection without its becoming an unwanted romance, the therapist commented that one of the advantages of therapy was that it provided her with the opportunity to talk about exactly what she was feeling without its having romantic overtones. The client apparently felt some release, because the "wish" kicked in and she began inquiring in a seemingly competitive way about the therapist's work with other clients.

In the following session the issue of closeness in a significant relationship was reintroduced. The two sides—the wish for intensity and the fear of the other becoming too involved, with needs becoming subverted—were no longer displaced. The therapist was the object of the client's concern. The therapist noted that his interest in the client reflected concern about what was important to her. The client asked, "Not as in falling in love with me, type of thing?" The therapist commented that such reactions had subverted her needs in the past. The client broke down and compared her disrupted relationship to her father with her attraction to older men, who were "a substitute for my dad."

In other cases a client may isolate the components of her conflictual experience and use multiple relationships to resolve conflict. Through multiple relationships, the isolated components are insulated, thereby inhibiting overwhelming anxiety. Because of the hysterical client's feeling that she has no inner core, she is vulnerable to being swept along by another person and, from her past experience, becoming drained and losing her tenuous self-esteem:

> Soon after therapy began with a male therapist, one client initiated six concurrent relationships. Five of those relationships spanned a wide assortment of male figures, and one was with a woman who seemed to play the role of female counterpart to the male therapist. Each relationship had a specific focus. The client noted that they were "all very different people; they're all very individual, and they all appeal to a different side of my nature." The client commented that it was a new experience to be involved with so many people at the same time. Her fear was that if she became "very serious with" one person "that means I'd be taking all of their aspects in and saying they're all attractive to me. . .and I'm going to deal with *you*."

If matters go awry in the therapeutic relationship, a hysterical client will introduce some interpersonal theme in an ongoing relationship that reflects the client's reaction to the disconcerting events. The hysteric's capacity to capture the essence of the conflict through some interaction or another in one of her relationships is truly astonishing. Even if the therapist is unaware of the hysteric's intentionality in her productions, the therapist will feel the impact of the communication.

Any therapist who dismisses the productions of the hysterical client as so much scattered talk misses one of the most crucial opportunities to understand the client and reset therapy on a more favorable course. In one case the productions of the client were accurate, albeit magnified, reflections of the therapeutic relationship and the therapist's frustration and anger. Unless those productions are attended to carefully and honestly, they portend unsuccessful therapy.

The client was repeatedly late for sessions, and following a progressive session, the client would miss a session or discuss the possiblity of terminating. Instead of perceiving the client's ambivalence as reflecting her sense of vulnerability about being dependent and her anxiety about being controlled, the frustrated therapist missed the dynamic determinants and attended to the repeated lateness in an abrupt way.

The client's own father had been a contolling, volatile man who rejected the daughter for noncompliance with his often arbitrary and self-centered demands. From the experience of the client, the therapist's "demands" became an issue of submitting to the demands of a controlling male authority.

Immediately following the therapist's abruptness and distancing behavior, the client produced a story from one of her recent interactions with a man—a relationship that was replete with displaced elements. In speaking of her reaction to the male acquaintance, who had been punitive and controlling, the client angrily commented that, despite her perception of him as a powerful person, he would "never, *ever* get to me!" The client reported telling the male acquaintance that "I'm just as strong as you inside, and just as knowledgeable about human nature as you are." The therapist got the message. The hysteric may look compliant, but she seldom submits.

The client's production was a vivid portrayal of the undercurrents of the therapeutic session. In magnified form, the story captured the emotional tone of the immediately preceding therapist—client interchange. Through her story, the client not only conveyed her anger at the therapist, but also provided a running account of what activates her anger, how she experiences the conflict, and her resolution—in this case, noncompliance.

In the following session, the client's anger intensified. She pushed the therapist, and the therapist became defensive, with ensuing interactions becoming a battle of wits. With a hysterical client, that is a losing battle. After the defensive therapist responded in a rather clipped way to one of the client's many queries about the usefulness of therapy, the client retreated to her inner thoughts. When the therapist inquired about whether she had cut off her feelings, the client mused that she had been thinking of a male acquaintance whose passionate advances had been "too rough" for her. She felt that he held a conception of her that was inaccurate and that if he had known her, he wouldn't have behaved in that way. The client immediately associated to her father, who had been physically abusive.

Again, the client made her point very ably through her stories. If the therapist thought that she was going to be the "good girl" that she had been during development and take any abuse, he was sadly mistaken. The client had accurately experienced the therapist's frustration and anger. Had he been sensitive to her anxieties, that is, had he "known her," he wouldn't have behaved as he did. His "rough" response was experienced as insensitivity to the anxiety she felt about trusting a male to be helpful instead of destructive and controlling.

No client provides a therapist with greater opportunity for insight into her problems than does the hysterical client. Moment by moment in psychotherapy, the stories, fragments of interactions, and other thematic productions guide the therapist in understanding exactly what the hysteric is experiencing in the therapeutic relationship. If the therapist attends to client productions openly and honestly, he will attend to the potential reality of the client's attributions and search his own soul. To do so, the therapist must feel secure.

An insecure therapist may blame the client for being resistant as a rationalization for the therapist's own contribution to conflicts in the relationship and to therapeutic impasse. An appropriate therapist stance consists of recognizing the client's feelings and accurately assessing the reality and transference components of those feelings. In recognizing the reality of a client's feelings in relation to the therapist's own inner reactions, the therapist also recognizes that those heightened client reactions can provide the opportunity for a powerful corrective experience. As in this case, the inevitable reenactment of problematic encounters has occurred. The conflict is reawakened. The scene has been reset in the present. The therapist and client are the participants, and it is the therapeutic task to alter the outcome.

Chapter Six

Countertransference Phenomena in Hysterical Disorders

In this chapter several concepts about the dynamics of counter-transference phenomena are reviewed and applied to psychotherapy with the hysterical client. In particular, such concepts as the transference/countertransference interlock (Wolstein 1964, p. 139), "complementary countertransference" (Racker 1974, p. 137), "projective identification" and "introjective identification" (Issacharoff 1979, p. 34), and "projective counteridentification" (Grinberg 1979, p. 177) are considered relevant to understanding countertransference themes in work with the hysterical client.

We specifically propose that the hysterical client's hypersensitivity, propensity for polarization, and exaggeration of affects interact to provide a therapeutic climate that favors countertransference reactions. Their effects in therapeutic interactions are elaborated in this chapter and then related to other recurrent countertransference themes. Case material is provided to illustrate the intricate interaction of transference and countertransference themes.

THE DYNAMICS OF
COUNTERTRANSFERENCE PHENOMENA

The dynamics of countertransference phenomena have been accorded an increasingly important place in the literature in the past few decades. Wolstein (1964) used the very apt phrase "interlocking of experience" (p. 141) in describing the situation in therapy in which the "problems of the one participant had interlocked with the problems of the other" (p. 139), producing a spiraling effect in which action and reaction are outside the awareness of the therapist. According to Wolstein, the therapist unwittingly reinforces the client's defenses, which have become interlocked with the therapist's own security needs. Psychotherapy is disrupted because the therapist no longer has the self-awareness to utilize material for the client's benefit.

The transference/countertransference interlock has been observed by other theoreticians, notably Racker (1974) and Issacharoff (1979), who addressed the dynamics of the interlock. Racker (1974) termed the phenomenon the "complementary countertransference." From a dynamic perspective, Racker suggested that the complementary countertransference was a function of the therapist's "identification of himself with the...[internal] objects" of the client (p. 137).

Through illustrative case material, Issacharoff (1979) carefully described two complementary mechanisms at work in countertransference dynamics: "projective identification" and "introjective identification" (p. 34). In the interlock the two mechanisms are used by both therapist and client in their interchanges. Essentially, the client's projective identification of the client's disowned parts provides the basis for the therapist's empathic understanding, and, through interpretation, the projected material can be reintegrated by the client.

If the therapist, however, incorporates the client's object, the therapist may then react defensively, essentially enacting the incorporated role and reprojecting. In this vital step in the interlock, the client becomes the depository of the therapist's own projective identification. The client may then reverse roles and enact the introjected role of some significant other toward the projected parts that the therapist has incorporated, thus completing the interlocking cycle (Issacharoff 1979, pp. 33–39).

In this process the therapist's reactions are colored by his own attitudes toward the incorporated client projections, with responses mediated by the therapist's own defensive modalities. Although Issacharoff (1979) noted the effects of a "continuous and powerful transferential stimulation" (p. 33) on therapist responsivity, Grinberg's thesis (1979) provides clarification. Grinberg noted that a therapist's reactions during therapy may also arise "for the most part, independently of his own conflicts," being determined by the "intensity and quality of the patient's projective identification." The concept of "projective counteridentification" suggests that the power of the client's elicitations "actively provokes a determined emotional response" that is received and felt "in a passive way" (p. 177).

Grinberg's thesis is akin to that of Leary (1957), who contended that the power of one participant in an interaction to elicit predictable responses from another is determined by the narrowness of the interpersonal response modality. In other words, the more limited the interpersonal repertoire, the more predictable the response. If helpless, docile stimulus behaviors are hypertrophied and rigidly employed in interpersonal relationships, their power to evoke strong, helpful responses intensifies (Leary 1957, pp. 126, 292–293).

In this chapter, those countertransferential concepts involved in the interlock and the eliciting power of client projections are applied to psychotherapy with hysterical disorders. We propose that hysterical dynamics and defenses, and the sheer eliciting power of the hysteric's communications, provide fertile conditions for the development of the transference/countertransference interlock (Wolstein 1964) in which projective and introjective identifications (Issacharoff 1979) and counteridentifications (Grinberg 1979, Leary 1957) flourish in the transactions of therapist and client.

It is further proposed that the hysteric is very adroit at reversing roles through a process of turning passivity into activity (Fenichel 1945). This role reversal takes several forms. In the simplest, the hysteric, in what has been termed the "myth of passivity" (Krohn 1978, p. 158), actively uses passive defenses to induce passivity and immobilize the therapist.

From a second perspective, the hypertrophied or exclusive nature of the hysteric's passive communications increases her stimulus power in inducing predictable responses (Leary 1957) and counteridentifications in the therapist (Grinberg 1979). A more complex form of role reversal as a function of introjective and projective identification was advanced by Issacharoff (1979). According to Issacharoff, role reversal consists of a client's conversion of the passive pathological introjects of significant others into an active stance against the client's own projections that have been incorporated by the therapist (see pp. 34–38). Issacharoff's thesis provides the opportunity to understand some of the complex role reversals that occur during psychotherapy with hysterical clients, and later in this chapter a dramatic example of this type of role reversal is presented.

EXEMPLIFYING THE INTERLOCK IN HYSTERIA

A concrete example of the intricacies of the transference/countertransference interlock in work with the hysterical client will illustrate the patterns and levels of therapist–client interactions. Because helplessness and control are recurrent issues in psychotherapy of the hysterical client, those issues will serve to demonstrate the interaction patterns.

In her later interactions with significant others, the hysteric converts the passive, helpless experiences of childhood into an active stance that provides her with several internal and external gains. The hysteric uses helplessness (1) to master her own inner sense of helplessness, (2) as an empathic communication of what that internal experience is, (3) as a way of controlling the "controlling other," and (4) as a way of discomfitting significant others by responding to them in the way they usually treat others.

In psychotherapy, these various functions are enacted with

varying consequences. The hysteric uses her passivity and help-lessness actively to control the therapist (Krohn 1978, Halleck 1967) and induce helplessness in him (Celani 1976). If the therapist feels helpless to help, overwhelmed, and controlled, then he is experiencing what the client feels. The empathic link has been established; discomfiture has been effected in the other; the controls are in place.

It is when the therapist reacts to the inner feelings that are aroused by the client's behavior that there is potential either for a therapeutic reintegration in the client or for activating and recycling through the transference/countertransference interlock. The power of the hysteric's helpless communication may arouse certain predictable reactions in the therapist, such as efforts at regaining control by controlling behaviors that in effect constitute the counteridentifications.

Drawing freely on the work of Issacharoff (1979), we can state that the therapist's sense of helplessness provides a potential empathic link, in that the therapist's experience resonates with the conscious experience of the client. If the therapist incorporates the client's experience and feels like a helpless child, however, he may disown the experience and react by escalating his own need to control the client. It is through the therapist's efforts at controlling his own sense of helplessness by controlling the client that the interlock is established. In essence, the therapist's modality is precisely that employed by the client in interaction with significant others in her life. So therapy is at an impasse—more exactly, the hysteric's style is reinforced in that she learns nothing about how to change those patterns.

The interlock is established, but to understand more fully the projective and introjective identifications in the ensuing transactions, we must analyze the sequential interactions. The therapist's efforts at control are often met with increasing helplessness, and the hysterical client may invoke such corollary traits as histrionics to intensify her demands. The hysteric escalates the interchange. The net effect is that the therapist may become frustrated and angry, perhaps accusing the client of being controlling. In his externalization of his own control issues, his anger, and his rejecting response, the therapist inadvertently reconstitutes the pathogenic family situation. To complete the cycle, the hysteric may then reverse roles and, echoing the pejorative strains of significant others during her adolescence, accuse the therapist of irresponsible, uncaring, and selfish behavior.

To view the multiple interchanges solely as defensive maneuvers by a client to immobilize and frustrate a therapist misses a crucial dynamic point. As noted earlier, the hysteric experiences her helplessness as overwhelming, and in communicating her helplessness to the therapist, she forges an empathic link. The more crucial dynamic feature of those interchanges is that the hysteric, in her overwhelmed state, loses self-observation. When she effects helplessness in the therapist, the hysteric's observing ego can view the projected part and note its enactment by a significant other—that is, she can observe how the therapist handles his own sense of helplessness.

The learning potential of such observations has tremendous therapeutic value. If the therapist brings into awareness the way he attempted control to reduce his sense of helplessness, he is no longer helpless, and, in his awareness, he regains strength. In his ensuing communications—whatever his style—he can help the hysteric see that there is strength in self-awareness, thus reducing her need to externalize. Such an interchange enhances the potential reintegration of projected material, because its overwhelming aspects have been neutralized. Using the strength that accrues from inner awareness, the hysteric can then look more deeply into her helplessness to discover what underlies it and to find more effective ways of communicating those emotional experiences. And often it is anger and the threat of retaliation that undergird the helpless behavior.

The interlock is complicated by a step intervening between the client's induction of helplessness in the therapist and his reaction. The experience of helplessness in the client is a conscious experience, and the disowned associated motives and emotions are submerged. Underlying the helplessness is a fear of becoming angry toward a powerful significant other. In the client's projective identification, the conscious helplessness and the less conscious emotional components—anger, frustration, and anxiety about retaliation—are packaged together in the projection.

When the therapist reacts with anger and frustration, he is enacting the less conscious and warded-off feelings. His reactions, therefore, thwart the goals of facilitating awareness of the submerged feelings. At the surface level, he is "having the client's feelings for her," but at a deeper level, his anger is passively experienced by the client as retaliation for her own unconcious projected feelings. The effect is that the client's own anger goes deeper underground, another defensive layer covers its emergence, and the passive, helpless, hysterical style of relieving anger is reinforced.

In the following sections of this chapter, several representative features of the hysterical character considered to heighten the potential for such transference/countertransference reactions are elaborated. Specifically, we propose that the hysterical client's hypersensitivity, tendency to polarize, and magnification of affects interlock to create a therapeutic situation in which certain characteristic countertransference themes emerge. We will first advance some general observations about the defensive and communication functions of those hysterical characteristics. Their effects in stimulating countertransference reactions are then elaborated through case vignettes.

HYPERSENSITIVITY, POLARIZATION, AND THE EXAGGERATION OF AFFECT

The hysteric communicates her hypersensitivity behaviorally through a fragile stance and through reports of such subjective phenomena as sensitivity to light and noise. Often this sensitivity is reinforced by accounts of psychic experiences. Of particular significance for psychotherapy is the hysteric's acute awareness of the underlying emotional attitudes and feelings of others despite their verbal statements to the contrary. In relationships the hysteric's sensitive, fragile stance leaves the other participant "walking on eggs" with her. Of more importance, the hysteric's rather uncanny ability to sense the contradictory underlying feelings and attitudes of the other participant, however minimal, stimulates an obsessive, self-searching and introspective attitude in the other.

This hypersensitivity serves multiple defensive functions. The sensitivity provides the hysteric with a finely tuned alert system that she uses to protect her vulnerabilities. Through her sensitivity to others, the hysteric wards off anxiety and controls others' behavior toward her, particularly confrontive, aggressive behavior. Paradoxically, the hysteric further uses her sensitivity to accommodate herself to others through compliant behavior. To avoid anxiety about what she "sees" and for the sake of relating to others, the hysteric mutes her sensitivity. The hysteric fogs her vision through a diffuse, global style (Shapiro 1965). She further counters her sensitivity through such manifest character traits as superficiality, and in an insubstantial self-concept.

Coupled to this sensitivity is a tendency to polarize what she senses in the other and in herself. The hysteric's constructs are framed in "either-or" propositions that preclude integration. As noted earlier, Chodoff (1982) contended that the hysteric's submissiveness is the flip side of a willful spirit. Allen (1977) referred to the hysteric's "inward dilemmas of omnipotence and helplessness and longings for merging and separateness," which become evident during therapy "in the form of demanding total gratification or nothing" (p. 297).

The hysteric's tendency to polarize is most evident in her interpersonal relationships. The hysteric seeks a relationship that is mutual and egalitarian, but she defines her relationships in unrealistic terms. This romanticized view of relationships is expressed in her search for a relationship that is completely honest and open, in which the partner is to be unwavering in strength and responsibility. Her constructs are brittle and include a partner who in never failing and omnipotent, and whose love is unconditional and platonic. Yet the hysteric has strong power drives, disavows her own submissive dependent stance, and seeks complete independence.

Because of the mythical character of her relationships, the hysteric's needs go unmet. She does not integrate the polar oppo-sites, and in her frustration she turns to a new relationship to satisfy the needs unmet in any given relationship. In this proc-ess the hysteric searches for someone to accept one or the other side of her teeter-totter, never integrating or centering in her-self. This tendency to polarize is communicated in her stance about power and control issues and in the hysteric's concerns about expectations and performance. The hysteric's relationships have the flavor of parallel play. She performs and the partner is the passive, receptive one, or she becomes the submissive, docile partner, demanding performance by the dominant partner.

Polarization of the hysteric's world is reinforced through the use of exaggerated affect, and the two defenses work in tandem. The interlocking of exaggerated affect and polarization is par-ticularly evident in the hysteric's use of the polar extremes of the dominant–submissive and the love–hate axes in relation-ships (see Leary 1957). Interpersonal themes are portrayed in love–hate terms and in extreme dominance or submission rather than in a balance of power and assertiveness or through appro-priate dependent behavior.

Such well-known character traits as histrionics, self-dramatization, emotional lability, and hysterical "bouts" bol-ster the hysterical propensity for exaggeration. The net effect of her histronics is that the partner feels forced to comply and may in anger withhold what otherwise would be freely given. The other's underlying anger may go unexpressed, but, in her sen-sitivity to underlying feelings, the hysteric correctly reads the other's intent. In turn, the hysteric then withholds, and because matters are often attached to sexual activity, it is sex that is with-held to frustrate the partner.

In her reports of relationships, the hysteric swings from depression at ruptures in relationships to euphoria in finding another "ideal male." Because of her polarizations, relationships fail to materialize, and the hysteric feels out of control and help-less to effect an impact. Her strident efforts at control may then escalate, and the hysteric ironically uses her helplessness to achieve these goals.

Each of these defenses has a communication aspect as well.

In a general way, the hysteric uses her sensitivity to induce sensitivity in others. She dramatizes her points for effect. And she uses polarities to communicate her own inner polarities. These modes of communicating are most evident in therapeutic work with the hysterical client and stimulate countertransference reactions.

The Effects in Psychotherapy:
Hypersensitivity and Countertransference Potential

The hysteric's hypersensitivity sets the stage for countertransference, paving the way for projective counteridentification and initiating the therapist's identification with the client's object. The hysteric is a master therapist in being able to read the therapist's true feelings, no matter how minor. The therapist may feel that the hysteric has a pipeline to his soul, that she knows him all too well, and he becomes wary and inhibited in her presence. This inhibition may then cause the therapist to become self-absorbed, experiencing self-doubts about his motives and in a general self-searching when interpretations may be appropriate.

With the male therapist, the client is sensitive to male chauvinism and male self-centeredness. There is always some truth to the hysteric's contentions, and any such feelings in the therapist may be blown out of proportion, for reasons that become clearer when the complementary defenses of exaggeration of affect and polarization are considered. The client's anxiety is reduced at the expense of the therapist's self-absorbed concern about his own motives. Essentially, the client has turned the tables on the therapist. This fact contributes to a therapist's accommodating to "the defensive system of the patient in order to keep the work on a smooth course" (Wolstein 1964, p. 139). To avoid accusations, the therapist may check his own motives, thus substituting self-analysis for the necessary therapeutic work.

Before turning to the complementary defenses of polarization and affect magnification, we can illustrate with case material the effects of hypersensitivity:

In his first session with a female hysterical client, the male therapist smiled in greeting her. The client responded, "You seem amused." The therapist commented that he was simply smiling in greeting her. After the session, however, the therapist recalled that prior to setting the hour, the client had assertively asked to meet him to arrange a time for sessions. When he met her to arrange matters, the client, although acting very assertive, had become very childlike, dropping her appointment pad and pencil. The therapist had been inwardly amused at her adult–child behavior and may have subliminally communicated his amusement to her.

The client's comment about the therapist's being amused then took on new meaning in relation to her hypersensitivity to his feelings. Although it was true that the client experienced herself as a child and felt that she was treated as such, her hypersensitivity to the therapist's internal responses set a reaction in the therapist in which he felt that the client could "see" his innermost thoughts. In short order, the therapist became quite defensive about any inconsistent attitudes he was experiencing. Essentially, he became introspective and as sensitive to his thoughts as his client was to them.

Often the hysterical client is aware of her sensitivity and attempts to mute it for the sake of relating. Fearful that her awareness will disrupt the therapeutic relationship as it has other relationships, the client may forewarn the therapist of her acute sensitivity:

At their first meeting the client warned the therapist of her sensitivity. She commented that in her previous therapy with a woman, she had felt comfortable, but she had "never worked with an older man." She mentioned that she was still very angry with her father and reflected that onto older men in "authority positions." "I get very...cynical, or I'm watching them through slitted eyes. Not necessarily that I'm going to do that with you, but I'm just letting you know kind of where I'm at." The client went on to say that "I tend to view them very skeptically. I don't trust what they necessarily say. . . . I will pick them out first for chauvinism beyond anyone else. I'm very sensitive to the dynamics." And then the client again repeated her concern that she wanted the therapist to know what she was thinking about "when I thought that we were going to work together."

In other cases a client may attempt to assure the therapist that she will use her sensitivity only in self-defense. Or, in the case of one very sensitive client, she attempted to mute her sensitivity through a diffuse, cognitive style:

At the outset of therapy, the client diffused her sensitivity through many affectively flat sentences that trailed off into nothingness or were punctuated with "Oh, I don't know." Yet at a later point in therapy, when her sensitive antenna picked up a slight anxious gesture in her therapist, the client left the session agitated. Within a day, the therapist had an "emergency" call from the client, who sounded as though she were decompensating. Essentially, the client sensitized the therapist to being more sensitive to her needs.

This hypersensitivity sets the stage for countertransference reactions and for the therapist to search his own motives, to doubt, and to react defensively. When this tendency is coupled with the hysteric's tendency to polarize and exaggerate affect, the therapist may begin to construct his world in terms of the client's constructs.

Polarization and the Magnification of Affect

As noted earlier, the hysterical client's world is constructed in polarities, and the polar extremes are punctuated with powerful affective reactions. When these complementary defenses are coupled with the hysteric's hypersensitivity, they have the powerful effect of drawing the therapist into construing his inner experiences in terms of the client's constructions. This begins the process of the therapist's "identification of himself with the... [internal] objects" of the client (Racker 1974, p. 137) and reprojecting (Issacharoff 1979).

In centering in the client rather than in himself, the therapist becomes vulnerable to unmediated reactivity. He may react reflexively to the eliciting power of the client, which is intended to evoke predictable and anxiety-reducing responses. Or, because of the conflicts aroused in him by the powerful projections, the therapist may react defensively. As Mueller and Kell (1972) have noted, a therapist may identify with significant others and react as they have to a client, or he may identify with the client's problems. Either position stimulates therapeutic impasse, but identification with the client's problems presents a more serious roadblock to resolution of impasse (pp. 67–74).

We will consider from several perspectives the inhibition in the therapist's normal response patterns that stems from the hysteric's dual tendency to polarize and to exaggerate affect. During the initial sessions of psychotherapy, for example, the hysterical client often parades past the therapist a series of relationships in which she was exploited. The essence of the stories is that she gave a great deal and received little in return, that she was treated as an object, that sexuality was of little concern to her but of prime interest to the man, and that she was rejected capriciously. Often the client will report wanting an intense, "real" relationship, one of depth and substance with complete honesty and openness as overriding characteristics.

Although seeking a genuine relationship in which honesty, openness, and love abound, the hysteric construes those emotional conditions in highly romanticized, mythical ways. She wants an intense relationship with unconditional, platonic love. Those "needs" are often voiced in intensely emotional ways, reinforced by histrionics and demands, and accompanied by reports of relationships characterized by such polarities as love turned into hate, victimization at the hands of an arrogant male, and feelings of total rejection for becoming too dependent.

Those reports, presented with such gusto and overwhelming evidence, are also factual. Their presentation, however, is couched in polarities and sets certain reactions in a therapist. The hysteric's view of relationships is inhibiting and portends a mythical relationship, one that is "always" honest, open, generous, loving, protective, and other directed. It should not include self-centeredness, defensiveness, errors, stress, or mixed feelings.

There are several immediate effects in the therapist: a feeling of intense pressure to repond therapeutically at all times, inhibited freedom to be himself, and a hypersensitivity to his own motives, feelings, and attitudes, and ensuing self-protective reactions. In being drawn into the client's polarized constructs, the therapist may find himself being careful to maintain eye contact and attending carefully to every nuance of behavior in the relationship. He may attempt to communicate that he is a trustworthy, honest person, and in his urgency to reflect his own openness, he may become inappropriately self-revealing.

Because of the way the hysteric magnifies feelings out of proportion, the therapist may deny in himself the normal feelings that occur in any human relationship. He may deny any angry reactions in himself, because they are equated with being hateful. Sexual feelings that are aroused during the course of therapy may be suppressed rather than evaluated in relation to client dynamics. In internalizing the client's concept of strength as being imperturbable and impervious to error, the therapist may "oversell his attributes" (Celani 1976, p. 1417) and attempt the herculean feat of being a never-failing source of strength. Chodoff (1982) calls such efforts on the part of the therapist "an exercise in megalomania" (p. 281).

In his awareness of his client's awareness of him, the therapist may become inappropriately introspective and inhibited. His self-consciousness may lead to self-doubts about his own motives, and he may defer interpretations for fear that they are boastful or arrogant. In short, the therapist denies his humanness. In his efforts to be very attentive, unswerving in strength, and denying of his personal feelings, the therapist creates a therapeutic relationship that is as unreal as the mythical relationships of his client.

The effects are manifold and we will describe them through a case vignette. Here we will note that in creating such a brittle relationship, the therapist reinforces the hysteric's polarized view of relationships. From a dynamic perspective, the therapist reinforces two complementary defenses in hysteria: isolation of the components of affective experience, and displacement. By enacting one side of the client's ambivalence toward objects, the therapist sets the stage and forces the client to displace the other side of her ambivalence. The emotional components of experience remain isolated, and the client must act out the other side of her conflicts in order to regain a homeostatic state.

THE TRANSFERENCE/COUNTERTRANSFERENCE INTERLOCK: A CASE VIGNETTE

To understand the power of the hysteric to pull predictable reponses from a therapist and set countertransference reactions in motion, we must closely evaluate the sequence of events in the transactions of therapist and client. A case vignette will be used to illustrate the intricacies of the interlocking effects, which begin in the first moment of contact with a client. In this case, which was referred to briefly earlier in this chapter, the client was extremely sensitive to any nuances of feeling in the therapist. Her immediate projection onto the therapist that he seemed amused with her was determined by her inner sense of being a child in an adult body. Yet the projection had a reality base, in that the client had accurately sensed the therapist's internal amusement at her behavior. The client's sensitivity set in motion a process of self-consciousness in the therapist and set the stage for later countertransferential issues.

During development, the client's relationship to her father had been stormy. The father's needs came first, and if the client rebelled or asserted her privacy, the father would become volatile. On one memorable occasion in early adolescence when the client defied her father, he became outraged and completely destroyed her room. The client had just cleaned her room to impress her mother. She felt that her father was trying to get at her "vitals," and she interpreted his aggressive actions as a symbolic sexual assault, feeling degraded, humiliated, and violated.

According to the client, the father was an addictive personality. The parents divorced in discord, and the father moved away. The client felt that she was at fault and spent considerable time trying to make amends to the father so that their relationship would end on a note of love rather than hate. In the process, she nurtured him and tried to rehabilitate him so that he could father her. But the father was impenetrable. He either saw the client as a childish brat or was threatened by her dependency. If she rebelled he would contend that she was a "brat." If she was sweet and tried to nurture him, he would cut her off because he was fearful of becoming overly involved.

The client wanted her father to accept her mixed feelings toward him and on occasion tried to convince him that she loved him but had hateful feelings toward him. He denied any such emotions in himself, which left the client feeling guilty about her hateful feelings, empty that she couldn't touch him, and helpless to work matters out with him. She felt that she must be the hateful one.

One would assume that, with knowledge of the client's history, the transferential potential would be clear and dictate the appropriate therapeutic process to help the client integrate her polarized, ambivalent feelings. Unfortunately, such was not the case. The client's hypersensitivity, tendency to polarize, and magnification of affect evoked strong defensive reactions in the therapist. In the ensuing transactions, the therapist and client replicated the pathogenic family with remarkable parallelism.

In opening sessions the client projected freely onto the therapist. She both nurtured him and saw him as a warm, responsive person who would be caring and understanding. The therapist had no trouble with those projections. But the client soon came to think that the therapist too had a "dark side," as all men did, and that he would come to hate her as her father did.

Instead of accepting the projection and helping the client to understand and accept her own ambivalence, the therapist introjected the projection and began fighting the feeling that he was "hateful." In internalizing the client's polarized construct that anger is equivalent to hate, the therapist denied his anger and frustration, which began to surface when the client's resistance became manifest.

The client was repeatedly late for sessions or would miss sessions without cause. The therapist's frustration began to surface, but he continued to deny his feelings. Instead, he took the role of the attentive, nurturant therapist who wasn't angry about the client's lateness, but who felt that the client was avoiding her issues about him and therapy. He further felt that she might be angry with him, thus reprojecting his own anger and reinforcing the client's tendency to externalize.

The client's resistance escalated. In sessions she contended that the therapist was most assuredly angry with her. When the therapist was no longer able to conceal his frustration, the client turned on him and angrily confronted him with his denial of his "dark side," which she knew had been there all along. The therapist felt like a reprimanded "brat."

In this sequence, several features of the transference/countertransference interlock stand out rather boldly. Of particular interest are the multiple interlocking introjections and projections and role reversals that occur during the therapist–client interactions. The work of Issacharoff (1979, pp. 33–39) provides a blueprint for interpreting the dynamics of these interactions. At the surface level, the client played the role of the dutiful daughter and nurtured the therapist, then switched roles and became rebellious. Her rebellious behavior evoked anger in the therapist, which he denied, eventually leading to impasse. In that sense the therapeutic relationship recapitulated the client's developmental history with her father.

At a deeper level, the client's initial nurturing attitude toward the therapist was an enactment of one side of her ambivalence toward objects. Of greater dynamic significance was the client's perception of the therapist as a warm, responsive person. That projection was a dynamically determined forerunner of her enactment of her angry, hateful feelings toward objects. In making the object safe, the client could potentially work through and integrate both sides of her ambivalence. That is precisely what she did in trying to convince the father "that she loved him but had hateful feelings toward him."

At that point in therapy, the potential for reintegration was solid. When the client began to think that the therapist had a "dark side," the second projection was in place and the opportunity for interpretation in the offing. The client's projection of "hateful" feelings onto the therapist was, however, introjected by the therapist, who then denied those feelings in himself, much as the father had. The transference/countertransference interlock was established.

The therapist then reversed roles and enacted the part of the "attentive, nurturant" daughter, leaving the client hanging with her feelings of being the hateful one. In that respect the therapist not only denied his anger but reprojected the disowned parts onto the client. When the therapist's anger was denied and reprojected onto her, the client acted the part of the rebellious child in order to flush out the therapist's anger.

In a sense the client regressed to an earlier adolescent state and reenacted her defiance of her father, with predictable consequences. When the therapist finally admitted that he was frustrated by his client's lateness, he replayed the role of the volatile father toward the "bratty" child. At that point the client re-reversed roles, and, taking the role of the introjected father, she reprimanded the therapist, who then felt like a brat.

COUNTERTRANSFERENCE THEMES IN HYSTERIA

Using the case just presented as a reference point, we can describe several features of the dynamics of countertransference phenomena in hysteria. A client's extreme sensitivity to the subliminal attitudes of a therapist and to the conditions of their relationship set the stage for the ensuing countertransference reactions. The therapist may become inappropriately introspective and inhibited in the presence of such a client. His wariness and obsessive preoccupation with his own motives in confronting issues constitute a self-protective reaction. In this self-absorbed condition, experienced as inhibition and guardedness, the therapist is vulnerable. In that vulnerable state, the therapist is more likely to internalize the client's objects and feel "treated as such; that is, he identifies himself with this object." The result is a "rejection of a part or tendency" in himself (Racker 1974, p. 135).

The client's hypersensitivity sets the process into motion: her tendency to polarize and exaggerate the associated affects contributes to the therapist's denial of the introjected parts, because they are experienced in extreme form. Although a therapist may admit anger and frustration in himself, he is less likely to tolerate a hateful self-concept. The power of the client's polarized and exaggerated projections tends to elicit predictable responses. The therapist's own vulnerable state, however, implies a tenuous observing ego, with consequential unmediated responses. In other words, in his vulnerability, the therapist's reactivity is likely to be a manifestation of his own defenses, which may be evident in avoidance of issues, denial, and "accommodations" to the client's "security operations" (Wolstein 1964, pp 139-140).

Under such conditions the interlock is predictable. The therapist's manifest reactions, however, are unpredictable, because they are mediated by the therapist's own security operations. Different therapists will respond to the same conditions in different ways, but the manifest defensive response reflects the underlying insecurity. One therapist may work harder; another may become controlling and patronizing; another may externalize and blame the client for being resistant, as did the therapist in the case vignette. Or a therapist may withdraw and become passive (see Racker 1974, pp. 135-139).

Issacharoff's thesis regarding projective and introjective identification in both parties of the transaction (1979) is particularly clarifying in work with hysterical clients once the interlock is established. When the therapist introjects the client's object and reprojects, he has already reversed roles and enacted the disowned part of the client. In introjecting and reprojecting the client's projected "hateful" self, the therapist is rendered doubly vulnerable to the client's reactivity. He has lost the therapist's observational chair, and, in the ensuing role reversal by the client, the interlock is completed and therapy reaches an impasse and recycles or ruptures.

Wolstein (1964) observes that the interlock is insurmountable and does not bode well for therapy unless the therapist is open to examining his role in the impasse. More optimistically, albeit paradoxically, the power of the interlock and the dramatic reenactment of the pathogenic family within the therapeutic sessions provides a most powerful vehicle for reintegration and change—provided the therapist is open enough to evaluate the interactions nondefensively and seek consultation. As Kell and Mueller (1966) noted, errors are inevitable and impasse is a prelude to change and can be "productive of therapeutic progress" if the therapist "can convert the dynamic, interpersonal consequences" of the behavior "into corrective measures" (p. 11).

Defending Against a Client's Inner Experience

According to the "participant–observer" role that Sullivan (1956) elaborated, to participate effectively, a therapist observes both his own and his client's inner experience, and his interventions are governed by the dynamics of those interlocking experiences. Neither his own nor his client's experience is distorted. In the case just cited, the therapist withdrew his observing ego from the client's internal experience because that experience produced anxiety in him that he defended against. He was doubly vulnerable because his own inner experience was blocked by anxiety. In another therapist, the same client's behavior might have evoked anger and frustration, which would have been consciously acceptable feelings. In his awareness of and acceptance of his angry feelings, the therapist would have been kept from distorting his inner experience. The therapist could have evaluated the meaning of the anger and the relationship conditions that triggered it, and the experience could have been turned into a potentially therapeutic one for the client.

Some additional examples from the case described earlier may be useful in delineating the difference between responses that may be more therapeutically productive and those that are encumbered by countertransference reactions.

The client projected readily onto the therapist, and the client began an early session by commenting that when she left their last session, she had felt that the therapist was symbolically patting her on the head. She felt that he thought of her as a little girl. Further, she thought that he looked sad about her situation and felt that she wan't going to make it. Variants on this same theme continued in several succeeding sessions.

The client communicated her pessimism to the therapist, who began to feel that the relationship might not develop. Had the therapist been tuned in to the client's inner experience, he would have had a beginning sense of the emptiness she felt in relationships. Instead of responding to that feeling state, he worked harder, essentially denying his own emerging feelings of pessimism. In his denial of his own feelings about the problems in their relationship, he recapitulated the client's experience with her father and set the stage for resistance.

The ensuing resistance, which was played out in repeated cancellations and late arrivals for sessions, was viewed by the therapist as the client's resistance to therapy. In fact, it was a strong transference reaction to the therapist, which was stimulated by the parallelism in his reactions to the client. Had the therapist been free enough to experience himself, he would have seen a communication link in those feelings. The therapist would then have seen what the client experienced in relation to her father. She struggled in that relationship, felt helpless, and saw no solution. Those were the therapist's feelings in relation to the client. The empathic link was there, but the therapist was too self-absorbed to forge it.

When matters escalated, the therapist interpreted the client's behavior as ambivalence. As Sullivan (1953a) noted, the self-serving function of interpretations must always be subjected to countertransference scrutiny. In his defensiveness, the therapist was blaming the client for problems in their relationship. Essentially, the message was that if the client was a "good girl" and changed, perhaps therapy would move on a better course. Ironically, male defensiveness, blame placing, and having been the "good girl" are central issues in the development of the hysterical personality.

To this point, it seems that the therapist has done no more than reproduce the client's history. As Kell and Mueller (1966) noted, such intensity and immediacy of the therapist's involvement do not augur well. All was not lost, however. Had the therapist been able to evaluate the sequence of events in the relationship, he would have had a clearer understanding of the processes of conflict in his client. Had the therapist been free enough, he could have "understood" how it felt to the client internally to struggle in a relationship and fail, how male defensiveness and externalization had contributed to the client's anger, and why she found it necessary to use a passive mode for expressing anger. Of more importance, he could have gotten insight into the hysterical style of communicating.

The client continued to exhaust her repertoire in efforts at communicating with the therapist. And she communicated exceedingly well. The therapist's observing ego was just not there to intercept the messages. In the relationship, the therapist felt many of the emotions that the hysterical client feels in development and in her adult relationships. He felt that he should have no angry feelings, that his freedom was circumscribed, that no matter what he did, the relationship would fail, and that he was completely ineffectual. And, after several exhausting bouts, the therapist knew something about the hysteric's willfulness. The client repeatedly wanted to change the hour for their meetings. Instead of viewing this fact as a clear index that he and his client were on a collision course in the locking of wills, he experienced that same willfulness and would not give in and change the time for sessions.

Hysterical clients are very forgiving people. Their thirst for a relationship is strong, and they readily give a therapist many chances to redeem himself (Allen 1977). In this case, had the therapist honestly approached his concerns about the relationship and attempted to negotiate some mutual goals, it is likely that the course could have been righted. Had the therapist converted his inner experience of what the client was feeling into an understanding of how the client must struggle to relate without loss of self-esteem, matters might have been redirected. And had that happened, a major therapeutic task would have been accomplished.

ACTING OUT IN RESPONSE
TO COUNTERTRANSFERENCE

Of continual concern in work with the hysterical client is the issue of acting out, a process that occurs in various forms. A client may act out by displacing her feelings from the therapist onto ongoing relationships, or as a way of countering the therapist's countertransference feelings about her. In the second case, the client's acting out may be a healthy resistance to an overprotective or paternal reaction in the therapist.

The hysterical client may tend to evoke a protective response from a male therapist, particularly if the client's own development has included an exploitative father. That protective stance, however, often runs counter to the assertive, independent strivings of the client and may in fact represent the therapist's own unconscious possessiveness of the client. In such a case, the therapist has merged with the possessive father, and the client's developmental plight is revisited. If the therapist inadvertently inhibits the client's freedom to grow because of his own needs, the client may need to take measures to break those chains:

> A hysterical client reported that she had cancelled the previous session because the weather was pleasant and she had instead decided to go to the beach. She said that she hoped the therapist wasn't angry and that she thought he would understand. On a manifest level, it appeared that the client wanted the therapist to excuse her and not take exception to her behavior. The therapist said he wasn't angry and rationalized his response by assuming he was

countering the role of the client's possessive and controlling father.

The therapist's posture with the client had been a protective one. At the conscious level, the therapist disidentified with the exploitative, controlling attitude of the client's father. He was intending to provide the client with a better "father figure." Dynamically, however, the therapist's attitude was similarly possessive. He was to be her self-appointed savior. From this perspective, the client's acting out could be interpreted as a response to the therapist's underlying possessiveness. It was healthy resistance to a benign but equally inhibiting guardian.

From another perspective, the therapist's protective attitude also confirmed the client's feelings of insubstantiality. When the therapist excused her behavior , he actually had not understood but, rather, colluded with her irresponsibility and confirmed her insubstantial character defenses. Later in the session following her missed appointment, the client gave the therapist another opportunity to address her unresolved feelings and rectify the relationship by introducing themes that suggested that she felt shallow and irresponsible.

Not only was the client's acting out a reaction to the therapist's unhelpful protective attitude, but it also presented the therapist with an interpersonal challenge. Would he care enough to take her seriously and work through the conflicts in the relationship, thus countering the superficiality she experienced in other relationships, or would he continue to treat her as if she were too fragile by avoiding confrontation, thereby precluding the possibility of a genuine encounter? The latter stance actually encourages continued acting out. The client's acting out reflects her disappointment and anger. It represents her attempts to mobilize the therapist to treat her as a responsible and substantial person. Of greatest import, the client's acting out is her only recourse in her efforts to free herself from the possessiveness that her father and the therapist both represent.

Part Three

The Process of Psychotherapy

Chapter Seven

Developing the Therapeutic Relationship

In the first section of the book, the developmental conditions that favored the hysterical personality were outlined. Consideration was given to the outcomes of those developmental conflicts in adult functioning, defenses, and interpersonal relationships. In that discussion the nature of the hysteric's interpersonal relationships and the recurrent themes that permeated those relationships were emphasized. In the second section those themes were recast as potential guidelines for therapeutic intervention.

In this section we attempt an integration. The focus is the therapeutic interview and the process of psychotherapy with hysterical clients. The interpersonal aspects of the therapeutic relationship and the dynamics of the therapist–client interaction are emphasized.

THEMES IN EARLY SESSIONS

The speed with which a hysterical client becomes emotionally involved, forms opinions, and intensely reacts to what her impressionistic evidence evokes in her can be a dizzying experience for a therapist. The client's reactions are unpredictable and irrational, and the therapist is without anchor points and stripped of cognitive control. The hysterical client also is without anchor points; her relationships have been replete with the inexplicable behavior of others. Her forte is her intuition. In these very early interactions, the therapist has made his first contact with the hysterical style of communicating.

During initial interviews, the formulation of an adequate differential diagnosis of the hysterical personality is based on intrapsychic and interpersonal functioning. The interpersonal themes during development and their outcomes in adult functioning that have been described in Chapters Two and Three provide partial assessment guidelines. More comprehensively, Baumbacher and Amini (1980), Krohn (1978), Blacker and Tupin (1977), and, to a lesser extent, Halleck (1967) have integrated the contributions of drive theory, character analysis, ego psychology, cognitive style, and the interpersonal-social-cultural school into a differentiating, dynamic definition of the hysterical personality.

The primary focus of this chapter is on the interpersonal-experiential dimensions of early interviews, their contributions to an assessment of the hysterical personality, and their effects on the developing relationship. Particular attention is given to the elicitation by the hysterical personality of predictable therapist reactions. The idiosyncratic nature of those elicitations contributes to a definition of the disorder. Ironically, the power of those elicitations to stimulate undue anxiety in a therapist may contribute to a more severe diagnosis.

The Experiential Aspects of Initial Contacts

The importance of the experiential aspects of the assessment of a hysterical personality has been voiced by Halleck (1967), who noted the interpersonal significance of the hysteric's helpless and irresponsible style as an important diagnostic feature. More generally, the tremendous interpersonal impact of the hysterical client on those who interact with her has been accorded significant prominence in the literature (Kell and Mueller 1966, Halleck 1967, Celani 1976, Chodoff 1978, 1982, Andrews 1984). That impact is felt immediately by the therapist during initial contacts.

Throughout those initial contacts, the interaction of therapist and client is rapid, intense, and unmediated on the part of the client. The client's unmediated experience is her problem and her privilege. Often, however, the therapist's reactivity becomes equally unmediated under the pressure of the client's affects and the power of her elicitations. Even during those early contacts, counteridentification and countertransference phenomena are evident. When the therapist's anxiety intrudes or his responses are reflexive, the therapist loses his observing ego, communication breaks down, the assessment task is subverted, the diagnosis is distorted, and the client at best may have second thoughts about continuing psychotherapy.

In the following sections, the hysteric's experience during the interview is somewhat artificially separated from that of the therapist. The reader must understand that the vital element is the interactive flow between therapist and client and the interlocking of therapist and client experience throughout the interview. The complexities of the reciprocal stimulating effects of that interaction are described through clinical material.

The Immediacy of the Hysteric's Experience
and Its Communicative Function

A therapist who attempts to obtain an orderly history of a hysterical client is apt to be frustrated. Hysterical clients simply do not provide chronological histories. Rather, they provide a much more meaningful history—an experiential one. Even when a hysterical client attempts to be rational and follow some developmental chronology, the orderly presentation of facts gives way immediately to the press of affects.

The hysteric becomes involved in her history and reexperiences the conflicts as she talks of them. Accordingly, she is easily derailed, and past conflicts, battles, and their effects become experienced in the present. The experience in the present takes on the semblance of a kind of "stream of consciousness," in which the flow of emotional experience provides the key to the inner experience. Through that spontaneous, freely flowing experience, the therapist obtains a deeper insight into problem areas than would be gained if the events had been recited in orderly detail by an obsessional client.

As history loses its historical perspective, it becomes the experience of the moment. Chodoff (1982) has beautifully described the way that the hysteric "is trapped in the present" (p. 282), thrashing about in emotional anguish without self-awareness. What seems to happen during the interview is that the hysteric attempts a chronological presentation because she recognizes that emotionality and subjectivity are her nemesis. Accordingly, the hysteric may attempt to mute her emotions, but logic is superseded by the emotional press of the moment and readily gives way to experiencing rather than symbolizing. The emotional experience becomes intense and awakens new associative links with past events, which propel the hysteric into new emotional reactions, recall, and additional reactions. The ego is momentarily overwhelmed but then recovers, a change that can be evidenced in a hysterical client's sudden awareness of her involvement.

That awareness may be embarrassing, and the client may note that she has lost track or may ask the therapist, "What was that question, again?" One client who repeatedly became intensely involved in the experience of the emotions she was describing turned to the therapist after an emotional outburst and angrily wondered "how we got onto that subject"—almost as though she had been manipulated into the embarrassing situation by the therapist. To some extent the client was correct in that the therapist's silence during the client's free-flowing emotional associations was intended to obtain a diagnostic picture of the client's strength to regress, become highly emotional, and recover without intervention.

The way in which content gives way to emotions is augmented by another unique aspect of the hysterical style. The emotional conditions embedded in the content of any hysterical production are often being enacted as the content is discussed. If, for example, the hysterical client addresses the question of why it has been necessary for her to lead a chameleonlike existence in relation to the needs of others, she may, in her sensitivity, be simultaneously fitting her content to her notions of what she believes the therapist wants to hear (see Masterson 1976). Thus, the client is enacting her compliance as she talks about her ongoing and previous relationships in which her needs were preempted by the needs of others who demanded compliance. This interesting phenomenon provides a unique validation for the contentual matter. But it does more. In enacting the problematic emotional conditions during the interview, the client's behavior suggests that even in the opening moments of her initial contacts, the client is already experiencing herself in a relationship with the therapist who is conducting the interview.

The inclusion of the therapist as a significant other is often expressed through accommodating, compliant behavior. Admittedly, such behavior is a major stumbling block in work with hysterical clients. The literature is replete with examples of the propensity of the hysterical client to meet the needs of others and fit in. Andrews (1984), for example, reviewed the clinical material about compliance and offered a psychotherapeutic strategy for countering compliance. In Chapter Four we have elaborated a number of the personality functions that are served through compliant behavior.

During early interviews, a therapist is more likely to note a client's compliant behavior as a diagnostic indicator than to take steps to counter compliance. Compliance is an overriding form of interacting that the hysterical client has learned as a way of integrating relationships and gaining acceptance. Thus, a therapist would not be inclined to tamper with that organizational principle in initial interviews. Rather, the interviews are facilitated if the therapist understands that the client's compliance subsumes an intense need to communicate and relate and an equally intense fear of failure to negotiate a relationship.

The immediacy with which the hysterical client incorporates the male therapist as a significant other (Allen 1977) is only partially explained by her need to relate and her fears of being unable to negotiate a satisfactory male relationship. The hysteric's neurotic conflicts and her competitive spirit play a major role in her rather irrational trust of the therapist as her new-found savior. The competitive factors arousing a hysterical client's immediate trust of the therapist are evident in a sequence from an initial interview.

The client entered psychotherapy because of conflicts in her relationship with her boyfriend. Rationally, she felt that she should terminate the relationship, but she couldn't do so. In the client's words, "My heart tells me one thing, and my mind tells me another." The conflicts with the boyfriend were intermixed with her conflicts with her parents, particularly her father.

The client's father was the dominant, controlling force in the family. He was purportedly a volatile, bombastic man whom the client feared. His irrationality was particularly pronounced on occasions when the client became romantically involved. The father was particularly antagonistic toward her current boyfriend. On one occasion when the client stayed out overnight, her father told her that she could "hook" as far as he was concerned and summarily rejected her. From the client's reports, her boyfriend was a duplicate of the father. He was possessive, volatile, and jealous. His well-being seemed contingent on the client's nurturing his ego.

According to the client's reports, her mother was subservient to the father, catering to his ego. She was a sweet person who loved her "flowers" and in general seemed compliant and insubstantial. Yet the marriage remained intact, and the mother seemed to be able to master the volatile father. The client's female relationships were practically nonexistent. She just did not get along with women. She felt "that there is some type of cattiness, jealousy, and...evil [laughs] about them."

Within the context of that abbreviated background material, the client's interactions with the male therapist during their initial interview were significant. Immediately after having reported her feelings about women as catty, jealous, and evil, the client noted that she had consulted two health professionals previously. Neither had been satisfactory. She felt that the last, a man, hadn't taken her seriously. She had talked with him because she felt that a female friend "was kind of screwing" her. The client couldn't remember much of what he said. In fact, she said, to tell the truth, she "didn't care to remember."

The male therapist commented that she seemed to be searching for something different. The client agreed. She commented that "I'm looking for someone, well, I think I found you. [Laughs.] When I talk to people, I tend to pour everything out. But I can't pour it out to just anyone. I have to develop a trust. Develop a trust—well, I'm sure you are aware. Develop a trust and to just feel comfortable, which I do now. I feel totally at ease." And then the client went on to talk of how her female friend had exploited her.

The immediacy with which the therapist becomes a significant figure in the life of the client during the initial interview is interesting. On the basis of the client's reactions, she would appear to be putty in the therapist's hands. She trusts him, feels comfortable, and has found the man she has been searching for. He has been chosen to alleviate her problems. The client's hidden agenda is not very well concealed. Her trust comes on the heels of her difficulties in relating to women. The competitive factors arousing that trust are apparent. The therapist is to rescue the client from the clutches of evil women. Other male professionals have not been able to do so. The therapist must prove himself to be the better man. Considering the competition between father and boyfriend, the therapist's task would be monumental if his own "ego" became involved in the rescue mission. Such ploys to activate a therapist to compete with and triumph over other males and win the favor of the client are repetitive themes.

The hysterical client is intensely aware of how she is being received. In particular, the hysteric is hypersensitive to the therapist's feelings about her, constantly alert to nuances in his behavior that reflect his subliminal attitudes about her. A hysterical client may leave an initial interview feeling that the therapist was cold or warm rather than that he was competent or lacking in insight.

In initial interviews, the client is provided with a sense of what therapy is all about. The client is extremely sensitive to how the therapist responds to her efforts at integrating that relationship, regardless of her circuitous mode of communicating. Accordingly, it is crucial that the client develop a sense of the therapist. If a therapist simply sits back, listens, asks questions periodically, and internally notes the client's defensive patterns, that client is unlikely to continue therapy. Chodoff (1982) expressed the issue well when he observed that the therapist must be flexible and interactive and that therapist neutrality may be ineffective with many hysterical clients. The therapist must be natural. He must let humanness guide his reactions.

That humanness is sometimes evident in the therapist's response to client behaviors that are intended to entertain and please. The hysterical client, in order to relate and communicate, often introduces humorous stories. If the therapist enjoys the bit of humor, the client may respond by escalating her entertaining behavior. Such reactions are the norm. The problem arises if the therapist feels that he must conceal the fact that the client has amused him.

One client, who had been seeing a therapist for some time, described her earlier internal experience to the therapist's "poker face." She said that she exhausted her repertoire in attempting to elicit a response from the therapist, but to no avail. As with most interpersonally oriented hysterics, her intent was to stimulate an interaction. She humorously described her interaction with the therapist as that of talking to ''a baked potato.'' The ideal lies somewhere between the two extremes of being ''a baked potato'' and becoming overly involved at the expense of attending to the dynamic issues embedded in the humorous reports (see Chodoff 1982).

The introduction of material and flow of emotional experience in the client's productions reflect, to a large extent, the immediacy of her experience with the therapist and her rather remarkable sense of the therapist's feelings and reactions to her. The client's associative links may appear disconnected and illogical, but when the person of the therapist is included in the equation, her stories and seeming illogic take on new meaning. If the therapist retains his center of gravity despite the rapid-fire interactions and attends to his feelings and reactions as the potential stimulus for the client's thematic productions, he receives a vital picture of the nature and process of conflict in the client. Essentially, he gains access to the internal mediating processes in the client.

The Hysterical Style of Presentation

Farber (1966) noted a curious phenomenon, frequently experienced in therapy with the hysterical client, in which the hysteric's ''mannerisms of body and voice, formerly inconspicuous, acquire a new and crude existence widely separated from what is said'' (p. 107). Essentially, the style of the hysteric's presentation can overshadow the content or substance of the communication. The net result is that the therapist may respond to the manner of the presentation rather than to the substance of the material, and accordingly the therapeutic task will be derailed. But if the therapist can accept the hysteric's style and work within it without becoming collusive or overwhelmed, then the foundation for understanding and continued therapeutic exploration has been established.

The hysteric's previously mentioned need to entertain is diagnostic in itself. But if the therapist responds in ways that suggest that he finds the hysteric entertaining, then the content and associated affects of the ensuing entertaining material gain added significance, because the productions are for the therapist's benefit. Careful attention to that material may reveal some of the client's underlying attitudes and feelings about the therapist and others whom she has found it necessary to entertain.

During initial interviews, it is crucial that the therapist maintain a balanced attention to the content and style of presentation. The stories that the hysteric produces about her experiential history may provide some insight into the relationship between style and content. In recounting conflicts in her previous and ongoing relationships, the hysteric takes two roles: she is at once an actor in the drama and the narrator. In the hysteric's role as actor, her histrionics and flare for drama, and the "as-if" character of her affects, are dominant. She lives the part of the victim, rescuer, angry child, or the like with affects that are overdone and "unreal."

The hysteric takes not only her own role in recounting dramatic scenes, but also the roles of significant others in relation to her. She may mimic the voices of her father, mother, or lovers in her elaborations of those interactions, revealing much about the emotional residue of those experiences. The exaggerated affects in those portrayals are often defensive maneuvers and obvious efforts at denying the impact of those encounters and their continuing importance to her.

The highly emotional scenes are interrupted at times by the hysteric as narrator. The narrator is a rather dispassionate observer of the scenario who intercedes to provide factual links in the stories for the benefit of the therapist. The switch from actor to narrator is dramatic in itself. In the role of narrator, the hysteric is matter-of-fact. She fills in the details in much the way that a reporter flashes the camera back and forth in describing a highly emotional scene:

> During her initial interview, the client launched immediately into a description of the way in which she had been

exploited by her father and mother. According to the client's reports, the father was a narcissistic man who denigrated the mother in the client's presence as well as in private talks with the client. The client was the father's confidante and traveling companion. The mother was perceived to be resentful but impotent to interfere in the father–daughter relationship or relate as a wife.

In describing vivid scenes of familial interactions, the client acted the part of both parents as well as that of the exploited child. She mimicked the voices of her father and mother. Throughout her portrayal of those dramatic scenes, the client's voice was strident and pleading, like the wailing of a child. In the midst of a rather histrionic description of one scene during early adolescence in which she was her father's drinking companion, the client's voice changed dramatically. In the rather matter-of-fact voice of an observer of the scene, she laughingly commented that ''from the sounds of things, when I'm explaining them to you, it doesn't sound like I had a normal childhood.''

Some of the seemingly factual links that the narrator interjects provide the therapist with crucial information about the precipitants of conflict and the hysteric's own role and neurotic gains. It is as though the narrator role is that of the observing ego that recognizes the drama for what it is but is helpless to drop the curtain on the interminable play.

Both the narrator role and the scenario provide the therapist with clues to the core conflicts. The content of the drama, with the assistance of the observing narrator, provides the therapist with clues to the events that aroused conflict, the conflict proper, and the neurotic outcomes. The magnified and fictitious affects displayed during the scenario provide the therapist with a sense of the unfulfilled emotional needs of the client.

The affects may be of several orders. The consciously experienced affect may screen unconscious affects of the same order. The hysterical client who contends that she feels so guilty about her mother's distraught state may in fact feel guilty because of her collusion with the father. In that case, the exaggerated guilt may ward off genuine guilt. The magnified affects however, may also screen a complex of sometimes oppositional affects. The client may contend that she is very angry with her father when in fact the intonations sound like anything but anger. The contention of anger may be expressed in a highly strident or pleading voice, or the whiny tones of the child who can't get what she wants. Although some genuine anger may be screened by the fictitious display of anger, that anger is often a thin veneer covering hurtful experiences, affectional needs, and neurotic gains.

In either case, the exaggerated affect, reinforced by histrionics and "acting," maintains a disconnected state between the experience and affective awareness. To some extent, the hysteric avoids knowing what she feels by "acting" or emoting, but she also avoids anxiety and conflict by stopping herself at the point at which she may understand. The insight is too traumatic; it may disorganize self-percepts and those of others. So the hysteric retreats to trailing-off sentences, using words like "I don't know" to avoid knowing.

The net effect is that the hysteric may report serious difficulty in achieving. Shapiro (1965) described the global, diffuse style of the hysteric, which serves to reinforce repression and works against successful mastery of the logical, the sciences. The hysteric has difficulty in the sciences because they are problem-solving ventures. For the hysteric, problem solving is associatively close to becoming aware of dissociated feelings. In initial sessions the therapist may not solve the analytic question of what undergirds the client's inability to follow through with feelings, but he may gain respect for the client if he recognizes the intense anxiety about "knowing" that has necessitated the development of her elaborate defensive structure. The pattern can be shown in a case vignette.

The client initially entered the sciences to appease her father, who had been collusive with her during early development but then rejected her when she turned her attention to other men. She had considerable difficulty in achieving, not because she was incapable of the work, but because something inside would stop her just as she was about to solve a difficult problem in one of her assignments. On one such occasion, the client reported that she had felt frustrated and had turned to a male friend for help. Despite his efforts to help her reach a solution, the client was unable to grasp the concepts. The friend became frustrated and left. The client later felt very apologetic and called her friend. They were reunited, and he responded in nurturant, caring ways, providing the client with warm, emotional support. The client's remorse as a way of gaining warmth and affection took its toll in renewed anger, and the cycle repeated itself interminably in various forms.

Only later in therapy did it become clear that the client couldn't win with her father. If she appeared too bright or attempted to solve the problems that led to familial discord, she was dismissed as a child. She was encouraged to enter the sciences, her father's field, but if she became too conversant in the subject matter, she threatened her father and was considered an intruder into a "man's" field. The client contended that she was angry with her father, but she did not feel the anger. The stakes were too high. She could not allow herself to "know" that he was a threatened man who felt inadequate. Rather, she reverted to frustrating the father by not understanding simple mathematics problems.

In his annoyance, the father would reject the client as stupid. To regain his affection and maintain the myth that she was in fact the stupid one, the client would constantly cater to his ego. The gain from frustrating the father was secondary. The primary gain was the denial of the father's inadequacy. In the initial interviews, the outcome of those developmental conflicts was evident in the client's anxiety about solving problems, her belief that she was stupid, her conversion of anger into frustrating the male, and her abject apologies as a way of winning affection and reinforcing her myth about males.

MULTIPLE EFFECTS OF THERAPIST REACTIVITY

The therapist's reactions, feelings, and attitudes about the hysterical client during initial contacts may facilitate the diagnostic process and set the stage for a productive psychotherapeutic venture, or they may contribute to a breakdown in communication and interrupt the development of an adequate clinical picture, and psychotherapy may end before it begins.

Perhaps the most crucial issue determining the success of early interviews, both in obtaining an adequate assessment and in setting psychotherapy on a productive course, is the therapist's attitude about the hysterical client. Chodoff's comments (1982) about the deleterious effects of pejorative attitudes on the therapeutic relationship with a hysterical client are as relevant to the initial phase as they are to the ensuing psychotherapeutic venture—perhaps more so, because these attitudes provide the hysteric's initiation into the process. A hysterical client will forgive many errors on the part of a therapist if she feels he is concerned about her and respects her, but she will not tolerate being disdained.

The hysterical style of relating and the associated defenses—exaggeration, dramatization, flightiness, and demandingness—can alienate a therapist and set into motion therapist reactions and behaviors that, no matter how carefully screened, are experienced in magnified form by the hypersensitive client. (A therapist who is immediately alienated by a hysterical client's style may have much in common with her. Such a therapist's reactions appear impulsive, unmediated, and feeling oriented. The therapist's impulsive distaste for the client is akin to the hysteric's reactions following an initial interview.)

The net effect of a therapist's negative attitudes is that the client's free-flowing style immediately tightens, and instead of revealing herself, the client becomes resistant. In her resistance, however, the client is apt to recall material that bears on her immediate experience with the rejecting therapist. Provided that the therapist is sensitive to the relevance of the material as an index of clients' reactions to their interactions, the potential exists for resolving the impasse and facilitating communication. At those times in the interview, it may be necessary to attend to the relationship so that matters can move ahead. In a very real sense, however, such attention to the relationship *is* progressive, because it provides the client with an encapsulated prelude to one of the critical issues in her psychotherapy: the working through of conflict in a human relationship.

If the therapist is insensitive to his own stimulus value in generating client productions and assumes that the client's resistance is her problem, the client may fall back on one of her major defenses: thwarting the therapist through passive control. A hysterical client is so immediately interpersonally reactive that her interests in solving her problems will become secondary to her possible gains from engaging the pejorative and patronizing therapist in a battle of wills—a clash that the therapist will lose. Hysterical clients have a way of activating a therapist's own willfulness, and unless the therapist can disengage himself from battle, the interview has terminated for all practical purposes.

Unless the therapist is so enmeshed in his own unmediated participatory behavior that his observing ego is obliterated, he may be able to sit back and be somewhat amused at what he has learned about himself. In doing so, he has a chance of recovering and getting the process back on track, with renewed insight and respect for the eliciting power of the hysterical personality. That insight may also help the therapist to modify some of his preconceived views about the shallowness of the hysterical character.

Therapist Reactivity as a Diagnostic Guide

When a therapist catches himself becoming overly involved, anxious, overwhelmed by the client's material, or engaging in a battle of wills with the client, he may be tracking a hysterical personality. The therapist's reactivity can be a useful diagnostic guide provided that he has sufficient grasp of the therapist's role that his own anxiety does not preclude observing himself in relation to the client.

But a therapist's anxieties may get the best of him. Levenson's observation (1972) that a therapist's diagnostic powers are inversely related to his anxiety level seems particularly appropriate to the problem of accurately diagnosing the hysterical personality. Although speaking more generally, Levenson provided some superb examples of the way in which the severity of the diagnosis escalates as the therapist attempts to rid himself of his anxious feelings—an event that seems to occur with regularity in the diagnosis and psychotherapy of the hysterical personality.

In an early session with a highly disturbed client, a therapist may experience anxiety because of his sense of imminent danger to the client's emotional state, his fear for the client, and his inability to forestall further debilitation. Such anxiety is appropriate; it is aroused by concern for another's well-being, and it is integrative and productive for the client. With a hysterical client, a distinction must be made between two types of therapist anxiety.

Anxiety can be aroused in a therapist by the hysteric's impulsive, self-destructive reports of her behavior. That kind of therapist concern about the client's well-being is integrative in that it arises out of concern for the client. Therapist anxiety that is destructive to the relationship is of a different order. Often, the anxiety that is aroused in a therapist in work with the hysterical client, whether during initial contacts or later in psychotherapy, is a sense of danger to the therapist's own sense of well-being.

The hysterical client is highly sensitive to a therapist's vulnerabilities and has a way of touching those tender spots with uncanny accuracy. Often a therapist's anxiety is aroused because his defenses are being penetrated, and he may take measures to dissociate himself from the client. Glazer (1979) made the very apt point that therapists are not inclined to see themselves as borderline personalities and may inappropriately use the diagnosis to distance themselves from the client. In the case of hysterical personalities, who tend to wreak havoc with a therapist's sense of well-being, such a misdiagnosis seems a simple way to settle one's anxiety.

During the interview a therapist may find other ways of retreating from the intensity of the hysteric's interpersonal sensitivities, particularly her angry demandingness. He may become inappropriately supportive and collusive, abdicating necessary inquiry for the sake of his own comfort. In either case, the issue reveals more about the therapist than the client. Apparently, such a therapist views his own anxiety negatively instead of as a diagnostic guide in an interview.

The therapist who views his own reactions—anxiety, anger, disdain, collusiveness—as diagnostic guides can be particularly effective with a hysterical personality. The therapist must constantly attend to his own reactions, noting the arousal of any feelings, no matter how fleeting. If the therapist can attach those feelings to the content, affect, or style of the hysteric, he has additional assessment information. When a therapist attends to his reactions during the interview, he may note the pressure he feels to respond in particular ways. He may feel that his freedom is attenuated and that he is cast in roles that he disavows. In Leary's terms (1957), the pressures to respond in given ways increase in relation to the limitations of the repertoire of the other person.

Those pressures reveal much about the anxieties of the client and her efforts to maintain the status quo. The therapist may feel forced into a controlling position because of a client's many pleas for help and her reports of her helplessness to master her environment. The trick is for the therapist to do what the hysterical client cannot do: step back and observe his participating behavior in the process. Once the therapist steps back, he can provide the client with information about his reactions and her stimulus value, thus giving her a prototype that may be useful to her in psychotherapy.

In other words, the therapist searches for the communicative aspects of the emotions that the client elicits in others. For example, the controlling features of a hysteric's helpless behavior have been greatly emphasized in the study of hysterical personalities. Certainly there are controlling features to a hysteric's contention of helplessness. It is also true that the hysteric communicates her anger, particularly at dominating, controlling males, through her passivity. But she does more: she communicates her anxiety about the direct expression of angry, aggressive feelings. She communicates a sense of hopelessness that she can have her needs met on other grounds. She communicates a vulnerability to being controlled that stems from unmet dependency needs, and a fear of exploitation if those needs are manifested.

When viewed dispassionately, the defensive character and underlying insecurity of such an intense need to control are apparent. But the complexity of the personality—the underlying substance, anguish, and need to relate—is often lost in the hysterical overlay of exaggerations, apparent shallowness, and control issues that may distract and draw a therapist into impulsive reactivity. The ability of a client to elicit such predictable responses suggests the power of the neurosis, the intensity of the anxiety, and the certainty of the diagnosis. Yet the very features that confirm the diagnosis become the conditions for misdiagnosis because of the reflexive reactivity of the therapist.

A therapist who is overly involved and nonobservant may discount data crucial to an adequate assessment. The stories that the hysteric produces may be dismissed as meaningless chatter. Yet those stories are rather remarkable indices of the client's experience of the relationship, they are the seeds for later transference reactions, and they foretell the pitfalls that the therapist must avoid if therapy is to be productive. In the next section, a sequential analysis of an initial interview with a hysterical client is provided to demonstrate the subtleties of interactions and the relevance of the material that the client produces.

SEQUENTIAL ANALYSIS OF AN INITIAL INTERVIEW

The contents and associated affects of an initial interview often predict the unfolding of the transferences during therapy. In an initial interview, through the many stories that she weaves, the hysteric demonstrates what she needs, the way she defends, and her predictions for therapy. In a similar vein, the therapist's thoughts, feelings, and initial reactions to the client embody the themes that may emerge as countertransference issues in later interactions. Much of the course of therapy is evident in the initial interview (Kell and Mueller 1966).

An initial session with a very sensitive hysterical client may help to illustrate a client's emotional swirl, massive projections, and hair-trigger reactivity to the ongoing flow of emotional conditions within the relationship. Throughout the session, the client speaks to the therapist primarily through the third person of a newly forming relationship with a male friend. Other subordinate male relationships are introduced periodically and serve similar functions. The client's hopes for therapy, her fears that therapy may leave her in a worsened state, the nature of her anxieties, and the regression she anticipates in order to gain more self-esteem are all expressed indirectly through those relationships.

The conflicts in those relationships not only guide the therapist in understanding the client's expectations for therapy, the nature of the conflict, and the anticipated outcome, but also reflect the client's inner processes during the session. One can note the ebb and flow of ambivalence and modified predictions about therapy through the changing contents and affects associated with the ongoing relationships reported. The rapid-fire changes in content and emotion reflect an uncanny awareness of the therapist during the session.

The client was a very attractive woman who exuded a kind of sexualized energy through which she communicated all of her needs. She breezed into the therapist's office in a charming way. The client was electric. She had a way of searching the therapist's face for reactions that suggested a highly tuned alert system. She tended to laugh when she was anxious, a rather unreal laugh that seemed devoid of any connection with a rich, inner fantasy life.

The client was somewhat late for the first session; she was anxious and extremely sensitive to the therapist and her surroundings. The therapist commented that he could provide the client with a little extra time because it was their first session, but he clarified their appointment time. The client countered that she would need to leave early because she had another pressing appointment.

Rather immediately, the client commented that she was reluctant to discuss certain problems and might better talk to a woman. With some mild encouragement, the client said that she needed to make a decision that day about whether to become sexually involved with an older man for what "could be just a fling." She thought that she might be able to reserve judgment about becoming sexually involved until she had a chance to "see how things feel and all." The rendezvous had been arranged a few weeks earlier, and the client was having second thoughts about how the relationship would affect her emotionally.

The therapist's initial thoughts were that he was in the presence of a most interesting woman. There seemed to be a significant parallel in the arrangement for the first session and the anticipated sexual rendezvous with a potential suitor. Through the safety of a third person, the client was speaking to the therapist of her anxieties about entering psychotherapy and her fears that the relationship may affect her adversely. The client's ambivalence seemed apparent in her tentativeness and in her likening therapy to a fling. The client seemed skeptical and skittish.

Because the therapist felt that the client's concerns might not be consciously experienced and that approaching them directly might simply meet resistance, he avoided any direct discussion about her fears about therapy. Rather, he attempted to uncover those concerns through a discussion of her fears and anticipations about her forthcoming encounter with her male friend.

The therapist asked the client what had attracted her to the potential suitor. She responded that the man was someone she had known for a while. She was attracted to him because they were both deep thinkers who shared an interest in psychic phenomena; the man had a good sense of humor and was very loving. The client felt that his being married was his concern and that the intimate course the relationship might take would be his responsibility. She didn't want to break up the marriage; she felt that the relationship was not going to be a "long-term thing" and hoped they could be friends afterward.

She was also attracted to him because he was patient and related well to his children. The client felt that she might be looking for a father figure. As the client described the latter quality, she seemed to be searching the therapist's face. She followed her statement with the comment that she didn't think he would "mind playing a little bit of that role." The client then went on to say that she was searching for physical affection and that she wasn't about to engage in the relationship "just for the sex"; she hoped the relationship with him would give her a chance to "explore a part of" herself and had a "feeling" that he was "the right person to help" her. Immediately thereafter, the client noted that she had had problems with sex before and that the man knew of her sex life and the troubles she had encountered in that area. She commented that knowing about her difficulties didn't "scare him off."

At that point in the session, the transparency began to crumple, the tense and person in sentences changed, and the client began to talk more directly to the therapist through the other male. She didn't want someone to erase her problems, because that would be "egotistical" of the male. She repeated her feeling of being "fond of" the man but noted that they had an agreement that if the relationship didn't "click" they would call it off. The important thing for the client was that she was willing to try the relationship because she wasn't feeling pressure.

This was an astonishing beginning. In the first few minutes of their contact, through her discussion of an impending relationship with a male suitor, the client spelled out exactly what she wanted from therapy, what therapist behavior would be helpful or inhibiting, and what her anxieties were that could dissolve the relationship. The previews of transference were embedded in needing a father figure, in confusing sexuality with affectional needs, in reacting negatively to egotistical behavior, and in showing resistance when pressured. The risk to the therapeutic venture lay in the client's ambivalence about a long-term agreement, in her impulsive behavior, and in the potential for "splitting" the transference and displacing transference feelings onto ongoing relationships.

A number of recurrent themes in the assessment of the hysterical personality begin to emerge during these opening interactions and client reports. The client's preoccupation with sex as a symbolic representation of a range of conflicts is typical of the hysterical personality. Sexuality appeared to be a vehicle for gratifying a range of needs yet seemed devoid of intrinsic genital gratification.

Issues of control were apparent even in the first moments of contact. The client's response that she, too, had other appointments when the therapist noted the time restraints of their meetings but offered some additional time suggested that she had a considerable investment in control issues. Her tentativeness about a commitment and her wariness about the adverse effects of the relationship suggested an underlying vulnerability to being controlled. The client's preoccupation in that regard seemed most evident in her repetitive statements about the freedom of either party to leave the relationship if it didn't "click."

The hypersensitivity of the client to the therapist's reactions was noteworthy. When the client commented that she needed a father figure, she seemed to be searching the therapist for cues to his internal reactions. Her following statement that she thought he wouldn't mind playing that role corresponded to the therapist's feeling at the time that the client seemed to have missed some fathering along the way. That type of hysterical sensitivity to the nuances of behavior and emotions in another can create problems in psychotherapy.

The problems arise because the hysteric's immense sensitivity is coupled with another recurring theme: the immediacy with which she acts on her internal judgments of the other person. In their brief contact, the therapist felt that the client was sensitively testing his reactions and then acting on her intuitive sense of him in providing additional information about her conflicts. The client's feeling orientation was evident in her unvalidated impression that he "is the right person to help." Such rapid internal processing in a client can provide a therapist with some lively moments. The immediacy with which the hysteric acts on her reactions can lead to a rupture in the relationship or to the displacement of conflicts onto ongoing relationships. In this case, the client seemed to have split-second emotional reactions to the therapist, as evidenced by the ebb and flow of her ambivalence about psychotherapy. This oscillation escalated as the session continued.

The client's fears become apparent if her positive statements are inverted. She feared that she would scare the therapist if he got to know her; she feared being pressured; she feared egotistical males. Those fears were coupled with anxiety and expressed in her musing about the emotional effects the relationship might have on her. The anxiety aroused ambivalence, which was expressed through repeated limit-setting on the length of the relationship. It was not to be a long-term one and was to be an open-ended contract.

After some mild intervention by the therapist to the effect that exploration of such conflicts seemed appropriate for therapy, the client introduced conflict in another male relationship. It seemed that the platonic nature of the second relationship, with a man her own age, was changing, and the client feared that it was evolving into a sexual relationship. The client felt that sex "sometimes spoils a relationship." She hoped that through her impending relationship with the first suitor, she would be able to gain self-confidence and be able to engage in more satisfying sexual relationships with men her own age.

Given the entrée of her wish to gain more confidence in herself, the therapist again intervened, pointing out the usefulness of verbalizing and exploring those feelings. The client interpreted the therapist's statements as emphasizing talking about feelings, whereas she wanted to experience them. The client wanted to engage in a relationship in which she could be "observing what I'm doing while I'm doing." The therapist was encouraged by that bit of observing ego. The client immediately retreated to an ambivalent state and wondered whether she should call off her pending rendezvous with the older man. Although she felt like a "little scared kid," she didn't want to cut herself off from the relationship because she "would be no better than I was before."

Because the client's attention to sexuality seemed to predominate, the therapist asked if the client felt that she had conflicts in that area. The client admitted that she felt inadequate even though she had often been reassured about her beauty. Apparently, the therapist's inquiry about her sexuality triggered a significant reaction in the client. She noted that she was not as attracted to the potential suitor as she was sure he would be to her. She felt that she might not "be able to get really excited *just about him.*" And she inquired of the therapist, "You know what I mean? You know what I'm saying?" The therapist responded that he did. The client continued to wonder whether she would have as much ardor toward the man as he would toward her. But she wanted someone just to care about her, laughingly calling it "unconditional" love.

The hysterical client is often inappropriately accused of being scattered and superficial. In this case, on the surface it may seem that the client is flitting from male to male and topic to topic. Yet when the sequential themes are analyzed, they reflect a rather remarkable unconscious and a solid intuitive grasp of a healthy developmental process. To paraphrase the client, she notes that because of her lack of a solid identity, she has conflicts in an age-appropriate relationship that has the potential to become a sexual relationship. She sees the resolution to the conflict in exploring those problems in a safe relationship with a man who is secure in himself. She is anxious and ambivalent about doing so. She recognizes that if she avoids the issues, she will be cutting off an opportunity for growth.

The therapist met resistance with his statement about verbalizing feelings, which the client construed as a reference to talking about feelings rather than experiencing them. She provided him with a fair definition of an observing ego and then questioned whether she should continue in the relationship or call off the rendezvous. This hypersensitivity was impressive and disconcerting, because the therapist began to feel that he had little room in which to err. But then the client settled her own ambivalence by suggesting that if she didn't give the relationship a chance, she would be "no better than...before."

The client's response to the therapist's inquiry about sexual conflicts provided significant assessment information. The client's fear that the potential suitor would become more enamored of her than she of him seemed directly related to the therapist's inquiry. The client apparently was fearful that because of her attractiveness, the therapist might become overly responsive and lose his objectivity, and therapy might be derailed. When the client repeatedly asked if the therapist understood her meaning, he commented that he did, hoping to alleviate her fears that his question about her sexual conflicts was motivated by sexual interest.

In his response, the therapist also wanted to communicate to the client that he would take appropriate responsibility for himself in the therapeutic relationship. Male responsibility was an apparent concern of the client, who had commented that the man with whom she was planning a rendezvous was responsible for his own actions in relation to his marriage. The theme of significant males who have behaved irresponsibly and its relationship to the hysterical preoccupation with sexuality has its roots in the father–daughter relationship, as we have discussed. When such concerns are expressed, as they were by this client, the therapist is most certainly tracking a hysterical personality.

Seeing another opportunity to gain some distance and uncover some relevant history, the therapist inquired about whether the client felt she had gotten unconditional love. The client began a tirade about her father, who hadn't attended to her except when she performed. She attached her constricted feelings to that relationship and again expressed a wish to be totally immersed in her feelings. A third man was introduced into the picture, a man whom the client had casually observed in a public setting. He purportedly had been flirtatious. Something about the man had disturbed the client, a "kind of feeling from him." She had been with another man at the time and had felt a strong need to be protected, to be held and feel loved.

The client wasn't sure whether she could be understood. The man with whom she was contemplating a relationship had seen only one side of her, her inhibitions, inadequacies, and uncertainties. He hadn't seen how deep she was or the better parts of her personality. But she sensed that he wanted her to learn to be more expressive, which confirmed her belief that he wouldn't mind being a father figure. And the client then expressed her anxieties about how other people viewed her.

Seeing a potential opportunity to connect the feelings to the client's concerns about therapy, the therapist commented that many of those concerns were "perhaps true of your coming here too." The client laughed and commented that she had been about to say that she felt the same way with the therapist. The client then expressed a wish to work out her feelings about her father. Immediately thereafter, she noted that the air was stuffy and that she wanted to open a window but thought that she could "survive" another few minutes. The client then commented that she didn't like being viewed as immature and felt that she had been "going in different directions." She began to think that the therapist might be thinking unkindly of her, her "affairs," and her "immaturity."

In this sequence, several additional features emerge. In inquiring about whether the client had felt loved, the therapist set off a series of reactions. He activated some anger toward and longing for the father. The intensity of the activated need to feel loved was so great that it almost took on the proportions of an hallucinatory wish as she described her reactions to a complete stranger's assumed flirtatiousness. Then, through the third person of another man, the client questioned whether the therapist was capable of providing her with what she needed. She had been inhibited during the session, unsure of herself, and wondered whether the therapist could see the depth of her personality.

Throughout the sequence, the client's ambivalence was aroused; she can be seen to fight it, make a tentative move toward the therapist, and then retreat. A dramatic example of that oscillation appears at the end of the sequence, when she directly expressed to the therapist her interest in working through the conflicts in relation to her father. Immediately thereafter, the air became stuffy and the client wanted to open a window. The depth of the client's anxieties about entering psychotherapy with a male therapist seemed most evident at that moment.

The therapist then commented that the proof of his attitudes toward her was in their work together and that he didn't think any reassurances would substitute for her feeling that they had accomplished something. The client immediately took the conversation back to her new relationship and discussed her fears that all males have a hostile side, some secret inside "that's just lurking beneath the surface."

She then described her father's irrationality and his volatility. Reportedly, the client's father was explosive, and no amount of rationality on her part could control his moods. The client's reports of her relationship to her father became intermixed with projections onto the therapist, and her affect became labile. She felt that all men were explosive. The client's basic fear was that there was something about her that brought out such reactions in men. She then turned to the therapist and wondered if she was "going to bring out" his "feelings of hate" for her. She felt that the therapist would think that she was weird, immature, and bitchy.

The therapist commented that if such thoughts occurred to her, they ought to be discussed in the therapeutic work together. The mood of the session changed dramatically again. As suddenly as the client had projected hateful feelings onto the therapist, she found him completely trustworthy. Immediately, the client reintroduced the topic of her new male acquaintance and said that she hoped that she didn't develop a guilt complex if the relationship didn't work out. She again repeated the man's promise that if it didn't "click, fine."

Another male acquaintance was introduced into the discussion. The client felt that he was very attracted to her and needed her. Despite her forewarnings and his agreement to the conditions of the relationship that she had set, in short order he had made sexual advances. The client then wondered whether the man she had just met would be sexually persuasive; she wondered if he would be coarse. She anticipated no violence.

Performance again became an issue. The client felt guilty about having a male attend to her without her reciprocating sexually. The client noted that she felt differently now than she had a few weeks ago, however. Her own sexual urges were at low ebb, and she thought she would give the relationship a try for a few weeks and postpone sex. Those feelings were countered by equally strong feelings that it was her duty to perform sexually, "to get it over with." She laughed and said, "It's like, I've committed myself."

In these passages the client's anxieties become more focused. Male aggression in the face of thwarted sexual drives undergird some of the client's fears. At the surface level, several aspects of the client's bind become somewhat clearer. She assumes that sexuality is the driving force in any male–female relationship and that all other needs are subverted by the male's sexual appetite. If she wants to express other needs, she can do so only through the medium of sexual performance. If she refuses, she arouses male hostility. Yet she is sexually inhibited, so she desperately tries to be eminently clear in a relationship that sexuality will have no place in it until her self-confidence is reinforced. But her experience has been that sexual advances are always in the wings, and so the cycle repeats itself.

Another feature of the client's bind is that she interprets all actions and reactions as sexually motivated. No needs, feelings, or behaviors have meaning or intentionality on their own merits; all are subsumed under the sexual oversoul. That construction of events suggests the need for a rather complex unraveling process during psychotherapy.

The recall of affect-laden material about the father became the experience of the moment. The intensity of the client's feelings overwhelmed her observing ego, and she became labile, projecting freely and massively. As immediately as the therapist had become the hateful object, his few supporting words turned him into a most trustworthy person. The impulsive, unmediated, and labile affect suggests the power of the client's disowned hostile feelings and the fear of retaliation.

The recurrent themes in those passages provide additional confirmation for an assessment of this client as manifesting a hysterical personality disorder. The performance theme that permeates the client's reports, and its intricate association to sexual performance, is characteristic of hysterics. Resentment about self-indulgent males is its corollary. The satisfaction of other needs—receiving "unconditional love"—is contingent on performing satisfactorily for the male's benefit. Is it any wonder, then, that the hysterical client often complains of being frigid or inorgasmic and uses her sexuality as an outlet for anger and resentment and as a means to frustrate her partner?

In the remainder of the session, a number of themes in the client's relationship with her father predominated. The father's volatility was well established. From the client's perspective, the father was self-centered, unable to admit mistakes, and irresponsible. The client apparently spent considerable energy in frustrated efforts to induce responsible parental behavior in her father. His defensiveness precluded the expression of any negative feelings about him.

Although the father was the source of many of the client's complaints, her mother was instrumental in stimulating conflict. The client saw her mother as immature and as exploiting the client for the benefit of her own well-being. The client felt that she was the family scapegoat, used by the mother, who was too frightened to confront the father.

Several of the developmental themes that have been described in Chapter Two as characteristic of the histories of hysterics are reflected in this interview. The client's perception of her father as volatile, irrational, self-centered, irresponsible, and defensive is a repeated developmental theme. The client's reports of her mother are classical. The mother is perceived to be inadequate as a role model and exploitative of the child for the sake of her own sense of well-being in relation to the father. Neither the mother nor the father seems adequate to the task of parenting.

Chapter Eight

The Dynamics of Change

The focus of the last chapter was the initial encounter with the hysterical client and the conditions which facilitate or impede a productive therapeutic venture. The intent of the present chapter is to follow the hysterical client from her entrance into psychotherapy through the conflicts that are aroused as the relationship intensifies and the therapist grows in significance.

THEMES IN EARLY SESSIONS

In the following case illustration, the client, who had prior experience with therapy and was highly motivated, provided the therapist with a rather full accounting of her developmental conflicts in their initial session. The associated affects, however, were inconsistent with the contents, and the therapist had only brief, largely inferential glimpses of the client's genuine reactions to her experience. The guidelines for the ensuing therapeutic work were embedded in that inconsistency.

The client was a woman in her mid-twenties. She had seen a number of professionals before her contact with the present therapist. The client's reactions to her former therapists were of considerable assistance to the therapist in understanding what had been helpful and what had gone awry in those relationships. Not only did the therapist have the advantage of the client's impressions of previous professional help, but her many problematic relationships fueled her eagerness to correct whatever it was that kept her from self-fulfillment. The client was highly motivated to rectify a very dissatisfying relationship with her parents. Unlike some hysterical clients, who reveal themselves through the derivatives of conflict in displaced relationships, this client provided the therapist with significant information about her development. Like all true hysterics, the client did displace during the course of therapy, but the therapist had some solid anchor points from her history to guide his interventions.

In the initial interview, the client described what she liked about her former female therapist. The therapist had interacted with her. She was responsive and "didn't just stare at me," something she had experienced with another former therapist. The client wanted "feedback" that gave her some "direction as to what's going on." Having established that ground rule, the client began to discuss a crisis she was experiencing. The client clutched in taking tests and developed flu-like symptoms.

The client experienced many of her conflicts as stemming from a still-active relationship with her father. She saw her father as dominating, capricious, and self-centered. The father was disdainful of the mother in the client's presence and formed an early unhealthy collusive relationship with the daughter. He was seductive toward her as a way of expressing his resentment toward the mother. The client, however, wanted to be on the "winning team," so she would "laugh at his jokes," "go with his flow," and "agree with his opinions."

During her adolescence, the client was discouraged from finding a job or stretching her ego in the usual developmental ways. Rather, she was encouraged to remain in the home and develop her musical talents. The father told her that if she did so, he would always provide for her. The client accepted the promise and remained the possession of the father. When she stopped attending to the father's wishes, however, he flatly rejected her. In mid-adolescence the client started dating. The irate father sexualized the client's normal developmental socializing patterns. According to the client, she felt that her father treated her as though she were "a whore and I, I was only 16" with no sexual experience.

The client's mother colluded in this disparaging attitude. Previously, the mother had been impotent to forestall the father's seductive behavior toward the client. Her impotence was evident to the client, as was her competitive attitude. The mother would not permit the client to identify with her or learn from her. She kept the client out of the kitchen, resented the client's preferred position with the father, and in other ways took her anger out on her daughter. When the client attempted to communicate her anxiety about what was happening to the parents' marriage, the mother, who was actively competing with her, dismissed her as a child. When she attempted to intervene in parental arguments, the father, who had groomed her as confidante, was irate and relegated her to a child role. The client felt anxious, impotent, frustrated, exploited, and deceived. She felt that she was "at the mercy of those two."

The onset of the client's socializing coincided with a rift in the parental relationship, and the parents separated. The inevitable divorce left the client without father or mother. The father, who had promised to care for the client in exchange for her catering to his needs, instead disenfranchised her. The break occurred because the client turned her attention to other men. The client noted that "my dad wanted to be the only man in my life, so much so that it angered him when I went out with someone." The father didn't like the client's boyfriends and played the role of the spurned lover. The client mimicked his voice after the divorce: "You'll never come visit me; you'll just forget all about me."

The father remarried a woman the client's age and, according to the client, provided the new wife with the support he had promised the client. The mother, who was supposedly frigid—

information the client's father conveyed in one of their intimate father-daughter conversations—became sexually involved with a man. The client "knew that she was having sexual relations" with the man and was stunned to think that her mother was not frigid.

But the "shock" was that the mother, who had condemned the client for her supposed sexual interludes during adolescence, was living according to a double standard. In frustration and confusion, the client ended the session by commenting on the double message from both parents: "Damn it, we had the same thing all over again, two things at once."

The Contents of the Session: Preludes to Therapy

The contents of the initial session reflect the history of many hysterical clients and in themselves provided the therapist with some intervention guidelines. The dominant, capricious, and self-centered behavior of the client's father represented her expectations for a therapist. The behavior of acceding to the wishes of another for the "promise" that everything would turn out all right, only to be deceived and abandoned, supplied a warning signal for the therapeutic venture. If the therapist in such a situation takes a dominant, diagnostic role and fosters or condones compliance, he echoes the promises of the father and reenacts the unhealthy alliance. In reenacting the role of the possessive, controlling, and inhibiting father, the therapist will most assuredly not be able to effect change. He will, however, gain first-hand insight into how effectively a hysteric's compliance works as a medium for expressing her willfulness, resentment, and anger.

This client's history provides insight into a recurrent problem in the psychotherapy of hysterical disorders. Others have observed that the hysterical client seeks a relationship in which she is totally gratified by her male companion. Allen (1977), Chodoff (1978, 1982), and Celani (1976) have observed variants on the theme of the intensity of the hysteric's interpersonal demandingness. The dynamics underlying such behavior are partially rooted in the implicit promises of the fathers of hysterics that they will totally gratify the daughters if they remain the possessions of the fathers. From such a perspective, the hysteric's demandingness is a role reversal, with intense anger as the motivating force. Such a dynamic construction makes the behavior meaningful and easier for a therapist to cope with.

In this case the client's pact with the father consisted of the daughter's giving up all outside interests for the sake of the security of being an extension of the father. In essence, the father's promise is that "I will gratify you completely" if you will center in me. When the client submits, as this client did, she accepts the conditions. When this client rebelled and attempted to assert her independence, however, the father rejected her completely. The pact was phrased in all-or-nothing terms.

In her later relationships with males, the hysteric reverses roles and demands the same conditions that her father extracted. The male is to provide her with complete gratification. If he withdraws from such a contract after having made promises, he experiences the anguish that the client experienced in her father's withdrawal. The male must submit completely to her will, as she did to the will of her father. The all-or-nothing polarities of the father become the hysteric's polarities—a rather interesting role reversal. The therapeutic guidelines embedded in such an understanding of the dynamics of the hysteric's search for total gratification are apparent.

The client in this case set some rather healthy ground rules that could be useful in bypassing the development of a dominant–submissive relationship. She wanted "feedback" and some "direction as to what's going on." If such a client provision threatens the therapist because he anticipates being expected to give feedback every step of the way or because he experiences the issue as one of control, he has missed the intent. The client's submissive stance in relation to her parents during development has left her helpless and vulnerable—"at the mercy of those two." The client's request is understandable and healthy and, if appropriately acknowledged, represents a giant step toward developing the therapeutic partnership.

This is not to say that the client may not attempt to use her own ground rule to abort therapy. If the client distorts the need for feedback by adopting a submissive stance that serves to reinforce her sense of insubstantiality, those matters can be addressed. Hysterical clients often do want immediate feedback. They may want to know what the therapist discovered after a first session. Those issues often have much to do with the client's resentment about being the one who has to perform, about being kept in the dark, about being vulnerable to exploitation, and about being in the subservient "client" role.

There are many preludes to therapy in the client's reports of her interaction with her parents. The tendency to comply, to "go with" the flow, seems deeply ingrained. The client resents such compliance, but noncompliance means rejection. The client was ill prepared for life because of the other-centered role she took in the family. When she enters therapy, the client is highly sensitive to her deficits in managing herself independently. Such feelings place the client in a particularly tenuous position. She has learned that help is based on conformity. Although she may resent complying, the alternative is anxiety provoking. Hysterical clients often become highly anxious if they experience angry feelings about a therapist.

In view of this client's history, one can anticipate her concern about the therapist's interest in her. If the therapist becomes overly responsive to the client, she may begin to question his motives. The father was possessive and seductive, and the client is apt to read those motives into actions that are unduly nurturant or protective. Among other things, a protective attitude runs counter to the therapeutic goal of assisting the client to become independent, to understand her inner processes, and to gain a sense of her own substance. Countering the paternal influence by substituting a more benign, liberating "father figure" may in itself do little to help a client expand her ego operations.

The client's reports of her mother reflect considerable ambivalence toward female figures. We can anticipate that the client sees other women as competitive and threatened by her. The client's collusion with the father, however, probably provokes guilt whenever she attempts to compete with other women. She may also view other women as self-serving and as living by pragmatic standards in the service of their own personal gain.

During development, the client was forced to split her loyalties. Her allegiance to her father cost her a mother. Later, when the father rejected her, the client was left to renegotiate a relationship with the mother. The effects of such a splitting contribute to the hysteric's sense of being incomplete. In dyadic therapy, such a client is apt to locate someone in her environment not of the therapist's sex who serves as the therapist's counterpart. The selected person may then play a complementary role to the therapist as the client reworks her development. This client was being seen by a male therapist. If the client introduces some influential female acquaintances during the course of therapy, and the therapist becomes competitive with the outside influence, he reinforces the developmental split. In contrast, if the therapist assumes that the client is attempting to forge an identification with a female figure, his work can be directed toward facilitating a healthy identification.

The Contents and Associated Affects: Dissonance

The contents of the session provide the therapist with some insight into the issues that are likely to be replayed during therapy. When the affects associated with contents are studied, the therapist has a more powerful tool for anticipating process. During the session, the therapist had a sense of the client's strong assertive drives, which were overlaid by two competing defensive structures, neither of which was working effectively. At the manifest level, the client assumed a somewhat pseudomasculine posture in the counterphobic sense described by Blacker and Tupin (1977). This posture was at considerable odds with equally strong evidence of compliance, histrionics, and a generally woeful attitude about her condition.

The client's language was graphic, highly colorful, and coarse. Hardly a sentence reached its final exclamation point without including one or another expletive. The language was vigorous and assaultive, but it lacked "punch." The words did not fit the character and seemed in direct contradiction to the underlying feelings. The client's efforts at a counterphobic solution failed miserably. When the client described how angry she was at the conditions of her past, the anger was strident and pleading. It covered anxiety and helplessness and reflected the client's sense of impotence.

Histrionics were intermixed with the rough language. The client complained in tones reminiscent of those of a wailing child who doesn't really think that she deserves or will get what she wants. The expressed emotions seemed generally unreal, like an over-rehearsed part that had been played many times before. But on a few occasions, the therapist gathered a sense of the genuine emotions and began to understand the necessary overlay.

Early in the session, the client began to talk of her anxieties about being tested. Her explicit reference was to some forthcoming examinations, but the real import may have had more to do with her ''client'' role. Prior to seeing the therapist, the client had undergone an assessment interview and rather extensive diagnostic testing. In the initial session, this client, experienced in the ways of therapists, anticipated having to repeat her history for another stranger who would sit idly by as she again performed.

When the therapist inquired about the history of her test-taking anxiety, the client interrupted him and, in the most compliant way, asked if this session was to be another intake or whether she would be seeing the therapist regularly. The therapist suggested that they use a few sessions to see if they could work together. The client then dropped her false-compliant front and stated some of her concerns about working with the therapist. The therapist commented that if those issues arose, their discussion would keep the communication open.

The therapist was encouraged by the client's directness. Toward the end of the session, after the client had repeated her history for the benefit of the therapist, he asked a question. The client leaned forward and asked him to repeat the question. He did so and she said, ''Oh, I'm sorry, you speak so low that I didn't hear. I'm sorry.'' The therapist got the message. The client wanted to feel that she was in the presence of someone with a little more gusto so that she didn't have to hold back in encountering him. And the therapist had his second insight into the pseudocompliance that covered the client's substance.

That same evening the client called the therapist. She was anxiety ridden and didn't know if she could get through the week. What should she do? The therapist felt that he was reaping the "angry" profits from the repeat performance the client had put on that morning in compliantly telling her history for his benefit. The therapist felt the call was critical. If he responded by inviting an intervening session, the assumed anger would be converted to guilt because of his nurturant attitude; he would most likely set therapy on a course of crises as a substitute for the submerged anger, and, of most importance, he would reinforce the client's sense of being insubstantial. Therefore, the therapist acknowledged the client's anxiety and commented that he felt they most certainly ought to attend to the source of its arousal at their next meeting.

The Emergence of Conflict

The client entered the second session in much the mood of the phone call. She felt she was "going crazy." She was "full of anxiety," got "sick for no reason," had "stomach problems," and couldn't eat or "go to sleep." The client abjectly apologized for calling the therapist because she "didn't mean to bother him or anything," but she was so distraught that she had had no alternative. According to the client, her anxiety was about her "performance" in her academic studies. The client was worried about "knowing what's going on," so much so that she couldn't "hear"; while busily taking "notes" she missed important material. The client felt that if she just "sat back and listened" she could understand. Taking a test was an "inquisition." She felt that perhaps she was taking on too much and should modify her goals.

The issue seemed clearly the client's needing to perform for the sake of others, her resentment about such performances, and her solution: to conform, withdraw, and take a passive role. The client felt that she should be submissive, sit back, listen, and take notes on the words of wisdom from others. Yet her anger, experienced as anxiety, argued for a more assertive posture. The conflict had to be addressed so as to avoid reinforcing the passive character defenses and insubstantiality. The therapist pursued the inhibited assertiveness.

The therapist inquired as to whether those same emotional experiences had occurred in the past. The client elaborated on her experience with her father. The father would become impatient with her lack of understanding about homework assignments. The more the client failed to understand, the more angry the father would become, and the more the client would "freeze up" and become confused. The father's tutoring sessions were of no help. The client recalled that this same situation occurred with her boss in later employment. His anger would escalate at her stupidity; he would "scream" at her, "swear" at her, and humiliate her "in front of other people." The therapist wondered whether her behavior had "frustrated him." The client felt that it did, and the therapist followed up with some comment about her anger having been "heard."

The therapist was trying to plant the seed that the client's own frustration and inability to perform provided her with some gains and permitted the indirect expression of anger. In noting that the client's anger, albeit indirect, was "heard," the therapist attempted also to let the client know that he had heard her anger and accepted it. The therapist's hope was that the client would be able to find some more direct and less self-destructive ways of managing those feelings.

The issue of the client's feeling respected and regarded as a person with some substance recurred later in the session. The client felt that she was "uncertain how other people" viewed her. She described herself as "extremely insecure." She felt "invisible with other people—like I'm talking but I'm not there. It's almost as if I feel like those other people can't even see me."

The client felt "stupid," as though she were the dense one. The therapist commented that her self-disparaging feelings might more accurately reflect the negative feelings she was having toward the other person. The client felt she was not important enough to be remembered, a concept that seemed clearly related to the reaction of significant males toward her. Her basic belief was that males were threatened by women of substance. The client graphically described how she could pick out with uncanny accuracy men who were threatened by women.

The client returned to the issue of performance. She felt her lack of self-confidence triggered her anxiety. She felt as though she had a built-in tape recorder that kept saying, "I can't do it." She wanted to suppress the recorder, but it played on. The therapist suggested that perhaps she was suppressing "I won't do it" instead of "I can't do it," and that the issue was anger. The client assented, but the felt anger was still distant from consciousness.

The session ended with the client retreating to the posture she had taken at the outset of the interview. The client pleaded pathetically for some help with her anxiety. It was again the question of what she should do to get through the week. The therapist again acknowledged her distraught state but stated that he felt that in the long run she might feel better if they continued on their course of trying to unearth its causes. The client's final "all right" was delivered in the tones of a submissive child. The therapist assumed he would hear those intonations again.

The Escalation of Anger

In ensuing sessions the client's anger became more direct, and themes of shared responsibility, performance, mutuality, and power came into the foreground.

The client's anger intensified, and so did honest anxiety, but the client was able to focus on the sources. In the process she provided the therapist with insight into her defensive maneuvering and some additional guidelines for their work together. While taking a test, the client had begun to experience anger. "I was so angry and frustrated that I was practically shaking. I was just so angry at having to take this test." The client's anger was characteristic of some tests and not others. If the client felt that the teacher was involved, interested, and putting effort into teaching, that "sits very well with me." But if she felt that the teacher was going through the motions, she became incensed, because "I have to put forth such an effort, why can't he?" Further, the client felt that she was the one who was always attempting to negotiate a relationship, to find a common ground, to "match up" so both people could "get the maximum out of the relationship." The client was pleased that she had discovered that insightful bit of information about herself.

Several themes are evident at this point. The client's anger was aroused when she felt that a relationship was one-sided and that she was expected to perform unilaterally. She wanted to know that the other person was struggling as hard as she was. The guidelines for the psychotherapy relationship seem evident. Performance is often an issue with hysterical clients. The anger that underlies having to perform for a self-absorbed other takes many forms. In initial sessions a client may demand that the therapist "do something," or a client may perform marvelously in a first session and then expect the therapist to perform for her in the second session. Whatever shape the demand takes, "it sits very well" with a hysterical client if she feels the other person is as deeply invested in the relationship as she is.

The hysteric's idea that a relationship should be defined by mutuality is a solid one. Unfortunately, the hysteric has not learned ways of effecting such mutuality, so she uses whatever means she can muster to communicate her desire for reciprocity. She may do so, as this client initially did, by having an anxiety attack after a session in which she performed. If residual anger from previous relationships is intense, she may demand a performance before she gives anything of a performance herself. Such occurrences are evident in some initial interviews, in which the therapist is left totally responsible for attempting to somehow understand what is creating such havoc in the hysteric's life and in his office.

One of the long-term therapeutic tasks is to help the client to attach her anger to its sources in the emotional experiences of the therapeutic relationship and to point out the ineffectiveness of its indirect expression. In early sessions, before the client feels secure enough to confront her anger, the experience of anger in other relationships is often safer for her. The first step is helping the client to discriminate the conditions under which the anger appears so that it does not spill over in destructive ways. In this case the therapist attempted to help the client to detach the anger from taking tests, because her career was at stake. He felt that if she saw that her reactions were to the personalities of different teachers, she might be in a better position to respond to the material despite her anger.

The client associated anger to feeling powerless, and powerlessness was associated with her father. She wanted to have power over her life, "where I'm going to go, how I'm going to feel, and most of the time it's not like that." Rather, the client felt that she was being molded by external forces. When she talked of wanting power, the client noted that she was always "very tactful with people" even when she didn't feel like being that way. She felt powerful when she didn't rein herself in and just "let out my feelings." The client was never open about her feelings with her father. She felt that he "deluded" himself into thinking he was an "understanding person." But when matters were brought into the open, he would become angry and rejecting. She wanted to see her arrogant father "humbled." She felt that all men were like that. The therapist wondered whether she included him in her generalization. The client felt "pretty comfortable" with the therapist and thought they were getting somewhere.

Returning to her generalization, the client stated that she felt that men didn't listen to women or take them seriously. She felt a woman had "to fight all the time." She didn't want "to carry a chip" around, but she didn't want to be taken advantage of. She feared, however, that given her characteristic style, she could see herself "rolling over" and "letting them roll right over me." The client described her pseudo-masculine posture as being in part a reaction to male dominance. The client said that "in order for men to take me seriously, I must swear like they do, look pretty much like they do. I gotta blend in." Further, she contended that "when I try to act female, no one takes me seriously."

Many of the feelings that the client was expressing about men in general and about her sense of powerlessness to be effective and assertive became the experiential contents of later sessions with the therapist. In a later session, the therapist did inadvertently strip the client of her power, and her reactions were those that she predicted: she became submissive and withdrawn. Those sessions will be described later.

Significant Female Relationships: A Crucial Development

The client's comment that she felt "pretty comfortable" with the therapist and thought that they were working well together may have been the triggering stimulus for the client's introduction of her competitive relationships with two significant women in her life.

The first relationship was with a colleague. The client felt the colleague had a strong personality, like her own. They were competitive, always vying for top position. The client, however, didn't want to compete, but in their conversations, the client would "get so uptight. I really like her, but I get so uptight" for no understandable reason. She thought the two of them worked "well together," but the client had a "smothered feeling around her." Although she sometimes disagreed with the other woman, she would "go along with things" to avoid conflict. But inside she was fighting. The client felt that her own submissive behavior substantiated the woman's feelings "that she is always right."

The client's feelings were less ambivalent in relation to the next woman she introduced: her father's second wife, a woman her own age. In that relationship, the client sensed that she had more power than the father's wife—that she "had a power over her, sort of." The discussion that led to the surfacing of those feelings was one in which the client had gloried in the knowledge that she knew more about her father than the other woman did.

The two women seemed to represent two conflicting wishes: the ambivalent wish to identify and the powerful neurotic gratification in having been the father's confidante and the better woman in the oedipal triangle. The client's sense of having "power over" the father's second wife was an accurate replay of her history in relation to the father and the gratification of knowing her father better than her mother did. The neurotic wish was, however, counterbalanced by the need for a strong female identification figure.

The colleague seemed to be an identification figure, representing the ambivalence the client felt toward her own mother. The client's own mother had been competitive with her, which worked against forging an identification. The client felt guilty in relation to the mother about her own collusion with the father. As a consequence, the client was constantly trying to make amends and to mobilize her martyrlike mother to find a better job and take care of herself. In the process the client avoided discussions about her own accomplishments or acquisitions. Those conflicts seemed displaced onto her relationship with her colleague. In that relationship the client did not want to compete but felt "smothered" and withdrew to "avoid conflict." She was submissive and reinforced the colleague's self-esteem at the expense of her own ideas.

The introduction of the ambivalent wish to identify with a female colleague provides the male therapist with a safeguard in his work with the client. Not only can the therapist follow the course of that relationship and help the client to complete her identification, but he can counter some developmental learnings. Developmentally, the client learned that she must split her loyalties between her mother and father. If she allied herself to the father, the client ipso facto disaffiliated with the mother. Through his attitude toward the conflicts in the client's relationship to her colleague, the therapist can facilitate resolution of the ambivalence or reinforce the split.

The matter is delicate. The relationship with the colleague is an ambivalent one for the client, with both positive and negative features. The therapist's attitude will surely be immediately evident to the sensitive hysterical client. If the therapist highlights the negative aspects of the relationship, the client's sensors may construe the reaction as disdain for the other woman. Dynamically, the therapist's attending to the negative features of the relationship reinforces the splitting of loyalties that the client experienced in development. Depending on whether the client's wish to identify with a strong woman outweighs her neurotic gains from being the preferred one, the client may become anxious about another potentially binding relationship with a man or may spend many hours luxuriating in the intimacies of another exclusive and excluding relationship. If, however, the therapist simply notes the client's ambivalence and searches for its meaning, the therapist can facilitate defrocking the client's relationship with her colleague of its displaced components. The therapist communicates that he is interested in the client's development of solid relationships with women, thus countering the developmental split.

Reenactment of Conflict

As the relationship develops and the therapist takes on greater significance to the client, conflicts are enacted in the therapy sessions. The contents of previous sessions preview these inevitable transferences, thereby providing the therapist with the guidelines to make such emotional experiences constructive for the client. In the enactment of such experiences with the therapist as principal, the opportunity for emotional relearning and integration is optimal. Early in therapy with this client, the issues of power, substance, lack of preparation for life, and male chauvinistic attitudes were repetitive themes. Submissiveness and compliance in the face of dominant male behavior were the learned modalities, through which frustration and anger were expressed. The underlying assertive power drives were countered by intense anxiety about confronting others, particularly men in authority roles.

In the following two sessions, conflict was activated by a self-serving interpretation. The client became depressed, reverted to her compliant modality, and began to withdraw. When the therapist drew attention to the behavior that elicited the response, the client at first displaced the conflict onto others but eventually directed her resentment to the therapist. After working on the conflict-arousing situation in the therapeutic relationship and her reactions, the client experienced herself as having increased power and put her insight to good use in an important job interview.

In the session immediately preceding the two sequential sessions under discussion, the therapist had pushed the client with regard to understanding her guilt feelings in relation to her mother. Until that time, the therapist had patiently followed the client, and sessions were gaining momentum. In pushing the client and in his premature interpretation, the therapist not only conveyed an impatience with the client, but essentially stripped her of power and mastery by his insightful interpretations. The client became submissive, assented to matters, and, as she had so often done with her father, "went with the flow," but she expressed her resentment indirectly by becoming somewhat dense. The most direct she became was in needing to leave the session early to go to the bathroom.

The next session began with a flurry of anger and anxiety about meeting others' expectations. Anticipating a job interview, the client was "scared." Quite hysterically, she noted that "I've never worked. That's scary. All these expectations people have of me. What they expect from me is not necessarily what you're going to get right off the bat. I feel like they want something, almost they want something for nothing. Experience without ever having had the time for it." The theme continued and es-

calated. The client felt ill prepared to make gigantic leaps. People
were going to "dump something huge" on her. The client had
felt "unsure of my abilities" all week. Other people are
"quicker," feel she is "too slow, so they grab the stuff from
me... I feel so stupid."

The client had laid out the conflict, the precipitants, and the
outcome. Expectations were unreal and triggered anxiety, and
she reacted by feeling stupid. In the last session, the therapist
had "dump[ed] something huge" on the client in his interpretation about her guilt in relation to the mother and collusion
with the father. He had done just what the client indicated; he
had "grab[bed] the stuff from" her and left her feeling out of
control. The therapist began the process of redirecting the anger and anxiety to the events of the previous session.

The therapist asked the client if she remembered their conversation of the last session about her mother. The client immediately remembered their speaking about it. The therapist inquired whether the client felt "that was something you came
to or did you think it was something that I came to?" The client wanted to think and replied, "I think it was something I unconsciously had been doing, but I think *you* were the one who
really verbalized what was happening, maybe." And then the
client chastized herself again for having blinders on. The therapist persisted, but the client felt that she and the therapist had
been "working together." To reinforce her point, the client expressed her anger at a woman who was trying to dominate her,
thus triangulating the situation, perhaps in the hope of drawing the therapist into a neurotic collusion. In any case, the intended effect was to create some safe distance between her anger and its rightful target.

The father was then introduced into the conversation. The client thought that he had wanted to "mold" her "into a second
him." He would push her beyond her limits, "things were going too fast" for her, but "I kept up, and I kept going. Somehow, I managed not to feel it." The client could not understand
why she couldn't "feel" what was happening in the relation-

ship with her father. "Why," she queried, "would I not feel the biggest thing that I was immersed in? I didn't even feel! Isn't that strange?"

The client continued to move closer to the object of her anger—the therapist. In discussing the preliminary appointment she had had regarding the potential job, she pointedly noted that the man was about "your age." And then the client began a tirade about being taken advantage of, noting that she became "instantly defensive" and was "angrier than hell" all day long. Later she became angry with her husband. The client felt she was "caught in a bind again." In a whiny voice, she contended that she felt "so mixed up. I'm sorry, I'm just getting really mixed up. I'm just so upset. I just feel trapped."

The therapist noted that she sounded angry and wondered if she was angry with him. The client could think of no reason to be angry with him. The therapist pursued the issue, asking about any feelings the client had when she left the last session. The question took the discussion nowhere, and the client began to discuss how fearful a person she was and how much she wanted to feel what was happening to her.

Taking a different tack, the therapist inquired into the feelings she anticipated having if her job application was accepted. The client thought it would be nice but wondered if she "would be able to feel it." On inquiry, she wanted to feel "triumphant," that she "really did do it." The client then likened it to an orchestra in which the soloist and orchestra work together, but the soloist controls the "tempo of the orchestra." She felt the soloist controls the tempo and the "mood." Seeing an opportunity to bring her feelings into the moment of the session, the therapist inquired how she felt "about the mood of the session" and wondered if she felt that she controlled the mood of sessions. The client responded that "right now, I don't for some reason. Right now, this minute, I feel very uncomfortable. I don't really know why. I'm just, I just feel like I want to run away or something. Yeah, I'm really itchy."

The therapist commented that he imagined the client did not feel she should have too many insights and was supposed to be the client. That comment activated accelerated anger, at first directed at her father, and then the client talked about how she had been living with herself for a number of years and had a good sense of what her problems were. The problem she contended that she was "trying to overcome is changing my behavior because I know what's...I know how I feel.... *I know* what's happening and I know that it is a product of the way I have grown up...."

The therapist commented that perhaps the client needed "to get more direct." The client wondered what he meant, and the therapist noted that he thought she was directing the question to him about how she could change her behavior but was "doing it a bit indirectly." The client then asked, "How do I change myself?" Then she softened the encounter by noting that "you may not have the answer, but I'm going to ask you at the risk of really looking stupid." The therapist thought there might be an even more direct question behind the verbalized one: What was his job?

The client said that she had often had such thoughts when she went to other therapists. With some additional help, the client eventually asked "so what can you do for me, that I can't do for myself?...You have all this education...what can you do for me that I haven't...already found out?" The therapist thought that sounded much better. The client was worried that her tirade might bother the therapist, but she noted in closing that "when I come right in straight, I feel better inside."

At the start of the next session, the client reported that the job interview had gone very well and that she "felt more confident about being direct." Further, she was stunned by the response of the interviewer, who liked her "frankness" and "directness." She didn't care whether she actually got the job; she felt good about the way she had conducted herself.

Matters were certainly not settled, but the client had a taste of her own substance and a thirst for more interpersonal power. In succeeding sessions the client continued to make progress, and despite setbacks and regression to well-learned modes of coping, the release of energy provided by more direct communication and the pleasure of recognition and respect counterbalanced the safety of less effective modes of interaction.

The client was certainly well motivated and provided the therapist with the help to help her. More importantly, the process of psychotherapy with the client provides some validation for the order of events in working with hysterical clients. At the outset, the client was compliant, falsely sweet, and mildly seductive. Those defenses were countered by a kind of counterphobic roughness in language. The two sets of defenses served similar functions: to enable the client to fit in and cope in a male-dominated world.

The early therapeutic goal was to help the client to counter her own feelings of insubstantiality. Until the client feels some sense of inner substance, attention to any defensive maneuvering will be construed as critical. Once it is clearly established that the therapist respects the client and will not be deterred from that respect by any show of disruptive behavior, the healthy and neurotic sides of the client begin their fight for dominance. Because the therapist is allied with health, or ego mastery, the sides are uneven and the healthy side has a better chance of winning.

Throughout the battle, the therapist consistently works to increase the client's awareness of her own inner processes. To this end, he informs the client of his thoughts, notes the source of interpretations in client productions, and plays a subordinate role to the client's insights. Nothing is mystical or magical. The curative factors are in the client. The therapist's understanding of human nature is available to the client and is freely given for her benefit. He does not hold back from what he "sees," but his observations are conveyed in the spirit of what is useful to the client at that time.

Within such a context, the therapist attends to the themes that are introduced into sessions. Sound dynamics suggest attending to substance as an initial and continuing issue with hysterical clients. Sexuality serves many substitutive functions, and attention to seductive, provocative behavior early in sessions places it in a preeminent position, thus simply reinforcing its function in subverting other needs. As noted earlier, there is a decided difference between a therapist's expressing considerable concern about a client's self-destructive, acting-out sexual behavior and focusing on such character defenses as seductiveness.

Once the client experiences some substance and interpersonal power in relationships, she may reintroduce sexual conflicts. Such a reintroduction is often qualitatively different from the first mention. Because many of the client's conflicts and needs have been mediated through sexuality, the therapist can, within the context of a solid relationship, help the client to liberate her sexual drives from their encumbrance by other drives and needs and their derivatives.

In the case just detailed, the client introduced some of her conflicts about sexuality in early sessions. At that time the client's sense of her personal worth was minimal, and directing attention to the gains and intentionality in sexual encounters would have been equivalent to attacking symptoms and would have fallen on deaf ears or incited diffuse anxiety. Focusing on the underlying needs provides a more solid foundation for effecting change. Much later, after this client had gained in self-confidence and a sense of personal power, sexuality was again introduced. Within the context of a safe relationship and with a solid sense of her own identity, the client's questions and curiosities about sexuality were directed more to the acceptability of her feelings than to their legitimacy.

THE THEME OF SEXUALITY

The theme of sexuality in the case just cited can be contrasted to its expression in the case presented in Chapter Seven. In the latter, the client overprinted all needs with sexuality. Her syllogistic reasoning and inner equation seemed to be that all needs are subverted to sexual drives. Because sexuality was threatening, the client's minor premise and conclusion caused great difficulty in negotiating interpersonal relationships and achieving need satisfaction. In the next case to be considered, sexuality was quite seriously contaminated by aggressive drives and served as the dominant means for expressing hostility toward males and concomitant self-destructive tendencies. The case was briefly introduced earlier in a different context, but highlights of the client's developmental history are reintroduced as they apply to the psychotherapeutic process.

The client was a woman in her late twenties. In appearance, the client seemed to be a contradiction. She was an attractive woman, but her face seemed to be that of someone who had weathered many stressful experiences beyond her years. She seemed both soft and hard. Her smile was engaging; her frowns were angry and resentful. The contradiction was reinforced in dress. Her blouse was old-fashioned and hid the upper form of her body. Her jeans were form-fitting and lacked any color coordination. The client's outer contradictions were soon discovered to cover her inner contradictory feelings and behavior.

The client began the session by commenting on her overly emotional reactions to matters. She stopped to check with the therapist about how she should start, and with minimal encouragement to begin with what was happening in her life, the client began to experience her conflicts as she reported them. The client did not perform well in the sciences; rather, she was "people" oriented. She was feeling oriented, getting "feelings about people when" she met them. The client's life had been one of intense inner turmoil, with extensive acting out of inner conflicts. In her relationships there was a "lot of emphasis on...sex" as a way to attract men. The client also felt that she had been close to becoming an alcoholic, but "something inside" had stopped her.

In late adolescence, the client had decided to toughen herself. She joined a rough crowd and was able to hold her own in the most difficult of circumstances, often humiliating others with her insensitive behavior. At about that time, the client had an abortion, which her father discovered. She became "promiscuous," spending much time in bars, enticing men and engaging in sexual relations with many of them. The client often initiated the sexual encounter, was very aggressive, and left the lover feeling that he was not the man he thought he was.

Mixed with those ephemeral sexual contacts were some longer-standing relationships with men. The client had lived with a number of men but had never been able to commit herself to marriage. At one time she had contemplated marrying a man. The marriage never occurred because her own parents' marriage went into a crisis when she planned to marry, and she returned to the parental home; the parents' marriage stabilized. The man with whom the client was living at that time was her father's age. In his turmoil, the father commented that the man "happens to be my age" and wondered if the daughter was looking for "a husband or...a father." The client was attracted to the potential "glamorous living" the man offered her. He showered her with gifts, and "money" was no problem. In return for the material things he offered, the client suppressed all of her own feelings and "would never talk back to him." Somehow, the client decided to rebel, became angry with her lot, and did a "180-degree swing" to a man who was the complete opposite.

At the time the client entered therapy, she was living with another man, her longest continuous relationship. The man apparently had potency problems and had experienced some difficult relationships. According to the client, he was gentle, loving, and long suffering. The client gave him a difficult time, having "affairs" on the side and behaving in disdainful ways toward him. She felt that she was trying to destroy his love for her and had wanted to flee the relationship on numerous occasions. She considered all conflicts in the relationship to be of her making. Only in later sessions did some of the more histrionic features of the client's behavior in that relationship, and the male's possessiveness, become clearer.

In opposition to the client's assaultive sexual stance with men, she had a very soft side. She was very sensitive to the downtrodden, particularly abused children. In relationships, if the client felt that someone was being demeaned, she would deflect the ridicule to herself by playing the role of buffoon. Similarly, the client was very sensitive to criticism by others. Given the slightest provocation, she would break down, cry, and feel that she was a failure. At those times the client would panic and begin to consider alternate, less lofty goals for herself.

The client entered therapy because she was scared. She felt that she was "fighting a lot inside" and "felt like...a failure." She was tired of running, having seldom stayed in the same place for more than six months. She did not feel tht she was "dumb" and felt there were possibilities for her but that perhaps she needed "more time than most people, maybe to catch on to something" so that she could feel "capable."

The client introduced little about her developmental history in the first session other than to comment on her father's volatility. The client would "get hit with his hand...never an object." The father would tolerate no "backtalk" or "smirks" and would use such classic expressions as "Wipe that look off your face." The first clue to the way in which the father projected his own conflicts onto the client came with her statement that the father would give her books to read on anger and tell her that she had "a lot of anger" that she needed to learn "to channel." Given the circumstances, the client found a way to hide her own anger. She would compliantly "break out in hives."

The client's behavior was of considerable concern to the therapist. In her enticing and aggressive sexual behavior with men, the client placed herself in a highly vulnerable position. The self-destructive tendencies were tightly interwoven with gratification from her conquests. The client seemed to have an intuitive knack, however, for selecting men who, despite their taking advantage of the opportunities presented, often felt nurturant and apparently guilty after their sexual encounters with her. They often wanted to continue the relationship on a more wholesome note. Despite that fact, the therapist felt that the client must learn of his concern about her welfare as they worked together on the underlying issues.

Whereas the client discussed earlier took a half-hearted pseudomasculine posture in her rough language, this client reversed roles and played a "macho" role with men, stripping them of their arrogance and achieving substantial neurotic gains from her encounters. In her aggresive, sexual behavior, she would "love 'em and leave 'em." This posture was in contradiction to the client's nurturing side, which surfaced in relation to those who had suffered abuse. The client seemed to be a very caring person whose counterphobic exterior was a thin veneer for underlying helplessness and vulnerability.

Contradictory, also, was the client's interpersonal modality and emotionality during the session. The client was compliant throughout, wondering often whether she was avoiding an issue or being scattered. She was immensely sensitive to the therapist's reactions to her. At times she would stop herself, sigh, and wonder, "what did you just ask me?" The client was very feeling oriented, sensing feelings in others, not good in "abstract" subjects but intensely interested in communication. The client's mood changed often. Content often readily triggered highly emotional distressed feelings and tears; at other times the client's laughter seemed genuine and robust.

The client's emotional state was tenuous; she had low self-esteem, but she was highly motivated to change. The client's tendency to flee situations that became stressful did not augur well for therapy, but the client's dissatisfaction with her life situation contraindicated a premature rupture in the therapeutic relationship. In addition, the client had been open and revealing about antisocial behaviors that she found embarrassing. Finally, there was an intensity and inner strength to the client. She had survived unusual ordeals, still struggled to find herself, and was willing to risk another relationship.

Developmental Themes and the Sexual Orientation

In ensuing sessions, the therapist was able to piece together some of the critical determinants of the client's ongoing behavior from her accounts of her developmental history.

At a very early age, the client had entered into a highly collusive and seemingly seductive relationship with her father. The client's favored position with the father stimulated a hostile, competitive relationship with a younger sister and set her into competition with her disapproving mother. The mother, however, did nothing to intervene in the father–daughter relationship and was subservient to him in all matters.

The mother became the brunt of the father's hostility, and the client was the unwitting pawn in the attacks on her mother. It was in such a context that the father inquired about the client's acquaintance with the mechanics of intercourse. Not only was the target of the father's hostility displaced, but the inappropriate inquiries were made during the client's very early adolescence before she was ready for such discussions under even the most favorable of conditions. The client was humiliated by the experience, confused, and overwhelmed by the content.

On prior and future occasions, the father would discuss sexuality with the client for reasons she could not understand. The sister was denied such access to the father and became resentful of the client, commenting that "Dad never gave me sex talks; he always used to talk to you." Such discussions were often conducted in a warm, collusive setting that left the client feeling drawn to the father but confused.

On one occasion, later played out in a dream during psychotherapy, the client ran away from home. The father followed and sat with her on a park bench. For no identifiable reason, the father talked with her about "not giving in to guys." Inconsistent with such behavior, the father was often volatile and rejecting. At times the client felt rejected, but "other times...I could run up and he would just embrace me." The client felt that the father was very aware of her development in adolescence. During that time, the client knew subliminally of the father's favoritism for another woman, whom the father would visit with the children along for the sake of propriety.

Sexuality became an overriding concern of the client. From an early age, when the father would sing to her in her bed or she would enter the parents' bed on the father's side, the client experienced sexual dreams and thoughts. The paternal invitation was suddenly turned to rejection, and the client, as a child, was left wondering why the father's behavior toward her had changed. Throughout latency, the client "reflected" the father in whatever she did. She would "hang on him" in front of the mother. She thought of herself as his possession. She became what she thought he wanted her to be. Unwittingly, she became the object of the father's own inner conflicts.

The client was very sensitive in preadolescence. Confused by the father's inconsistent behavior and with an unhelpful mother, she retreated to her own inner world, watching soap operas and playing with dolls. The father objected and suggested she play with friends. The client did so and the father objected again, wanting to know why she didn't stay home more, because he liked talking to her. The client complied and would often sit with the family because she felt it was required. But when she retreated to her room, the father would wonder what she was doing and would call her "very selfish." In reporting that incident, the client cried deeply at the father's contention that she was "just thinking about" herself, not caring "about anybody else," and acting like "the queen bee."

During that time, the client was given to crying easily. In school, if she was addressed harshly, she would break into tears. The father wanted to toughen her. He was too rough on her, and when she was hurt, he would ignore her honest pain. In turn, when the client attempted to roughhouse with the father, he would reject her at his whim. The client was confused about whether she was reared to be hard or soft, dependent or independent.

One time in her early adolescence, when the father was entertaining another woman, the client jumped onto his lap, and the father summarily rejected her with some hostile comment. The client was humiliated. Matters took a turn for the worse, and the client eventually began drinking heavily and leaving the evidence for anyone to see. The father recognized the behavior but assured the client that he would not tell the mother. Rather than discuss the meaning of the deteriorating condition of the client, the father ignored the obvious warning signs.

The client became more deeply involved in bizarre behavior, but the father, perhaps out of anxiety about his role in the behavior, did not interfere. The father was aroused to action only when the client planned to marry. At that time the parental marriage went into a crisis, the mother pleaded her case with the client, the client returned home, and the parental marriage stabilized. The parents "started making love again; you could hear them." The client was happy but had "mixed feelings about it."

Throughout the client's development, the mother remained a shadowy figure, deferring to the father's judgment and refraining from interference. The mother's feelings, concerns, or disapproval was relayed to the client through the father. The client felt that the mother was a loving person but that she was fearful of the realities of life. After the client experienced the seamier side of life, she tutored her mother in some of life's stark realities. The mother would listen with rapt attention.

After the client left home and her sister married, the mother began to assert herself more, took a job, and played a more dominant role in relation to the father. Although the father was threatened, he found himself sharing the power base in the family. On a visit home, the client noticed that the mother "spoke back to" the father and "that was the end of" the argument. Unfortunately, that changing state of affairs occurred too late to benefit the client.

The therapist became acquainted with the client's developmental history over the course of a number of sessions. Fragments of her history were evoked by incidents in the client's current life and by a dream. In one session the client began to feel angry at males but couldn't "figure out why." The client thought that it might have something to do with having been treated, and allowing herself to be treated, as a sexual object. She berated herself for the problem and then recited a number of sexual dreams she had had about her father. The client's association to having such dreams occurred immediately after the therapist inquired about whether the father had spanked her. The client reported that she had often been spanked on the bare bottom by her father and finished the sentence by noting that "I used to have a lot of dreams about him, very sexual dreams and when I was very young."

The client reported dreams about having sexual intercourse with her father during her adult years. One such dream occurred after she had returned home because of stress in the parental relationship and heard the parents "making love again." The dream "really bothered" her. The dream took place in a hotel room, and she and the father were in bed together. The client didn't know "if I seduced him...that's not really clear." They "did end up having intercourse and my mother was there...sister was there." The client had awakened feeling terrible "that I was sneaking, that my mother didn't really know I was doing that with him at the time."

The circumstances surrounding the dream were that the parental relationship had stabilized and the parents' love making had been rekindled when the errant daughter returned home. The client must have experienced awesome power over her father's feelings, power that was at once gratifying, frustrating, anxiety provoking, and guilt producing. In a way, the client had irrefutable evidence of being the better woman in the father–mother–daughter triad.

The crucial issue, however, was that the client's return to the family dwelling was a function in part of her mother's entreaties because of the anguished state of the marriage. Whereas during development the mother had taken a noninterference role in the father–daughter collusion, her later pleas for the daughter's return to the fold symbolically gave that collusion her blessing. The mother placed the daughter in an intolerable position with no maternal control. The client's report of the dream during therapy suggested that the same conditions existed in her current life. The dream represented that state of affairs. The client's sexual behavior was out of control. Her superego was overwhelmed by her sexualized aggressive impulses, and her ego was the passive observer of her own impulsive acting out.

Following her report of the dream, the client flagellated herself for her many sexual feelings, thoughts, and actions. Because the client conveyed most of her needs through sexual symbols, the therapist attempted to intervene so as to distract the client from her self-punitive reactions and perhaps evoke some of the feelings that were covered by her obsessive preoccupation with sex.

There was an aspect of the dream that the client had glossed over: her own passive observation of her act in the form of her mother and sister. The therapist pursued the anger and anguish that must have been felt after being left unprotected by the mother. The therapist asked the client to return to the dream for a moment and wondered if it were possible that "it wasn't a sexual dream...but had more to do with wishing that your mother had intervened more between you and your father." At that point in the session, the mother's passive, observational stance within the family, the father' disdain for the mother, and the father's surreptitious behavior with other women emerged. The therapist wondered aloud about whether those experiences related to the client's fears about a commitment to marriage.

At the outset of the next session, the client reported feeling as though she would "just crack up any minute." She had felt as though she was "disconnected" in a conversation with a peer and "almost started crying." The client reported "berating" herself. Internally, the therapist wondered whether the client's reactions were an escalation of her need for control, a function of the arousal of anger and hurt feelings, or whether his interventions and the ensuing themes during the last session had been overwhelming, generating diffuse anxiety. Because of the client's history of having been overwhelmed by information she wasn't ready for, the therapist was particularly sensitive to monitoring her readiness. But the therapist also considered the possibility that the client's reactions were unconsciously motivated to forestall intervention and reinforce the client's feelings of fragility.

The therapist commented that some feelings could have been stirred by the last session. The client responded that she felt "kind of funny...when you just sit and listen" and that it felt "awkward" to have someone listen for that period of time. She then commented that "you brought that one point up" about her fears of committing herself to a relationship, and "that helped me. I feel like something kind of cleared up inside." The one thing the client carried away with her was the therapist's comment that made sense to the client in terms of her current dilemmas. The client's response was encouraging and was reinforced by comments that suggested she wanted to search deeper.

Effects of Premature Remarks

In many of those early sessions, it was evident that the client had a highly tuned sensor system. She scanned the therapist for reactions and seemed easily alarmed. The historical determinants in relation to the father seemed evident.

In one session the client introduced many torturous experiences in which she had wanted to disagree with teachers but feared their disapproval and was too frightened to do so. The therapist internally recalled an earlier incident in which the client had a startled reaction to one of his comments. At the time the client had been attempting to justify her father's conversations about sexuality. She thought that the father might have been able to predict that she would become promiscuous. In the hope of dispelling the belief that her "promiscuity" was genetically determined and unchangeable, the therapist had commented that he didn't think that the father could have foreseen such occurrences. The client seemed visibly to "jump," but her reaction had been lost in the ensuing discussion and was not addressed.

The therapist was uncertain about whether his comment at that time bore on the material the client was now introducing about her sensitivity to disapproval. He commented that the client had shown a rather startled reaction to one of his observations in a previous session. The client clearly recalled the incident and the content. The therapist asked what her internal reaction had been to his comment. She had thought that she "was saying the wrong thing" but had justified the therapist's comment by noting that she had to be open with him and that he wasn't "going to make a moral judgment" about her.

The meaning the client attached to the therapist's remark and her internal reactions were exactly opposite to what the therapist had intended. It was a lesson for the therapist in the unpredictable effects that a remark can have unless the groundwork is laid in understanding. The therapist saw an opportunity to correct his error for the benefit of the client. Because the client's history was replete with incidents of poor communication in which she was left with her own speculations about what the other person thought, the therapist told her that "the reason I said that was that it seemed to me that some things got attached to sex in your life" that did not "belong there."

Genuine Concern for the Client: Containing "Acting Out"

In ensuing sessions the client seemed to be gaining more self-respect, her alcoholic consumption lessened, and her sexual activity seemed under better, although brittle, control. The client reported that she was making progress. She had a serious setback, however: although the client had begun to feel that bars posed a strong sexual risk and were destructive to her, she became drunk one night and engaged in sexual intercourse with an unknown man.

Following that incident, she had a nightmare that had occurred in the past and that began recurring whenever she was with her steady boyfriend. The dream was about bugs. In the most recent variation, the client dreamed that she was in bed with the boyfriend, but it didn't seem to be him. She saw a slimy bug that the boyfriend noticed by her head. The client wanted him to "get it away, take it away from me." She wasn't sure but she thought he said no. She felt frozen, couldn't move, and at that point awakened and threw back the covers, screaming at the boyfriend, "Why didn't you help me? Why didn't you get it away?" She remembered talking as she got out of bed, but it took her a few minutes to "get my bearings."

During the session the client introduced her father's inconsistent behavior toward her, and his double standards. The therapist asked whether the father was inconsistent in protecting her. The client felt that if he had said no to some things "a little more often, that maybe some of these things I wouldn't have gone, you know, off like I did." The client felt that her mother "didn't agree with a lot of things" and wanted her to have "supervision." But the father's attitude was one of denial of what was happening to the client. When she was 14 and drunk, he would tell her that he was "not going to tell your mother about this." When the client left her bottles in open view in the family car, he would simply tell her to "clean out the car. But he never really talked to me about it, why I was doing it." The client then commented that during her childhood she sometimes faked being hurt to get attention, but at other times she really was injured.

This client's recurrent nightmare and her associations in the session to her father's denial of the self-destructive aspects of her behavior are significant features in hysterical disorders. Many years ago, Janet (1929) noted that the hysteric experiences an *"incapacity of stopping"* (p. 315) an act once it has begun. Janet noted that the act "might have been very easily stopped at the beginning" (p. 315), but once begun it accelerates out of control. This client's sexual promiscuity was out of control. Had it been attended to by the father at its inception, matters might have been different. But the client never got the protection and understanding that she sought through her acting out behavior.

The client's carousing was a serious problem, and its causes needed careful attention. Exploration of the genetic sources of a client's behavior must take place in the context of the client's awareness of the therapist's concern about her. Within such a context, the therapeutic alliance is formed in mutual recognition of the ego-dystonic behavior and the common search for its sources. The client begins the search if she recognizes the therapist's concern.

But protecting the client from the anxiety she must experience to change is a different matter. In this case, the client warned the therapist about confusing her faking "being hurt to get attention" and her real injury. The therapeutic task is to differentiate between the character defenses and neurotic gains from appearing fragile and the client's genuine anxieties. In this case, the overstimulating conditions of the client's childhood suggest sensitivity to the arousal of overwhelming anxiety. Pacing matters so that the client can integrate emotional information becomes important if developmental learnings are to be countered. But inordinate therapist sensitivity can lead to the reinforcement of character defenses and the inhibition of growth.

The Formative Stages in Psychotherapy

The client continued to discuss her father's inconsistent reactions to her in the following session.

Rules became an issue. The client knew that she could bend the rules and that her father would "just let it slide." She knew that she wanted rules but not "phony" ones. Toward the end of the session, the client said that she was "learning more things" and "already" felt "better." It had become interesting to search the past about the things that had happened. And then she gifted the therapist with the laughing comment that "those dreams about the bugs stopped too."

Another dream was introduced, a dream in which one of the client's girlfriends was on a bench with the client's boyfriend. The client had learned that they were "sleeping together" and she showed a "little bit of anger, but...not a real type of anger." She tried to appear "upset about that" and remembered slapping him, but it was just "bouncing off." "And then in the dream I got conscious or I said, 'Why am I doing this?' I said, 'This isn't worth it,' and I walked away." In her dream the client felt that "hitting him was not resolving the problem, and I stopped and said, 'It's over; it's done.'" Then the client associated to feeling that there were ways of talking out her anger instead of physically expressing it and that she didn't need to do the latter anymore. She wanted to talk "things out more" but feared that some people could "not handle to much honesty." Then the client expressed a feeling that she needed "a little more breathing space to be around people" her own age.

The therapist inquired further into the client's recall of the dream. It occurred "up on a hill," not a "ledge, but kind of close." There was another person in the dream, a female acquaintance. The client remembered asking her if "she noticed anything funny going on." The girlfriend had been "reading a book" and wasn't observant. But the client persisted. The other woman seemed to have "kind of lost balance" and after direct inquiries admitted that she knew what was transpiring between the lovers.

The contents of the dream seemed to mirror some critical developmental themes. When the client was running away from home, the father had followed, and in the ensuing warm discussion on a park bench, the father for no apparent reason had introduced sexuality and warned the client about "giving in" sexually to men. The warmth was inviting, the sexual conversation confusing. The client had abandoned her premature bid for independence and returned home, compliant and subservient to the father. In the ensuing years the client was exploited by the father in relation to the mother and rejected by him in favor of other women. The father used the client to express his resentment toward the mother. Hostility toward the mother was the affect; inappropriate curiosity about the client's sexuality was the content. The client wedded the two, and in her own relationships, sexuality was the vehicle for her own hostility.

The client was bound in the relationship with the father, and when she made bids for independence, she was drawn back into the father's sexualized, possessive net with the assistance of the mother. The mother had been a passive observer of the father–daughter relationship, "off balance" as a mother. The only time the mother had turned to the client was when the marriage was threatened, and the client had returned to the parental roof. In the dream, the client forces the female acquaintance to put her book aside and admit that she had been aware of the events that were transpiring.

The therapist had many thoughts about the dream, but the crucial issue was the meaning of its introduction into psychotherapy at that moment. The dream suggested that the client was in the midst of reworking some critical issues. Some anger was "passing" and not worth the investment. The physical expression of anger was giving way to verbalization. And, through the other woman, there was an internal admission of collusion. In addition, the client's attenuated adolescent socializing was reawakened. The client needed "breathing space" with people her own age.

Earlier in the session, the client had commented that she felt more self-respect and that "going out to a bar...doesn't hold any allure for me anymore." She reported feeling shy around men. The dream had actually occurred before the last session, and the client had held onto it until the dream about the "bugs" had stopped. Only after the therapist had attended to her need for guidelines and had shown a discriminating sensitivity to her genuine needs did the client introduce it. If the therapist now construes the client's dream and associated reactions as indicative of resolution of her conflicts, he will be badly mistaken. The client's dream represents a transfer of conflicts from the father to the therapist. The relationship has been formed, and the client now trusts the therapist. She feels safe enough to undertake a reconstructive venture.

The client's mixed hopes and anxieties about the potential risks in such an undertaking are reflected in the dream, which occurred "up on a hill," not a "ledge, but kind of close." Through the dream, the client essentially communicates that she will now rework the past in the present through the person of the therapist. The therapeutic relationship now takes on new meaning as the vehicle for change. The person of the therapist, his attitudes, and his behavior become critical determinants of the change process. Attention to displacements in ongoing relationships as mirrors of the therapeutic process becomes critical. To understand that process, it is necessary to follow some ensuing sessions with the same client.

Progression and Regression: The Process of Working Through

The client had made sufficient gains in personal strength in psychotherapy to risk the anxieties of reworking the emotional learnings of the past. Such a client's willingness to risk the venture must be complemented by the therapist's commitment to go the route with her. If the therapist wavers in that resolve, the client's last state is worse than her first. Commitment must be coupled with competence, but competence in the sense of understanding the hysterical personality is insufficient. Compassion and humanness are essential. Compassion arises from "feeling for" another person, although that person is separate. Humanness means "feeling like" another person. Although the therapist's conflicts may be different, people are, as Sullivan (1953b) noted, more alike than different.

Humanness begets naturalness in relationships, and there is nothing that a hysterical client prizes more than feeling that she is in the company of someone who is natural: honest, open, concerned, unbiased, and with the strength of personal convictions. A therapeutic relationship built on such a solid ground is very useful in helping the hysteric to drop her protective facade and face her anxieties. From a therapist's point of view, such a relationship is equally relieving, because it allows for errors, for corrections, and for the working through of the conflicts that permeate all human relationships.

No human relationship, certainly not a therapeutic relationship, sets a course and works in unwavering fashion toward some preset goals. Progress occurs. Setbacks follow, and there is a regression to well-learned modalities for need satisfaction and neurotic gratification. Regression may occur because the client's forward movement activates anxiety. Regression is as likely to occur because of some therapist behavior that the hypersensitive client has experienced and that she communicates through her regressive behavior. The therapist as stimulus in client regression is apparent in the ensuing sessions with the client under discussion.

In the session following the one in which the client stated that the dream about the "bugs" had stopped and reported a seemingly progressive dream about searching for more constructive ways to mediate her feelings, she seemed hypersensitive and highly reactive to therapist interventions. The client's vulnerability and readiness to rework matters was apparent in the next session. She began by noting that her communication skills had atrophied. At one time she had been considered talented in writing and had read voraciously. The client felt that she needed to go back and recover those communication skills. She was ready.

The client felt that she held back in what she could accomplish. She feared competition; she would hold back and not follow through, whether in sports or in academics. In the ensuing discussion, it became evident that competition with her sister had taken its toll. The client had been in a favored position with the father. The sister had resented her private talks about sexuality, and a competitive rivalry for the father's attention had ensued. Out of guilt, the client had held back and allowed the sister to achieve at the expense of the client's own achievements. The client was particularly guilty about some early sexual play with her sister, which the client had initiated.

In response to the client's quandary about competitiveness, the therapist began a theoretical sojourn about the relationship between the client's issues about competing and the early sexual episode with the sister. The client thought the theory was interesting and agreed that events in early childhood were important. For the remainder of the session, the therapist had other insights with which the client seemed particularly impressed. Essentially, the therapist came to stage center, as the father had done, and the client was the overwhelmed child who was given information that she was not prepared to assimilate. The developmental scene had repeated itself.

During the week, the client "fell apart." She had a very emotional week, crying "very easily." She felt "incompetent" in school, angry, and frustrated. She became angry with her boyfriend. She felt "very insecure," and the "awful feelings" that she had had before returned. She felt "blocked." She began to feel that she wanted to be "independent" of her relationship with the boyfriend and "move along on" her own. She felt like "running away." The client felt that she and her boyfriend were alike in that they both wanted "to be in control or power at times."

The unfortunate boyfriend had become the convenient scapegoat for some of the client's feelings about the therapist and the transactions of the last session. To free that relationship of its displaced components and to direct the conflict back to its rightful target, the therapist inquired about any leftover feelings the client might have about their last session. The client submissively questioned whether the therapist was referring to the issue of competition with her sister. In that regard, the client felt that "I had a hard time still seeing how I was competitive" and felt that she had "missed getting to the real meat of the situation...pulling out that root and getting rid of it." She finished her statement with an assertive, "That's how I felt last time." The therapist felt the client's anger rather keenly. The client's graphic, metaphorical language conveyed a clear message.

After her assertive statement, the client reacted typically for a hysteric: she retreated to the safety of being the helpless one. The client noted that she was menstruating and that at those times she felt more depressed. She let the therapist know that she was feeling "very helpless right now." The therapist pursued the issue of mastery, and the client noted that with authority figures she deferred and would "accept" their position; then she wondered if the therapist noticed her "doing that." He did. The therapist talked with the client about letting him know if sessions were not going the way she wanted or if she felt that his comments did not fit with her experiences. Matters then took a different course, and the client complimented the therapist on helping her in the past, noting that she felt like "growing up."

The issue of being dependent was introduced by the client, who felt that therapy was "almost like a drug." Her fears about being dependent and needing weekly sessions were cast in terms of some soap operas she had watched in which women were in therapy for years. The therapist felt that such a dependent relationship would be out of character for her. The client's laugh seemed to be one of relief.

In the following session, the client reported that she and her boyfriend had had a discussion about their relationship. The client was always the accommodating one in the relationship, sacrificing her weekends—and needs—to be with her beau. She had centered her life around him. She felt that she needed to grow. Following the discussion with him, the client had felt "really depressed; I was sobbing, and I was very upset." But after the boyfriend left, the client had begun to recenter in her needs and goals. "Something clicked inside" regarding her own goals, and she felt that "something fell into place inside" as far as her own career was concerned. She felt that her relationship with the boyfriend could survive but that she needed, in her words, to keep "issues centered or ego centered." She had begun to recognize that she had "some intelligence."

In general, the client felt that she was making progress and had a sense of mastery. She noted that it was "becoming harder and harder to. . . put up those facades about faking a situation." She began to resent being touched in bars, finding it "degrading." And she talked about "self-respect." She thought that, contrary to the scratching that she did with the hives, she was letting some of her anger out. She then took the conversation back to her parents and seemed to have a renewed picture of her anxious, albeit nurturant, mother.

During a later session, the client spoke of a conversation she had had with a man in which she had "looked at him in the eyes" and had felt that she was talking to him as a "real person." Internally, she recognized some strong opinions she had and "felt like inside I was trying to struggle with stating an opinion." Although she felt she had gone to an "extreme," she began to express herself more directly.

In work with hysterical clients, the issue of mastery is preeminent. If the therapist, in however subtle a way, takes control of the session, the backlash is intense. Manifestly the hysteric invites an external control, but inwardly it stirs anger and resentment. That anger is very indirectly expressed and often takes the form of self-destructive behavior. Such behavior, however, takes its toll in the reaction of the significant other, who is left feeling guilty and helpless. The significant other then overcompensates, and the conflict simply recycles, with no relief to either party.

The issue of control must be addressed directly. If the therapist has taken control, as in this case, then he must be open to an admission of his role in the subsequent behavior. If that admission is advanced through a sense of guilt about what has transpired, therapy suffers a setback. But if the therapist recognizes what has happened and can acknowledge his role in the client's regressive behavior, then he is in a position of strength. In his awareness, the therapist can attend to the emotional conditions that triggered the client's reactions.

In this case, the therapist took control from the client and provided her with theoretical insights about her conflicts about competing that were of little help in allowing her competitive spirit to reach consciousness. In preempting the client's own associative process, he communicated to her that she was incapable of reaching a reasonable solution to her own conflicts about competing. The client reacted appropriately: she reverted to her learned modalities for effecting discomfort in another. She "fell apart" during the week, leaving the knowledgeable therapist to pick up the pieces. Fortunately, the therapist redirected her indirect expression of anger and displaced feelings to the conditions in the relationship that triggered the regression.

Identity Conflicts:
A Critical Stage in Psychotherapy

When the hysterical client finds that some of her usual ways of coping have become less effective, psychotherapeutic sessions become the scene for the experiencing of intense anxiety. The hysterical client's development was devoid of parental help in centering in herself, who she was, what she wanted, or where she was going. She did not master the usual developmental tasks that contribute to ego integration and autonomous functioning. Such a client often feels that she is floundering and in need of guidelines. She may fight the therapist in his efforts to instill inner guidelines, because external prohibitions and rewards are more to her liking.

The hysterical client is caught between healthy integrative strivings and the safety and comfort of known modalities for survival. The client's identity "confusion" (Erikson 1963, p. 261) and anxiety are often in balance with the inviting prospects of a regression to a dependent state. A therapist's understanding of that tenuous balance is crucial if the balance is to be tipped toward reorganization at a higher level of personality integration. In the following passages, taken from two sequential sessions with the same client, she can be seen struggling with those issues.

The client had made some gains. Her "bar hopping" dropped off, she felt better about the control she had achieved in her sexual acting out, and her reactivity in relation to her parents dissipated. The client no longer felt like "fighting so much with them" or proving her points, but the loss of that reactive stance left her wondering if she really had "the courage to do what" she believed in. At that point the client began to experience a great deal of inner distress. She felt confused, anxious, and uncertain. Like many other hysterical clients, she wanted power but not the "consequences." In an ongoing relationship, the client began to think about commitment, which stirred some real anxiety. As the client stated it, "it wasn't a reality; it wasn't something I had to face at that particular moment." She had begun to face some real anxiety and wondered what was "so frightening."

The client recalled that as a child, she had been "very conscious of watching, like to take cues...about what was the proper way to behave." With people her own age, those cues were not there. In her sensitivity to others' reactions, the client had aptly read the underlying feeling states, despite the words. She had relied on the "tone" or "looks" of others as a guide to her behavior. As a child, she would "fall apart" if called on in class, fearing that she would be "wrong, not trusting" her own feelings. The client then reintroduced the way she had centered in her father as a child, trying to mirror him in whatever she did. She described the father's sarcastic manner and her sensitivity to it. And when she turned to her mother, the mother likened the client's sensitivity to her own.

The therapist could sense that the client was in balance between facing her anxiety and retreating. The client's search for cues as to how to behave had been based in the reactions of others toward her. Those guideposts no longer were adequate; the client was at the crossroads of deciding to search internally. Inwardly, the therapist thought that one of the client's comments that she "had a very deep fear of getting involved in a relationship" because it could become "complacent" probably reflected a deeper wish to return to a dependent relationship, in which she would not have to face her anxieties.

In the next session, the fears emerged. The client felt that she didn't have the "money" to do things. She felt "blocked" and wished "sometimes I didn't have to. . . I wish I had somebody just to take care of it." The first part of the session was replete with statements of feeling incompetent, incapable, and overwhelmed by circumstances. Crying, the client reiterated her sense of inadequacy and pointed to situations in which her competitive sister had been punitive and humiliating. The client internalized the abuse and said she felt "really screwed up." The therapist suggested that the client retreated to feeling inadequate because it was safer than feeling angry.

The client feared "expressing" her anger, and the therapist suggested that she had trouble "feeling" angry. The client introduced an incident in which she "got angry," walked out of the room, and "cried, I started to cry, that's what I—I usually cry. I don't think I got angry." The client felt unsure of how she should express anger. The therapist commented that she seemed to express it through withdrawal and tears, but wondered what there was about the client's anger that was so frightening. The client's feelings began to escalate. She feared losing control and had done so in the past.

In one of her "fits of anger," she had been frightened at the "power that came out" and the "damage" she could have done. There had been a number of incidents in the client's early development in which she was thoroughly decimated by the destructive hostility of significant others. In one of those extremely frightening situations, the client was the target of the neurotic rage of a trusted female relative who had confused her, much as her father had done, by being seductive and then turning on her with a vengeance. The therapist began to understand some additional sources of the client's anger, the sexualization of anger, and the intense fear of being destroyed if she expressed her anger directly. Of greater importance, the therapist had a deeper sense of the identity confusion that his client was experiencing.

The therapist attempted to help the client differentiate the helplessness she felt in those situations as a child from the illusory power she ascribed to others in her adult interactions. The therapist's comments were an intellectual exercise, but he felt the client's anguish about the events she was reporting and wanted her to know that she deserved support in her struggle. The client showed some gain in personal strength and noted a somewhat ambivalent compliment that a woman had given her about her decision to return to school after a considerable hiatus. Immediately, however, the client again felt "dwarfed" by the accomplishments of others. The therapist noted that the client did not seem to take compliments well. The session ended with the client feeling that perhaps she should get "a little more cocky about it."

The events of these two sessions must be considered together. Both sessions reflect the client's identity confusion. In the first session, the client informs the therapist that she has given up her reactive stance against the parents, much as she did in the earlier dream. She is left feeling frightened and uncertain of the future. The client's fright intensifies in the second session, and she reverts to the helpless stance that often characterizes initial sessions with hysterical clients. But the issues are very different.

If the therapist assumes that the client has come full circle, he has made a gross diagnostic error. The client has reached the point where she is no longer simply reacting against others; she has turned inward. And when she does so, the client is in the midst of a genuine identity crisis. The therapist, in his work with the client, has helped to precipitate that crisis, necessary if the client is to grow. It is, in Erikson's terms (1963), a "nuclear conflict" (p. 270) with inevitable progressive and regressive features.

Since early adolescence the client had been highly reactive, behaving in counterphobic ways to toughen herself. Those behaviors were attempts to compensate for the sensitive spirit that left her vulnerable to the capricious assaults of others. Among other things, those behaviors reflected the client's willfulness.

The client reflected Farber's thesis (1966) concerning the way that the hysteric resists the will of others to the detriment of learning. And it was precisely that learning deficit that haunted the client and activated intense anxiety. The client was not prepared for life. Given the client's options, however, her willfulness was her saving grace; without it the ordeals of her childhood might have taken a greater toll in personality functioning.

Understanding the traumas of the client's childhood provides the therapist with the endurance to work patiently with her in her reconstructive work. As noted earlier, in the initial therapeutic session, the client had commented that "I feel like there's a possibility that maybe I need more time than most people, maybe to catch on to something." In their work thus far, the therapist has been effective, else the client would not risk suffering the intense anxiety that she was experiencing in her efforts to integrate at a higher level of functioning.

Working Through the Identity Crisis

In succeeding sessions, the therapist's responsibility is one of being there for the client, suffering through her anxieties with her, and fighting her neurosis with her. If the therapist's own anxiety interferes and he is unduly protective, overly responsive, or fostering of the unhealthy dependency that the client may attempt to elicit, the battle is lost. The therapist must walk a fine line between reinforcing old defenses and responding to genuine anxiety.

In the sessions that followed, the client often felt like running, but she remained and continued to gather strength. The client employed her full repertoire in attempting to sway the therapist from the course they had set together. But the messages were always mixed. The client felt that she didn't "like school," but she wasn't going to quit. Her sexual behavior was a problem that seemed like a "compulsion," and she would revert to old patterns. Symbolically, the client relayed her wish to be rejected by the therapist. In an ongoing relationship, the client felt that she kept "pushing" the male, as though she were "waiting for him to reject" her, "waiting for him to say, 'Enough. I can't deal with you anymore.'" Her fantasied response would be, "Oh, good."

The client's sexual behavior was a continuing problem for her, because so much anger was attached to it. But each time the issue was introduced, the client seemed to gain more insight into her motivations. She wanted to say no to offers of sexual intimacy but felt that she needed to apologize for her changing values. Under scrutiny, the apology was a defense against changing, and the client's angry sexual encounters became clearer to her. When she was with men who were resistant to a sexual encounter, she would push, as she did as a child with her father. But the client began to feel the anger in her seductions and saw the anger in her thoughts that despite the man's potential bragging about a conquest, he would know that it was she who "really got the better" of him.

Associations to such behavior reverberated back to her father's overwhelming her with talks about sexuality, and her humiliation and confusion. She wasn't sure whether his actions were a "form of abuse," but she did feel his behavior was "weird." An essential feature of many of those earlier father–daughter interactions had been that the client was "left hanging" with her feelings. The therapist asked the client whether she had felt that same way in sessions when topics were not worked through. Amidst some fears of being rejected, the client said that at times she would "just go away" from sessions with leftover feelings. In a following session, the client rejected a thought the therapist introduced and felt that she would "have to think more about that." She persevered and still was "not sure" the material was accurate. The therapist commented, "Then maybe it's not right," and suggested that the client had a good sense of what was on target.

A sequential analysis of these interviews reveals much about the process of psychotherapy as it reflects the process of development. Again, in the sense of Erikson's developmental model (1963), the client is in the midst of a crisis. The intense anxiety associated with the client's identity crisis reflects the inadequate resolution of prior developmental conflicts. As Erikson noted, confusion and anxiety are the necessary antecedents to change. In her crisis the client is balanced "between progress and regression, integration and retardation" (p. 271).

The therapist must be consistent and must resist the temptation to reduce the anxiety inappropriately or to be swayed by the client's resistance. Of most importance, the therapist must be careful not to assume that the behaviors represent lack of progress. On the contrary, they reflect good progress, or the client would not have returned to the conflict-ridden arena. In this case the client "pulled out all the stops" to deflect the therapist from the necessary work. If she was successful, the client would experience temporary relief, but the setback would make future therapeutic work much more difficult.

The client's ambivalence is understandable, and she often helped the therapist by mixing her messages about wanting to terminate with an ambivalent resolve to continue. The client was also learning to substitute feeling for action. Through her stories about hating school and seeking rejection, she communicated how she felt about therapy. The first therapeutic task is simply to accept those feelings. In doing so, the therapist counters the client's experience that she cannot feel certain ways. In itself, that acceptance changes those feelings.

The second task is to enlist the client's help in searching for the conditions that stimulated the feelings. If the client's feelings were a function of conditions in the therapeutic relationship, those conditions can be discussed. If the feelings were a function of anxiety about change, then the sources of anxiety become the focus.

In either case, some important emotional learnings accrue. The client learns not only that it is acceptable to feel negatively about things, but also that her feelings have validity. She sees causal relationships between inner states. A major problem in hysteria is that the client does not trust her feelings—what she senses has no validity. In addition, the hysteric does not see causal relationships between seemingly disparate inner emotional states; thus, she feels no control and her life seems to be a series of unmediated euphoric and depressive experiences. In the present case, the client's sexual behavior had the quality of unmediated action and served substitutive functions. For that reason, the therapist felt that some progress was in the offing when the client "felt" her anger as a motivating factor in sexual encounters. The conversion of affects was no longer functioning smoothly.

The Client Comes into Her Own

As the client became more assertive, she grew impatient with her progress. She began to talk about feeling that her boyfriend was trying to mold her, wanting her "to dress and to behave and act" in certain ways, which she resented. She seemed to have begun an adolescent rebellion. In relationships, she began to have opinions and to make her points with a great deal of vigor. She felt that she had to start having opinions but thought that she was "going overboard." She again became unhappy with school but still intended to finish. It was something she was committed "to complete." She reported "feeling" like calling and missing sessions, but she felt she was "avoiding." She still had a "barrier" that she wanted to "punch through." The therapist commented that her remark sounded pretty aggressive. With a laugh, the client said that "I am just tired of a lot of this crap. I feel like it's just time to get on with it."

The client also developed a relationship with a woman friend at this time. The woman was more knowledgeable than she in some areas. The woman had helped the client to further her career plans, and she offered to "teach" the client some ways of increasing her effectiveness. The client felt that "she's motivated me." At first the client looked to the woman as though she were on a pedestal, "perfect," as she had felt at one time about her mother. But then she began to feel that the woman was "not always right."

The client was experiencing other conflicts in relation to some female friends with whom she was sharing an apartment. Instead of running, as she often had done, the client felt that she needed to "face" the issues. The client noted that, as she did other arrangements in life, she treated her living situation as though it were temporary. Her room didn't "look like a room" because she had never unpacked—"like I'm going to take off any minute." The therapist commented that "maybe you ought to unpack." The client laughingly added, "and relax."

Matters were far from settled. A series of conflicts began to take shape in her relationship to her male companion. The relationship was a long-standing one. During its early phases, the man had been kind, loving, and helpful to the client, who was often spiteful in return. The client began to feel that the man was trying to mold her into his likeness. That theme escalated.

The client wanted freedom to date but felt guilty and unable to leave. She did not want to hurt the man, but she found the relationship stifling. She felt that she had used the relationship as a safe haven but didn't like the frustration that she experienced. She was not sure that she "wanted a man" in her life "right now." She had always leaned on men and felt that she wanted to "try being very independent and standing alone for a while." She tried to talk with her boyfriend about her feelings, and he felt hurt. He told her that she was the "first woman" who had responded to him or been concerned about him.

As tactfully as possible to avoid hurting him, the client tried to convince her companion that it was better to have the truth come out and be a "little" hurt than "hear a bunch of lies" and experience greater hurt later. The boyfriend was "willing to wait" while the client experimented with other relationships. That response simply intensified the client's sense of being stifled, as did the male's encouraging the client to return to him whenever she became upset.

The client's emergence into "adolescence" was heralded by her growing impatience with her progress and her feeling that her male companion wanted to mold her according to his likeness. This time around, however, the client prepared herself in a better way. In her environment she found a mother surrogate to whom she looked as a teacher and motivator. Whereas her own mother had been insufficient in her development, her woman friend provided a good identification figure. The woman was competent and giving. The introduction of that figure into therapy spoke well for the client's own sense of what was important if she was to complete herself. The therapist acknowledged her pleasure in that relationship, and implicitly encouraged the client through his comment that perhaps she "ought to unpack."

Adolescence came into full bloom when the client began to experience a desire to be independent and stand on her own feet. The issue is a complex one. If the client construes her need to be independent as rupturing ongoing relationships to gain such freedom—starting from scratch, so to speak—then she is still externalizing the conflict. Such behavior is akin to someone throwing away a perfectly good marriage for the sake of finding excitement in another person instead of working to create those conditions within the relationship.

The client became dissatisfied with the conditions within her relationship with her boyfriend. It was too easy to fall back on him instead of asserting her own will. She felt that he was molding her, feared hurting him, and felt that she was bound by guilt to continue the relationship. The companion's willingness to wait understandably intensified her feeling of being bound.

In her conflicts with her male friend, this client reflects a repetitive theme in hysteria. The reported interactions between the client and her boyfriend were replete with displaced components and were reminiscent of the developmental histories of many hysterics and their fathers. The father of the hysteric, despite his controlling behavior, provided a safe haven during the hysteric's preadolescent years. There is something very appealing about being the preferred child and being so wanted that the parental marriage becomes stormy or dissolves when one asserts one's independence.

The hysteric senses the power that she holds over her father's feelings. She does not want to hurt him, feels indebted to him, yet is inhibited by the relationship. When the hysteric reaches adolescence and wants to explore and find herself, her drives are countered by her indebtedness to the father, who will not give her up. His possessiveness is coupled with hostile rejection if she asserts her natural tendency to grow beyond him. This client played out that scene with her boyfriend.

Several things stand out in the client's reactions. Some of the emotional conditions in the client's own development vis-à-vis her father have been displaced. Whether the male's feelings and behavior are dynamic equivalents of those of the client's father is a moot question. The issue is that those conflicts are active in the client, and the therapist needs to work toward her understanding of the dynamic replay. Once the client is aware of her inner conflicts and how they relate to her past bondage, she is in a position of control. Then, with a foundation in the reality conditions of that relationship, her decision to stay or leave will be unencumbered by action based on unconscious motivating forces.

There is a more pressing issue that relates to the client's behavior. During psychotherapy the client had expressed her fears of becoming too dependent. The therapist had helped her during a number of anxious moments, and she was probably also careful about hurting the therapist's feelings. The client's transference feelings toward the therapist were probably tightly interwoven with the displaced feelings in the ongoing relationship. Both the transferred and the displaced feelings circled back to the client's relationship to her father. The conflict, however, was experienced in the present, and that had to be the starting point.

Because the transference occurs in the therapist's office, it seems reasonable to attend to the client's relationship to the therapist instead of casting some shadow over an unsuspecting male in the client's environment. Therefore, the therapist began with his impressions of what happened when the client became more assertive and then reverted to a submissive role. He noted that whenever she spoke of being assertive, she seemed to come alive, and when she felt as though she were stifled, she started feeling exhausted and tired. The therapist wanted the client to know that he was not particularly enthusiastic about the client's being submissive on his account.

The client attributed the problem to the "people I've surrounded myself" with, and for some time it seemed that she was planning a wholesale slaughter of her relationships. Eventually, however, the discussion turned to the client's inner conflicts in relationships. When the therapist suggested that the client might be "carrying" some feelings and attitudes over from the past, the client responded that "what you said touches on something." She couldn't put it into words—"a vague feeling" about things she no longer wanted.

But the client apparently did still want a touchstone as she grew. She still had some anxieties and did not want to have the door slammed on her. She then described her inner ideal, picturing herself as "capable," as speaking out and not stuttering, as she tended to do. The therapist thought she had some "good pictures in there." As therapy continued, the client had her "ups and downs," but she caught herself and would associate to the conflicts and note the ways in which she resolved them.

In her relationship to her male companion, the client became direct in communicating what she wanted and often felt that their talks were productive. The client achieved her goals academically, and after a number of sessions in which she felt that she had not regressed and was in solid control of matters, she suggested that she take a month off to consolidate some things for herself. She returned a month later to report that things were continuing to go smoothly; she had experienced anxiety on a number of occasions but felt that she had handled herself well.

Chapter Nine

Conceptual Integration

The focus of the present chapter is the therapeutic interview and the processes of psychotherapy. There remains the task of integrating the concepts and interpersonal themes involved in the psychotherapy of the hysterical client. Material from a number of sessions will be compressed in portraying one client, her affects, cognitive style, history, and interpersonal conflicts. The crux of the chapter, however, consists of an analysis of two sequential sessions that embody many of the issues in psychotherapeutic work with hysterical clients.

INITIAL IMPRESSIONS OF THE CLIENT: HYSTERICAL STYLE

The client's reasons for seeking psychotherapy centered around difficulties in her interpersonal relationships. She had developed some extended relationships with men, but internal conflicts precluded commitment. The relationships were riddled with the residue of unresolved past conflicts, and as a result the client could not understand her own behavior. The client also had a rather serious problem with alcohol and believed herself to be an alcoholic. Later in therapy she joined a group to control her alcohol consumption. Previously, the client had sought the assistance of another professional, but the relationship was a limited one and became confused with her father's need for help. The father accompanied the daughter to a session. Following that, the father "took" her appointment, and she "never went anymore."

The client was an attractive 21-year-old woman. She had a mildly seductive, whimsical air about her. The client's voice was husky—sensuous—and her manner intense. She had a body language that seemed to flow with the expressed emotions of the moment. The client had a way of avoiding self-exploration through her questioning manner. Her questions fell somewhere between rhetorical and internal musings. It was difficult to determine whether she wanted an answer or was attempting to validate the normalcy of her feelings by identifying them in the therapist.

In cognitive style, the client was reminiscent of some of the other hysterical clients who have been discussed. The client had a curious way of saying that she "forgot" important matters. In the first session, the client described some of her father's rituals about cleanliness, which she now performed as well. "In fact," she noted, "that's what I think my major problem is. I forgot to tell you." Later, when the question of guilt arose, the client said that she felt guilty, "but I try not to remember that I feel guilty and that's why I try not to think about it." Because of her sense of guilt, the client "stopped, I think I stopped dreaming for a long time." In a later session, when the therapist inquired about the reason for some action or another, the client said that she didn't know the reason, "I only know the emotion. And even after a while, I forget about the emotion. I've thought about it so much, I can't remember the emotion either." She added that "on top of not knowing why I think something, I forget what I'm thinking too. It's really—it's a bind."

Shapiro (1965) discussed the substitutive function that the hysteric's cognitive style serves as a repressive mechanism. Such a mechanism appears to be at work here. There are some peculiar features to this style, however, that shed light on a hysterical client's experience. Sullivan's work (1953b) on experience in the prototaxic and parataxic modes applies. Sullivan noted that in the prototaxic mode, experience is immediate and unobserved by the ego. Such experience does not have the benefit of recall and foresight. In the parataxic mode, meaningful symbols associated with an experience function in recalling past experience and provide the basis for foresight of similar experience.

In areas of considerable anxiety, the hysterical client seems to revert to the prototaxic mode of experience. She eradicates recall, and the experience becomes the experience of the moment. Because foresight is based in the recall of symbolized past experiences, the hysteric, by eradicating recall, loses her capacity to foresee events. This phenomenon is most evident in a hysteric's relationships, which she enters into blindly.

This "immediacy" has been noted by Chodoff (1982) in relation to the present orientation of the hysteric's relationships. It has been noted by Allen (1977) in relation to the way that the hysterical client immediately experiences the therapist as a significant other in her life. In one of the cases considered thus far, a client whose "experience" in previous relationships had been disastrous told the therapist in the initial session that she had been searching for a strong man all her life and had found him in the therapist. The hysteric's unique style of shutting down her recall provides her with the optimism to try, try again; otherwise, she would experience intense depression.

Returning to Shapiro's thesis (1965) that the hysterical style functions as a repressive mechanism, we can add that the cognitive style is equally efficient in replacing the functions that the defense mechanism of denial ordinarily serves. But the hysteric's cognitive style does not function smoothly. Again, the process is most apparent in interpersonal relationships. Although the hysteric operates in the present tense in relationships (Chodoff 1982), her tolerance for forestalling recall is limited. At some point in a deteriorating relationship, the hysteric suddenly is flooded with emotional insight into the reality of the relationship. And when a therapist inquires into the process of such a relationship, the hysterical client can elaborate the events with total accuracy.

The hysteric's cognitive style is evident in her sentence constructions. A nonhysterical client may simply say that she forgot something. The hysterical style is decidedly different. One of the clients considered earlier, who was concerned about having wasted time in her career plans, said, ''I didn't really remember that I wanted to study'' some particular subject matter. Another client used similar convoluted language in describing her loss of self-centeredness. The convolutions in language are revealing of the hysterical process.

In the case under consideration, the client's comment that ''I try not to remember that I feel guilty'' suggests a powerful mechanism for forgetting that is *in process*. The client also noted that she ''stopped'' dreaming for reasons of guilt avoidance. The sheer power of such control is impressive and is representative of the willfulness that Farber (1966) ascribed to the hysterical personality. That willfulness is a roadblock to psychotherapy and accounts for some of the control issues that permeate early sessions. But, as we have noted, the client's willfulness has saved her from becoming more severely disturbed.

THEMES IN THE CLIENT'S DEVELOPMENT
THAT SHAPED CONFLICT

The genetic basis of this client's strident efforts at self-control resides in her history. That history parallels the development of other clients that have been considered, so we will delineate only unique aspects.

Controlling the father's behavior was a paramount issue for this client. At one time the client went with the father to see a therapist ''to make sure that he didn't lie to the doctor.'' The father was a monumental ''contradiction'' to the client. She never knew ''where he [was] coming from.'' From an early age, the client had found the father to be inconsistent, at once angry and affectionate. The client, for whatever reasons, had been the one selected to emulate him. In a session that will be fully discussed later, it was revealed that the client had often entered the parents' bed for seemingly harmless games. But on one such instance when the father was ill, he apparently embraced her in such a way that the client felt that she had been mistaken for the mother. Her discomfort was such that she never entered the parental bed again. Later, the client supplanted her mother in her father's social and business affairs. She became his dance partner in the presence of the mother, and on business trips she was his advisor and drinking companion. Within the family, the client assumed the role of sole confidante to the father. The client said that "I was the only one that he would listen to" because "I don't think he respected my mother."

The father had rules, the basic tenet of all of which was that the father was supreme. Everyone in the family either fit into the father's scheme of things or was rejected. The client catered to the father. It was the father who took the client shopping and bought her clothes; the mother was a meaningless fixture around the house. In her preadolescence the client adored the father. But when the client reached adolescence and decided to become a cheerleader, the breach occurred. In defiance of the father, who was violently opposed to her decision, she became a cheerleader. She was suddenly "sleazy, cheap, stupid"—a whore. The client plaintively noted that after her decision to defy the father's wishes, he "stopped loving me." She felt that her defiance was the turning point in the father–daughter relationship, and his changing attitude contributed to her feeling "unsure of" herself, as though she were "totally" on her own and "against him." The client, who had centered in her father, was suddenly left rudderless and uncertain. The client described her plight poignantly by saying that "I could never do anything for myself" and that "I was his child and a reflection of him." Like so many other hysterics, the client was left totally unprepared for life.

The parents separated, and the client was caught between the two. If she accepted money from her mother, the father became furious. If she attempted to negotiate a relationship with the father, the mother was irate, would become melancholy, and in other ways forced the client into choosing between them. Subterfuge, deceit, and manipulation characterized the family interactions. If the client distanced herself from the father, he would contact the mother and complain that she was turning the daughter against him. The mother in turn would contact the daughter and report the father's untoward reactions. Out of guilt, the client ambivalently aligned herself with the mother and put distance between herself and the father. The father felt used if the client asked for anything. He would accuse her of wanting only his money. The client was split between two opposing, neurotic parents, and that split became evident in many of the client's conflicted relationships.

One of the most destructive events in this client's development occurred after the divorce. The mother, who had nurtured the client away from the father, reversed herself and rejoined the father. When she did, she urged the client to join the parents and live with them. In colluding with the father in his attempts to have the client join them, the mother participated in efforts to rebind the client in an unhealthy relationship, apparently for reasons of the mother's own security. That turnabout in the mother's attitude had a serious effect in the emotional well-being of the client, who felt completely deceived.

The developmental themes that were discussed in Chapter Two are clearly represented in this client's reports of the intrafamilial dynamics. For reasons that are not clear to the client, she was the "selected" one. It was her task to mirror the father, to satisfy his needs, and to be the projective target of his conflicts. This early alliance with the father was not founded in affection for her. At best, the alliance was one in which the client had to merge with the father and sacrifice a personal identity. Of even greater impact on development is the fact that the child becomes the weapon that is used by the father in his anger at the mother. The father's disdain for the mother, in this case as in others, is evident to the child. The mother is denigrated in public when the father ignores her to dance with the daughter, invites the daughter on business trips, and seeks her advice.

In some cases the mother accepts the resigned role. In the present case, the mother countered by using her influence to draw the battle lines. The client became the pawn in the parental struggles. Such exploitation leads to the eventual feelings of the hysteric: that she is an object with no intrinsic value. In this case the parental game led to the client's own feelings that life was filled with "mind games" and pretenses. Deceit, subterfuge, manipulation, and skepticism became integral parts of the client's dictionary of the motive forces in human interaction. For example, the client missed the second session. She was amazed and anguished that she received a call reminding her of sessions. The client noted that "I think usually if you don't make an appointment, they just forget about you and that's it." She felt that she would "sort of be more comfortable with you not caring at all." The client's skepticism was not easily laid to rest. Finally, she reverted to her best defense: "I'm not responsible."

The coming to adolescence in this client's history is classic. When the client asserted her will over that of her father, she was summarily rejected. But the bruised father was not satisfied with simple hostility; it was wedded to a sexualization of the client's normal developmental pursuits. She became a sleazy whore for becoming a cheerleader. The client realized only later that the issue was one of turning her attention to other men and no longer catering to the father. Thus, anger is wedded to sexuality and other affiliative needs are subverted. Sexuality becomes the medium for integrating relationships as well as for frustrating others and indirectly expressing anger. Sexuality becomes a survival technique. The hysteric must be perceived as a sexual, seductive person if she is to receive.

The fathers of hysterics do not give up their possessions easily. In her book on father–daughter incest, Herman (1981) noted that the incestuous father will pursue the daughter after marriage. Although the hysteric's fathers are not overtly incestuous, their narcissism demands that they retain what was once rightfully theirs. Thus, this client's father continued to pursue her and encourage her to join him. The disastrous turn of events

occurred when the mother colluded with the father in the un-
holy alliance.

It is not that the hysterical client is unambivalent about break-
ing her bonds; the paternal behavior is tremendously binding.
First, the hysteric's history leaves her unprepared for an independent existence. Second, the sense of power that the hysterical client experiences from supplanting the mother and being the confidante of the father is not easily defused. The
oedipal arena is enticing, despite its ultimate frustration, and the
client will return to it many times, particularly when the anxieties of responsible, independent behavior are considered. The
fantasy of being so desired by the father that he will go to
any extreme to keep his possession is a powerful one to combat. Unfortunately, a male therapist may play into the power
of this fantasy by attempting to provide the hysteric with a better father.

THE MALE THERAPIST AS "OEDIPAL" FATHER

In work with the hysterical client, there is always the temptation for a male therapist to consider himself to be a better model
of masculinity than the father of the hysteric. Such an attitude
sets the therapist in competition with the father and does very
little for the hysteric other than providing her the opportunity
to play one off against the other. Alternately, if the hysteric has
had enough of her hysteria and wants to change, such therapist
competitiveness sets anxiety into motion, and the relationship
is likely to terminate. The countertransferring therapist who becomes competitive with the father may share in his dynamics,
exacerbating the client's conflicts. It was the self-centeredness
of the father and his possessiveness that created the havoc. In
having to reflect him, the hysteric lost her self-centeredness. Underlying a therapist's struggle to be the better man is the need
to be recognized for those traits in himself—a variation on the
self-centered theme of the father. Such a therapist is suscepti-

ble to feeling possessive about changes in the client, as reflecting his work—a variation on the possessive father who wanted the daughter to be a reflection of him.

To some extent, the hysteric gains freedom from bondage by identifying with a strong woman. That is not to suggest that hysterical clients should work only with female therapists. On the contrary, if a male therapist holds the attitude that a client's identification with women is crucial to her development, such therapy can be a powerful vehicle for change.

The cases reported thus far have reflected similar themes. Developmentally, the clients learned to center in their fathers, who supplanted the mothers and relegated them to a secondary role. The mothers accepted that role and either became the servants of the fathers or competed with the daughters for the favored position. In either case, the mothers emerged as inadequate role models, and the fathers emerged as being the power bases in families. Under such conditions the clients allied themselves with their fathers and colluded in denigrating their mothers. As adult women the clients are left with the fate of their mothers. They assume their insubstantiality and are intensely fearful of venturing on their own without the protective shield of a controlling male figure, to whom they surrender their power.

In the following sequence, the therapist inadvertently enters the competitive arena by attempting to provide the hysteric with a contrasting male model—one in which attention, sensitivity, and understanding play a role. But the therapist's interest in being seen as having those traits recapitulates the developmental scene. In his sensitivity, the therapist avoids encountering the client's irresponsibility. His understanding takes the form of collusiveness. In being overly responsive, the therapist reinforces the oedipal conflicts of the client. The oedipal scene is replayed—with a better father, to be sure, but the conflicts are simply transferred and unresolved. During successive sessions with this client, one can almost hear the intense inner battle between the client's healthy strivings to identify with a woman and the neurotic pleasures of being the exclusive and excluding one.

The client's history had been such that the male therapist was drawn to protect her. He was understanding and sympathetic and attempted to be sensitive at all times. His apparent motives were to counter the client's binding experience with her father. His preoccupation with being intense, omnipresent, and non-judgmental had the ring of collusiveness. He was overly concerned that the client see the therapeutic relationship as different—and, one may infer, see *him* as different.

In one session the client was describing some of her conflicted relationships with women. The first such conflicted relationship was with a roommate. The woman was demanding and irresponsible. The client catered to her but was resentful. The client felt that the roommate was counting on her to take ''care of her things for her.'' The client felt that she was unable to deal with so much ''irresponsibility'' on the part of the roommate. The woman would not carry her fair share of work and seemed frankly exploitative of the client, playing on guilt to manipulate situations.

At this point in the session, the therapist made the assumption that the issue of ''responsibility'' was one that might relate to the client's feelings about the therapeutic relationship. In defense of the therapist, it was certainly true that the father had behaved irresponsibly. Further, the client had been thoroughly exploited by the father for his own gains. Apparently wanting nothing of that kind of shadow cast on himself as therapist, he inquired into the client's feelings about how she thought responsibility was shared in their relationship. The client felt that therapy was her ''favorite thing'' of the week. She felt that it was ''absolutely equal,'' and she praised the therapist for his endeavors on her behalf.

In deflecting the issue to therapy prematurely, the therapist reinforced the basic excluding and exclusive oedipal battle. Essentially, he communicated that the therapeutic relationship was the higher-order relationship. The therapist's question came while the client was discussing her conflicts in relation to a female roommate, a conflict that was a clear displacement of her feelings about her mother's problems in negotiating a relationship with the father without her help. The client felt that she was taking "care of [the roommate's] things for her," a thin veneer for the client's role as confidante of the father and mediator in parental conflicts. During her development, the client had been the one who negotiated the settlement of family quarrels. As the client had noted earlier, she was the "only one" to whom the father would listen, because he had no respect for the mother.

The pleasure that the client derived from her powerful and usurping position in the family was evident in a later session, when the therapist questioned the client's reasons for not pulling "away more from" her mediating role, because it seemed to cause her much discomfort. The client summarily dismissed the therapist's intervention as superficial, noting that matters were "pretty complicated" and providing irrefutable supporting evidence. The client had considerable investment in her neurosis, and she netted some real gain from the splitting of loyalties that plagued her.

Had the therapist attended to the conflicts related to the female roommate and tried to help the client to examine the dynamics underlying the surface conflict, the client in all likelihood would have seen him as a nonunderstanding person. But the client and therapist would both have known that he was allied with her against her neurosis. When the therapist deflects the issue to his relationship with the client, he reinforces her strivings for exclusiveness with the father, activating neurotic wishes as well as guilt. How the client responds in succeeding sessions can be an index of which side is more heavily weighted and how much she will fight the alliance.

The effects of the therapist's intervention were evident in a later session and suggested that the client's healthy strivings outweighed her neurotic power gains.

Despite her conflicts with the roommate, the client reported that she was pleased that the two of them had begun to talk again. She introduced a third party, however, another female roommate who was interfering in that relationship. The client felt that the third party was "really disappointed" that she and her roommate were on speaking terms. The therapist addressed the issue of the split loyalties. He noted that in the client's own family, her relationship with her father led to her mother's feeling excluded, and vice versa. The client followed the therapist's lead and reported her dilemma in relation to her parents. In particular, the client's guilt seemed evident from her reports of the many times that the father turned to her as a dance partner or drinking companion in the presence of the mother.

The client's feelings about her mother's inadequacy seemed clear from her projections. The client, whose temporary home was distant from that of both parents, wished that her mother would live with her. "I think she'd probably like the idea that she was in a place that I was in. . . . And I'd feel better, too." Those statements were a commentary on the client's favored position with the father and the mother's supposed envy of her role. They also embodied the client's ambivalent wish to re-create the family in a more wholesome way. Immediately following that statement, the client's dilemma in relation to the father was evidenced in her comments that she had to fake enjoying what he did "so he would feel good." The client was truly caught between two rather immature and competitive parents. Consequently, the client felt extremely insecure. Symbolically, the client conveyed her sense of being uncared for. She commented that "if I have a lot of money and I know it's in there, then I'm less likely to spend it, for some reason." In other words, if the client felt secure, there would be less need for her to liquidate her assets.

The client's ambivalence about her mother also emerged. She wanted her mother to stand on her own feet and not to engage in activities that "are organized by somebody else." This theme continued; the client felt that if she visited her father, there would not be time to "get back into the swing" of that relationship. Further, she thought that the father would object to her visiting him for the sake of renewing old acquaintances with her peer group. Her ambivalence was evident, and therapy stood at the crossroads of progression and regression.

RISKING THE THERAPEUTIC VENTURE

In succeeding sessions, the client turned to the therapist and began to intensify the therapeutic relationship. She protected herself in several interesting ways before deepening the interaction. She joined a group to combat her alcoholic tendencies. The group was led by a competent woman, and the client reported many insights she had gained from the woman, who held a significant place in her life. Like so many other hysterical clients who see male therapists, this client found a surrogate mother whom she perceived as strong and capable.

The client prefaced the intensification of therapy with another safeguard: she projected strength and nurturance onto the therapist. In a session soon after she revealed her ambivalence about the mother and her concerns about becoming reentwined with the father, she reported that she had called her father and deferred an extended visit with him. She projected the decision onto the therapist and empowered him with strength even greater than that of the father, whose hostility and potential rejection she feared. In describing her decision to resist visiting the father, she said, ''I didn't tell him that you said...'' and trailed off, only to add that ''he doesn't know I go to see you.''

With a strong maternal figure in the form of the group leader and a therapist who could successfully combat her father, the client was ready to reenter the oedipal arena and rework the conflict.

The client began the session with a dream in which she had begun to notice some things about herself that startled her. In her dream, she was on vacation with some peers and noticed that she had seven toes on one foot. The client couldn't believe that she had lived her 21 years not having noticed that aberration. She felt that a trick had been played on her by some of her friends. She thought that perhaps the extra toes were glued on. In her dilemma about the dream, she turned to the therapist and inquired into his thoughts about its meaning. The therapist commented that she was beginning to ''notice'' things about herself, but he did not comment on the dream. Rather, the therapist asked whether she had had other dreams that she found more embarrassing to report. The client noted that she had had a dream about a male friend, had forgotten it, and felt that she didn't like to talk with a man about her dreams about other men.

The client then began a monologue about a male peer who was selfish about being open and giving but who demanded that she attend to the things that were important to him. She noted that he, like other males, "expect something, but then don't give anything back." The client reported that his attitude filled her with rage. The therapist commented that she didn't seem to reflect the rage that she verbalized.

The therapist erred in not working with the client on the dream that she presented. Whether the therapist could help with an interpretation was not the issue; the issue was that the therapist demanded more without having given any help. In so doing, the therapist recapitulated the selfish father, whose own needs were always paramount. The client was expected to reveal her dreams about a male friend under circumstances in which she could only feel that the therapist's intentions—like those of her father—were to discredit her other male relationships. In the face of this, the client's resistance was laudable. Typically for the hysterical client, this client immediately drew on some material about an ongoing relationship with a selfish male to punctuate her anger at the therapist.

Later comments the client made in the same session finally reached the therapist's consciousness, and he began to attend to the issue that the client expected some help from him with the material she offered. Although his comments about the client's reactions to offering material and receiving no help were belated, the client, as most hysterics do, readily forgave him and provided additional material. In the material, the nature of the transference was illuminated. The client had withheld some crucial information because she thought that the therapist would consider her a "whore" as her father had. The nature of the withheld information suggested to the therapist that the client was very conscious of presenting herself in a good light and that those relationship conditions needed attention if the client was to progress.

To this point, the client must have felt some skepticism mixed with trust. The therapist had often missed the intent or erred, only to recover and belatedly address issues before the emotional experience was sealed. The client tested the therapist in a rather unusual way. In a much earlier session, when discussing her father, the client had made an offhand remark about his lack of understanding of her needs. The context was one in which she was describing the father's possessive, demanding, and self-centered behavior. About her father, the client commented, "I don't think that he can understand the idea that anybody would just want to go to the beach" to relax and "rest a little bit."

The client then missed a session. In the following hour, the therapist did not question her absence. The client introduced the matter. She said that she had been "at the beach." She followed the comment with an elaboration of excuses, but with each excuse, she would counter with some comment that she "could have come" to the session. In the remainder of the session, the client's dissatisfaction with therapy was the issue. She was "anxious" and "waiting for something to happen." She felt superficial and that there really wasn't "much behind that. . . beneath the surface." The client hated being seen as "shallow." She had internally struggled during the week with thoughts about whether the therapist would be "curious about why" she missed the session.

The session was a lesson for the therapist in working with a hysterical client. The client had set up the test at least a month before it was enacted. In that session, she had conveyed the idea that her father would not be understanding if she wanted to take some time and rest at the beach. If the therapist questions her missing the session for the sake of sitting on the beach, he is not understanding. If he lets the issue pass without attending to the client's responsibility to attend sessions, he is treating her superficially. In accepting the client's definition of "understanding" as allowing crucial issues to pass without attention, the therapist is behaving irresponsibly. The therapist's behavior in letting issues slide for the sake of a conflict-free relationship may not be so different from that of the father. Underlying a therapist's behavior in not confronting issues is often a wish to be "liked" by the client, to be regarded favorably, or to have the client think of him as "ideal." In the main, the therapist's personal needs take precedence over the therapeutic task—and that is an exact replica of the paternal attitude that helped to shape the hysterical personality.

There is another crucial component embedded in the therapist–client interaction that touches a basic issue in hysteria. As Andrews (1984), Eichler (1976), and others have pointed out, the manifestly accommodating and compliant attitude of the hysterical client provides a protective cover for underlying anger and aggressive impulses. If the therapist is very accommodating, he provides a poor role model for unearthing the angry undertones. Evidence of the client's dilemma emerged in this case when the therapist inquired into the conditions of the relationship that contributed to the client's feeling shallow.

The client commented that she didn't know what she could "talk about, that I'll feel comfortable talking about." Underneath, the client felt that many issues were "embarrassing" to her and were points of discomfort. In working with a hysterical client—or any client—the therapist can err in trying to make the relationship so safe and comfortable for the client that disagreeable matters must remain submerged. The by-product of such therapist behavior is reinforcement of the client's sense of herself as fragile, insubstantial, and unable to cope with "real-life" issues. The deleterious effects of the therapist's oversolicitous attitude were evident in the client's opening comments in the following session. Life lacked challenge. The client felt that "everything is just basically pretty easy." Those feelings, however, were coupled with feelings of "deceiving everybody."

AN ANALYSIS OF TWO CRITICAL SESSIONS

Again, the therapist was sensitive to his own errors, the relationship continued, and the client gave the therapist another chance to be of help. She introduced an issue of considerable concern to her. The client's conflicts about her sexuality became the focus in two successive sessions. Because a number of issues involved in work with hysterical clients emerged in the second of those sessions, it is considered in extensive detail.

The Fathers and their Phallic-Narcissistic Organization

The first of the two crucial sessions began with the client's introduction of some of the historical determinants of her sexual conflicts. The client's father was the focus in the early part of the session, and matters later turned to her mother's contribution to her uneasiness about sexuality.

The client's father was very observant of her body. He wanted her to exercise with him to remove the excess fat that he observed. When the client was in a bathing suit, he would appraise her and comment on her being somewhat overweight. The client felt that the father wanted her to be in top physical condition, but not for "anybody else besides him." The father's comments often took the form of condemnation: the client's clothes were too tight or her bathing suit too revealing. The father's possessiveness and the client's ambivalence about him and fear of hurting him were evident in one situation in which a man she liked wanted to date her. The client turned down the offer. In the client's words, she noted that "I said no...because my father was there, and I was..." The remainder of the sentence was left unsaid.

The mother was apparently equally observant of the interaction between daughter and father. Despite her anxiety about discussing sexual matters, she finally approached the topic with the client. The implication of the mother's indirect question seemed clear to the client. The client was open with her mother. There had been no physical contact, but the client felt that the father might have such thoughts, as evidenced by his negative reactions to sharing her "with any other men."

The client said that she had always been of the opinion that her mother "thought that something funny was going on between my father and me." When the client was young, the father had encouraged her rubbing his back, brushing his hair, and romping in bed with the parents. At one point, when the client was 7 years old, the father, who was apparently ill at the time, had put his arm around her, and the client thought that he had mistaken her for the mother. She felt strange and "never, ever liked to sleep in his bed anymore." The client reiterated that the father was sleeping, so he couldn't have known that he was holding his daughter to himself.

Immediately, the client turned the discussion to her problems in relationships with men her own age. She didn't feel she had "normal" relationships with them. If she felt that someone was attracted to her, she dropped the relationship. She feared both sides of the coin. She couldn't be the object of male pursuit without anxiety. In turn, if she pursued, she feared that her feelings would discourage the relationship. Part of the client's dilemma was that she never knew what the male's intentions were. She felt that she was a weekend affair or, as in her experience with the sleeping father, she wondered if she was pursued because the "guy has had too much to drink."

The client's sentiments seemed characteristic of many hysterical clients. The hysteric never knows whether she represents some kind of displacement, an "object" with no intrinsic value. She also experiences conflict about the overly responsive reactions of others. She seeks attention, but, in the words of this client, "then I don't want it when I get it." Developmentally, the client was unable to pursue the father and learn about her own sexuality without the fear of his acting on it. The fathers of hysterics seem not to be incestuous, but they are seductive and inviting. They activate sexual conflicts in the daughters and then reject what they have stimulated. One interpretation of the paternal behavior is that the fathers become anxious about their own sexual impulses, project those impulses onto the daughters, and gain control by condemning the daughters' behavior.

There is certainly evidence to support that position. The fathers' controls seem to become particularly shaky when the daughters reach adolescence. At that time, the fathers' possessiveness and competitive behaviors become manifest. Loss of control occurs when the daughters interact with other males. At those times, the fathers' rage is expressed in assaultive sexual language, which suggests that the rage is to some extent a by-product of sexual frustration. The fathers of hysterics seem to be sexually frustrated men. Hysterics are aware of the sexual orientation of their fathers. They are also very aware of the lack of sexual satisfaction in the parental relationship. Despite the mothers' blindness to events, the clients sense the fathers' "affairs." After all, the father sensitized the daughter to sexuality and later sexualizes her relationships. As this client noted, the father "likes having a lot of women" around, "different" women, with no continuing commitment. After the divorce, for example, the father invited the mother to live with him without their entering into a remarriage.

The effect in the hysteric is that she is confused about whether she was groomed to be sexual. Sexuality seems to hold a pre-eminent position in the father's hierarchy of need satisfaction. The daughter learns that being sexy is rewarded, but when she applies her skills toward a suitable male, the father becomes infuriated. As this client noted about being a sexual, sensuous person, "I'm supposed to be, but I'm not supposed to be...and the not supposed to be is a hell of a lot stronger than the supposed to be." The client missed the point. She was "supposed to be" so long as the object of her strivings was the father.

There is, however, a more compelling argument that might be advanced regarding the fathers of hysterics and their daughters' dilemmas about sexuality. Sexuality, in the sense of genital sexuality, is not the major issue. An overriding motivating force in the fathers' sexual frustrations, "affairs," and condemnation of the daughters' interests in other males is bruised narcissism within a phallic personality organization. The fathers are possessive and wish to retain control over their possessions. In case after case, the daughters are nonentity extensions of the fathers. During development the daughters must constantly "stroke" their fathers. That stroking may take the form of "back rubs" or keeping the fathers' possessions clean, shiny, and always in place.

The fathers express their conflicts about control, power, conquests, and narcissism in phallic terms. It is the manifest sexualized orientation of the fathers that contributes to the hysterics' sexually provocative ways of attempting to gain satisfaction for other needs. And it is the hysterics' awareness of the underlying narcissistic trends in the fathers that contributes to their wariness about males, fears about commitment, and use of sexuality to express hostility and resentment.

The Client's Sensuousness

Considering the hysteric's belief that sexiness is the way to her father's heart, it is not surprising that the hysteric is often very conscious of her mother's appearance and tries to encourage the mother to dress in more provocative ways for the father. If the mother were more appealing, it would free the daughter. In the case under consideration, the client took her mother on a shopping tour. The following sequence from the session demonstrates the role reversal that takes place because of the mother's inadequacy as wife and the daughter's favored position in relation to the father. The sequence also heralds a theme that was to be of considerable significance in this client's therapy.

The manifest theme in the client's reports consisted of her efforts to teach her mother to dress in feminine, alluring ways. The client described her shopping excursions with her mother, during which she attempted to help her mother to purchase more exotic garments. Again, she described in unabashed terms the slinky look that she was trying to create. The client's reports of her efforts on her mother's behalf seemed nurturing of the father–mother relationship, but two underlying themes were evident. The more obvious theme was that the client felt that the mother was drab and was not a particularly apt pupil. Despite the mother's ineptitude, however, learning did take place. Unfortunately, the father did not like the change and preferred the mother in drab attire.

The manifest content of the client's reports also carried a second, somewhat more subtle theme. The client's vivid description of the slinky undergarments was rather erotic. The detail with which the client repeatedly contrasted her mother's attire with her own sensitive concept of what was alluring was apparently for the benefit of the therapist. But the therapist did not address that critical theme. On the contrary, the therapist encouraged the client in her desire to be more feminine and complimented her on her courage in revealing some of her conflicted feelings about sexuality. At the close of the session, the therapist experienced a pang of anxiety—perhaps guilt—when he commented that the session had been a good one and the client quipped that they had finally gotten to "sex."

During the session, the client reported a number of disturbing events during her development that had affected her views about her own sexuality. On the surface, it appeared to be a productive session. After all, the client was open in her reports of the events of the past. Superficially, it appeared that the oedipal arena had been reopened. The client's productions had a competitive ring to them. She was the better woman. Symbolically, the client was considering the mother to be an adversary of little note and attempting to excite the father in the person of the therapist. It thus appeared that the session provided the opportunity to work through some previous deficits in development.

Actually, the session could represent a setback for therapy if the motivating dynamics for the thematic productions are missed. In her recounting of events, the client confirmed much of what a therapist may want to hear about the way that sexuality entered into her early development and affected her adult attitudes. The client was providing the therapist with what she anticipated would fascinate him. She was being compliant and accommodating. She was "other directed" and was providing information that she thought would be pleasing (see Andrews

1984). In doing so, she chose the topic that was most likely to please—her sexuality. In the session she had regressed to her typical way of gaining attention and being appreciated: she was being sexy. In the recounting of her history, one could almost feel the sensuous silkiness in her graphic descriptions of what purportedly is enticing to a man. At the end of the session, when the therapist commented that the client had been courageous in revealing herself, he reinforced the client's ideas about what is rewarded: sexiness. The client's final quip that they had finally gotten to "sex" must have been a rather depressing revelation to her.

The Therapist's Reactions
as Reinforcements of Core Issues

The ensuing session is worth considering in detail. In that session, the client reveals her dilemma about continuing therapy. Manifestly, the client is ecstatic. But the undercurrents reflect her hopelessness about reworking her conflicts. Because many themes in work with hysterical clients are embedded in the interchanges, the session is described in detail.

The session began on a light note. The client's intonations were sensuously appealing. At last, the client felt that she was being appreciated. To add to the client's pleasure, the therapist had rescheduled the appointment time to accommodate the client, who had a pressing issue that demanded immediate attention. As it turned out, the client commented that the issue had not been as pressing as she had anticipated, and rescheduling had been unnecessary. The client immediately turned to another issue. She had missed a number of classes where the rules were fixed: three strikes and you're out. She had appealed to the instructor, who not only made an exception, but also conveyed his impression that the client was talented. The client felt that she had a renewed attitude about therapists, instructors, and people in general.

These initial passages are revealing. In the last session, the client had introduced sexual material for the sake of furthering the relationship with the therapist. In turn, the therapist accommodated the client by adjusting their session time. Both of those events were likely to be outside the awareness of client and therapist and are reminiscent of the transference/countertransference interlock (Wolstein 1964). Wolstein's comments about the way that a therapist will "accommodate" a client's security operations for the sake of keeping therapy "on a smooth course" (p. 139) seem particularly appropriate to these events. The reinforcing aspects of the therapist's responsivity to the sexual content must have been dramatic, because the client's light-heartedness at the outset of the session had the distinct flavor of seductiveness.

In her plea to the instructor for reinstatement, the client had "confessed" that in missing classes, she had no excuse. The instructor had understood. In the changing of session times for no good reason, the client encountered the same kind of understanding from the therapist. Because both events followed on the client's reverting to sensuousness as a modality for furthering the therapeutic relationship, the effects in the client must have been both exhilarating and depressing.

Hysterical clients often plead for exceptions. They request changes in appointment times for reasons that sound solid. In sessions, they sometimes ask for an abbreviated session because of some pressing matter that competes for their time. If the therapist makes such exceptions or ignores a missed session so as not to appear rigid, he misses the intent of the client and reinforces the client's sense of her own insubstantiality and fragility. Despite their pleas, hysterical clients do not like exceptions to be made. In this case, the therapist made an exception immediately following the client's accommodating "sexual revelations," thus reinforcing simultaneously her basic modality for achieving need satisfaction and her sense of being insubstantial.

Sex: The Roadblock to Need Satisfaction

The therapist missed the dynamic issue and interpreted the the client's behavior in approaching the instructor as having taken considerable risks. He then inquired into the client's reactions to their last session. The therapist wondered how the client felt about addressing the issue of her sexuality. The client responded that "it was better than any other time" that she could recall. The client felt that sexuality was an important issue for her and indicated that she needed help in that area. Turning the question on the therapist, the client asked whether she had been "complete." The word "complete" confused the therapist, and he wondered what the client meant. She was not sure if she had told the therapist "enough" of what was "going on" for him to help her. The client must have experienced a healthy brush with anger because she quipped, "Like, you tell me." The therapist repeated his comment at the end of the previous session. He felt it had taken "courage" to introduce the material she had, and he thought they should "keep moving."

The client's language was symbolically interesting in light of her use of her sexual orientation as a modality for need satisfaction. She felt that she had "opened up" in the last session. She trusted the therapist but not enough to discuss some matters that caused discomfort. But the client felt that other material could not be attended to so long as there was "something as heavy as that inside me." The client's graphic language continued. She felt that her conflicts "get pulled back in." Essentially, the client felt that she could not feel better until such matters were addressed.

The client apparently had some pressing issues that she wanted to resolve through psychotherapy, but she must first get "sex" out of the way in order to receive help in other areas. In the last session, she chose that route. The therapist missed the dynamic and attended to the content. Sexual conflicts are not the core issue; they are the overlay. The client must feel that if she accommodates males by appealing to their sexual appetites, they may be responsive enough to attend to her more basic needs. The client wondered if she had been "complete" enough for the therapist to help her. That question is very poignant. In other words, if the client made herself completely vulnerable, would she then receive help?

The hysterical client often feels that sexuality interferes in relationships, and in the cases noted earlier, that theme is recurrent. It may be recalled that one of the clients commented that the man's ego is in his penis. In this case, the client symbolically conveyed the same message. So long as there was "something as heavy as that inside" her, she could not resolve her conflicts. The preeminence of sexuality as a learned modality for satisfying other needs is evident in her statement that her conflicts "get pulled back in." The client's only modality is to do what she did in the previous session—become sensuous as a way of being appreciated and receiving.

The therapist's rejoinder that they "keep moving" when the client directly questioned what he had to offer—"like, you tell me"—simply reinforced the client's beliefs about what was important to him. In addition, in telling a hysterical client that what she did took "courage," one always runs the risk of reinforcing the client's sense of being insubstantial and fragile, that is, that she is not perceived as having "guts." In fact, in most human interactions, telling someone that something took courage is often quite patronizing and belittling unless the event was truly heroic.

Displacements: Guides to the Emotional Conditions of the Therapeutic Relationship

In the next section of the session, the client reported that she had felt very appreciated by her male friends during the week. She wasn't hesitant about being nice to them, and she commented that she liked "to do things for other people that they will like." She recited a litany of domestic tasks she had performed, including baking and preparing a dinner for her friends. Mixed with her reports, the client commented on her ability to bring men out of their shells.

The client's next association was to a conflict she had: she could not tell a man "I love you" unless the man said it first. She could show her love in many ways but feared that if she stated her love, the man might think she was "coming on" to him, become scared, and back away. In addition, the client felt that the male "wouldn't want that." Further, she felt that if she exposed herself, she might be rejected and feel hurt and "foolish." She then noted that she was fearful of investing in one man because it would make her too vulnerable. The therapist inquired about whether she was seeking a sexual, romantic relationship. The client responded in a whispery voice, "Oh, yeah, romantic kind of relationship, sexual, any kind, all of them put together."

At that point in the session, the client introduced the topic of a male friend. The relationship with the man had been on friendly, nonsexual terms. But the client had begun to feel that there were sexual undercurrents entering the relationship. In her words, she felt "that something strange was going on between us," that "there was something more to our relationship than either of us had expected" except that "it was not physical at all—it just turned out to be like [pause] we were involved with each other [pause] deeply." The client talked to the man about her feeling that such a shift in the relationship would not "be a good idea" because she was "scared" and feared the exclusiveness it implied. The therapist commented on her feeling vulnerable, and the client noted that "now, even when I talk about it now, I get nervous about it. It's a little bit overwhelming. It's scary, really."

The therapist inquired into why it was "scary." The client began to resist talking further about it, but she continued. She was afraid to give the relationship a chance. She commented that "if I say, okay, I don't think this is going to work, but we'll try it out," she would be going against her intelligence and be having negative thoughts that "it's not going to work out." Whereas the client started the conversation with fears of being hurt, she then changed her mind and felt that she would be the one to hurt the man.

The client then began to explain herself by introducing another male figure. During her adolescence, the client had loved a man whom she had dated for two years. She felt that she had hurt the man badly because she had cheated on him and dated another fellow briefly, a man who was her "dream" guy, her "ideal," who was "gorgeous." The long-standing boyfriend was devastated, and the client felt "sick" about it. The boyfriend wanted to know if the other man meant anything to her. The client lied and said no because she didn't "know what" the boyfriend "wanted to hear and I wanted to say what he wanted to hear." The boyfriend wanted to forget the incident, but the client terminated the relationship "to punish" herself for her misdemeanor. But the boyfriend wouldn't accept the client's answer. Again, in the client's words, "I said we couldn't go out anymore, but he wouldn't let us break up. He said, 'No, we're still going out.' "

The client turned to the therapist and wondered if he had any idea about why she hadn't become seriously involved with another man since that time. She noted that she felt incapable of that kind of relationship and after the breakup hadn't dated for a long time. The client mentioned the number of months that had passed before she risked another relationship—a period exactly as long as the time that the client had been seeing the therapist. In the previous session, when the client had quipped that she and the therapist had finally gotten around to sex, she had noted the length of time that had passed since she started therapy. And, in the current session, she said that time was important to her for reasons she couldn't fathom. The client completed the story of her relationship with the past significant boyfriend by noting that she had missed the way they would lie on the "couch" together.

These passages can be viewed from several perspectives. The parallel between the progression of themes in the client's reports of extratherapeutic relationships and her experience of the therapist may be a useful starting point. The emotional conditions that the client reports in those relationships are of interest in themselves. When the emotional conditions are viewed as displacements from the past, the motivating force for conflict becomes available. Then, in studying the order of associations within and across relationships, the therapist gains even greater understanding of the process of conflict in the client. Finally, when their meaning as a reflection of the client's experience of the therapist is taken into account, they provide critical guidelines for constructive intervention.

The client began by describing her behavior during the week and the male reaction to her "feeding" the male ego. She is appreciated for catering to men. Men seem to warm up to the client when she gives freely of herself on their terms. So long as she takes the initiative, matters go along smoothly. But she takes all the risks and seems to await some risk taking in return. She can show her love in many ways but wants the male to take some initiative. She is afraid of exposing herself further, is unsure of how she is being received, and would settle for "any kind" of relationship.

The therapist was noncommital to that point in the session. Often when the client reported some material, the therapist would encourage her to continue or ask why she felt certain ways. The therapist revealed nothing of himself, his reactions, or his thoughts about the meaning of the material the client produced. The client was doing all the work, as she had done in the past session. Because the content was sexual material, the client was under great stress to know how she was being received and what the therapist had in mind in encouraging the discussion of sexual material. In addition, despite his noncommital responses, the therapist was being empathic and soft in his inquiries. In such a context, the therapist asked the client about the kind of relationship she wanted. Given that the question was asked after the therapist had changed sessions to accommodate the client after their sexual discussion and within the context of the present session, the client in all likelihood felt a seduction close at hand. The material that the client introduced about a male friend suggests that she found the prospect both anxiety inducing and enticing.

Her anxiety was expressed in exactly the same words she had used in the prior session to describe her mother's concern about her relationship with her father. She had come to the realization "that something strange was going on between us" and that the relationship was taking an unexpected turn. The client made clear that her current relationship "was not physical at all," which was again the message she had given to her mother about the father–daughter interaction. With the male friend she ambivalently wished for and feared a sexual encounter. Even in talking about it to the therapist, the client was "nervous" because the prospect was "overwhelming."

In these passages the past, the present, and the therapeutic session interlock. The transference is deflected to an ongoing relationship, which in turn is a displacement of the identical emotional conditions in relation to the father. The therapist pursued the issue of what was "scary" about the reported turn of events in the client's male relationship. In doing so without understanding the dynamics of what was occurring in his office, the therapist apparently increased the client's fright. Whereas earlier in the session, the client had been concerned about being rejected, she then reversed her opinion and feared that the relationship was "not going to work out" and that she would be the rejecting one.

The client's explanation of why she might hurt the man was particularly revealing. She had gone with a male friend for two years and at that time had turned her attention to another man, who was her "dream" man. The boyfriend was devastated and insisted on her revealing how she felt about the other beau. The events that followed were an exact replica of an earlier encounter with her father. She had noted in the last session that she declined an invitation to date an eligible male in the presence of her father. In this case, she again denied any affection for another male because she told the boyfriend what she assumed he wanted to hear. Then, converting her desire to be free of the man, she used self-punishment as an excuse to terminate the relationship. The boyfriend, however, like the father, was not inclined to give up his possessions easily and made the unilateral decision that they should continue.

In this past male relationship, as in her ongoing one, the displacements are blatant. One of the differences between the two relationships is that in the past relationship, possessiveness occurred when the client turned to another man. Through the displacements in an ongoing relationship, the client informs the therapist of her intent to terminate the therapeutic relationship if she experiences the therapist as possessive and binding. Then, in the last section, the client turns to the therapist and essentially asks him if he got the point of all this. The client is still ambivalent about continuing therapy and notes that she missed the warm times that she and the boyfriend had together. Essentially, the client seems to be indicating that she needs a warm, reciprocal relationship, and, although she finds sexuality enticing, the real needs cannot be met through sex.

Displacements and the Isolation of Affect

Within these passages, one can observe a unique feature of the hysterical personality. If one juxtaposes the picture and views the relationships that were introduced as indicative of the developmental process in the client, an interesting picture emerges. In the ongoing relationship, there is an ambivalent fear and wish expressed that is reminiscent of the oedipal scene. It is as though the current boyfriend represents the "oedipal" father. Something "strange" is transpiring, but there has been no physical contact. The potential sexualization is inviting but dangerous and overwhelming.

The past relationship reflects the coming to adolescence of the client and the conflicts of that era. The boyfriend is possessive and draws the client back into the net when she wants to test herself with her "dream" man. The client is left feeling that she hurt the male who had been very significant to her. The boyfriend represents the father of the client's adolescence. His behavior parallels the father's actions. The father–daughter relationship had been close so long as she didn't turn her attention to another man. The father was hurt and stopped loving her when she defied him, as occurred with the boyfriend.

The inverted order of those relationships reflects the course of therapy. In the ongoing relationship, there is a regression to the oedipal arena that parallels the client's regression in therapy. The displacements in the earlier relationship had the ring of an adolescent who fails to break free of her bondage to the father. In her current relationship, the client ambivalently tries again to rework the past, in the hope, perhaps, of finally finding freedom.

What is not so evident in this particular case is the way that a hysterical client isolates the components of an affective experience and works out her conflicts in manageable packages. In those cases, the client often reports multiple relationships, with each relationship representing some aspect of an overwhelming experience. In the case under consideration, the client isolates the emotional experiences of different developmental epochs and plays those out in sequential relationships, a variation of the same theme.

At this point it seems that the therapist embodies the oedipal father, and her fears are that if she lets herself go in that relationship, he, too, will want to retain his possession. Through her stories, the client has laid out with startling accuracy the guidelines for what would be therapeutically productive. In the remainder of the session, the client provides the therapist with an even richer picture of the needs that require attention and the pitfalls he may meet along the way.

The Client's Needs and Submerged Features of Personality

As the session continued, the client introduced aspects of herself that she thought would be disruptive to a relationship with a man. She felt that the man might not know "what he's getting into," that there were parts of her that weren't all that likeable. She didn't know what she had in mind but vaguely felt that she wasn't aggressive or glamorous. The therapist, in keeping with his interest in helping her to accept her attractiveness, wondered if she "held back" on the more glamorous aspects of herself.

The client agreed, but she wasn't sure if what she felt was acceptable. She noted that she didn't mind being glamorous if she could turn it on or off at will. She felt that being glamorous "would only be a part-time thing. I wouldn't want to be like that all the time; it's just too much work." The therapist laughingly agreed. The client felt that glamour was "just a surface thing, but it's important" because she was concerned about "looks." She didn't want others to know that she had psychological problems, however. The therapist didn't understand why, and the client had another brush with anger, questioning, "well, what does that mean?" The therapist apparently experienced the client's anger and responded rather tersely that its importance was in what it meant to the client.

The client then began a monologue about normality. Although she didn't feel normal, she didn't think many people were, despite their lack of realization of their own conflicts. The therapist responded that the client had some issues and was trying to attend to them, a quality he valued. The client's feelings heightened. She responded, "Yeah, okay, then sex comes into this, too." The client's next words carried a refrain that many hysterical clients echo. She said, "I never think of myself with guys that I like or am attracted to. I always think of them with somebody else.... I'd imagine they had a different girlfriend. I couldn't picture myself going someplace with them. Even though I have a pretty good imagination.... And all the girls that I imagine they would date or be attracted to would feel comfortable about their sexuality and sex, but I don't, and that makes me feel again like I'm not normal." The therapist followed the client's comments with the query that the client seemed to feel that she wasn't "the one involved." The client emphatically said, "No." She could imagine it, but "it's not real. It's not a real possibility."

Several features of this passage are noteworthy. The client made clear that there were submerged aspects of her personality that weren't all that likeable. She wanted to feel what she felt without restrictions on it. In a sense, she was countering her surface "niceness" and expressing the dissonance between her manifest nurturing attitudes and her underlying frustration with that character defense. The client then played out some of her real feelings in becoming angry with the therapist for his constant questioning of her statements without revealing himself. She directly questioned him in her abrupt "Well, what does that mean?" The client's anger, however, was met by the therapist's own impatience and irritation. In a sense, that was the moment of real contact and could have been very therapeutic if attended to. But the therapist reverted to being a "therapist" and couched his anger in noncombatable terms. He noted that matters were important insofar as they were important to the client. That is a neat double bind: the therapist is angry because of his concern for the client.

But the client was not dissuaded, and her monologue on normality was directed at the composed, self-assured therapist. The target of the anger was immediately under the surface, and some few words from the therapist might have heated the session and changed its mood. But the therapist simply reiterated that the client had some issues and they had work to do. The client's next rendition about not feeling that she was involved in a relationship was ominous. On the surface, the client's statements about feeling that the males she was involved with "had a different girlfriend" might be construed as a variation on the theme of oedipal guilt. Perhaps; but there is an alternate construction to the client's reactions that is a repetitive theme in work with hysterical clients.

The hysterical client feels—and often with much evidence— that all men are interested in is sex. If other needs are voiced, they are met with impatience, and the ability to perform sexually takes precedence. In this case the client felt that her deficit was related to her sexual anxieties. She could not imagine a man being interested in her with such a deficit—it wasn't real, "not a real possibility." That statement is particularly poignant because it embodies the hysterical client's experience that she is an "object," interchangeable with any other object that happens to meet the needs of the other party of an interaction. As one client expressed it, "It's not *me* they are interested in," but, rather, some image in the other person's mind that may have little relationship to the person of the client.

In the few remaining minutes of the session, the client continued to criticize the intolerance in others toward her sexual abnormality; she was tolerant of imperfections in others. The client wanted to be comfortable with her sexuality but felt "unsure" of herself and wasn't comfortable with the "idea of sex." The client assured the therapist that the issue was not that "I don't have it, but I don't like it, the idea of it." The therapist felt the client had issues about her sexuality and they could work on them. The client felt "stuck." And, in what was her most direct moment in the session, the client asked, "You think we can get places with that?" When the therapist responded in the affirmative, the client queried, "How?"

The therapist's suggestion was a repeat performance of his previous observations that work needed to be done together. The client reminded the therapist of what she had said at an earlier time in their relationship: "We progress and then we regress." The client took the blame, however. She noted that when she begins to think that "no, we're not going to get anywhere, then we don't get anywhere, because I think we're not going to and I convince myself that you can't accomplish anything by just talking about it." Those final comments echoed the client's sentiments about her ongoing relationship with her boyfriend, who symbolized the oedipal father: "It's not going to work out." The client did not return for continuing sessions despite efforts to contact her and schedule further appointments.

FINAL OBSERVATIONS

Psychotherapeutic intervention in hysterical disorders is challenging work. Therapeutic interactions are exceedingly complex and rapid. Moment by moment, the hysteric will introduce conflicts in current and past extratherapeutic interactions that are nearly exact replications of her feelings and reactions to the therapist. The seemingly disjointed material that is sometimes introduced is often an accurate reproduction of the emotional tone of sessions and their impact on the client. As noted earlier, the unconscious associational process of the hysterical client is worthy of deep respect.

No therapist can expect to run the course of therapy with a hysterical client without making a great many errors. Those errors can be turned to genuine therapeutic gains—if they are recognized and acknowledged by the therapist. In the case just cited, the therapist's behavior triggered the activation of seductive character defenses and reawakened ambivalent oedipal strivings. The subsequent reenactment by the therapist and client paralleled her disappointing and conflicted relationships with her father and other males. Such conditions are inevitable in psychotherapy with the hysterical client and are not easily forestalled or avoided, nor should they be.

The critical issue for the therapist is not the avoidance of becoming unwittingly enmeshed in a reenactment of the client's distressing relationships but, rather, the recognition that he has done so (see Kell and Mueller 1966, Levenson 1972). With this awareness, the therapist can better decipher just how such a situation evolved and what his behavior activated in the client. Herein lies a main curative aspect of psychotherapy with the female hysterical client: the potential for working through a relationship with a significant male. In recognizing his contribution to the interaction, the therapist does not respond out of guilt; rather, he uses his awareness for the benefit of the client. The problems in psychotherapy with the hysterical disorders often reside in the arousal of therapist defenses. That is not to condemn the therapist; it is, rather, to empower the hysteric with an interpersonal sensitivity and understanding that makes interacting with her a growth-producing experience.

References

Abse, D.W. (1966). *Hysteria and Related Mental Disorders: an Approach to Psychological Medicine*. Bristol, England: Wright.

Alarcon, R. (1973). Hysteria and hysterical personality: how come one without the other? *Psychiatric Quarterly* 47:258-275.

Alexander, F. (1946a). The development of psychoanalytic therapy. In *Psychoanalytic Therapy*, ed. F. Alexander and T.M. French, pp. 13-24. New York: Ronald.

———. (1946b). The principle of corrective emotional experience. In *Psychoanalytic Therapy*, ed. F. Alexander and T.M. French, pp. 66-70. New York: Ronald.

———. (1952). Development of the fundamental concepts of psychoanalysis. In *Dynamic Psychiatry*, ed. F. Alexander and H. Ross, pp. 3-34. Chicago: University of Chicago Press.

Allen, D.W. (1977). Basic treatment issues. In *Hysterical Personality*, ed. M. Horowitz, pp. 283-328. New York: Jason Aronson.

American Psychiatric Association. (1980). *Diagnostic and Statistical Manual of Mental Disorders*, 3rd ed. Washington, DC: American Psychiatric Association.

Andrews, J.D.W. (1984). Psychotherapy with the hysterical personality: an interpersonal approach. *Psychiatry* 47:211-232.

Baumbacher, G., and Amini, F. (1980). The hysterical personality dis-
order: a proposed clarification of a diagnostic dilemma. *International
Journal of Psychoanalytic Psychotherapy* 8:501–533.
Blacker, K.H., and Tupin, J.P. (1977). Hysteria and hysterical struc-
tures: developmental and social theories. In *Hysterical Personality*, ed.
M. Horowitz, pp. 95–141. New York: Jason Aronson.
Blinder, M.G. (1966). The hysterical personality. *Psychiatry* 29:227–235.

Celani, D. (1976). An interpersonal approach to hysteria. *American
Journal of Psychiatry* 133:1414–1418.
Chodoff, P. (1974). The diagnosis of hysteria: An overview. *American
Journal of Psychiatry, 131* (10):1073–1078.
———. (1978). Psychotherapy of the hysterical personality disorder.
Journal of the American Academy of Psychoanalysis 6:496–510.
———. (1982). The hysterical personality disorder: a psychotherapeutic approach. In *Hysteria*, ed. A. Roy, pp. 277–285. New York: Wiley.
Chodoff, P., and Lyons, H. (1958). Hysteria, the hysterical personality and "hysterical" conversion. *American Journal of Psychiatry*
114:734–740.

Doehrman, M. (1976). Parallel processes in supervision and psychotherapy. *Bulletin of the Menninger Clinic* 40:1–104.

Easser, B.R., and Lesser, S.R. (1965). Hysterical personality: a reevaluation. *Psychoanalytic Quarterly* 34:390–412.
Eichler, M. (1976). The psychoanalytic treatment of an hysterical
character with special emphasis on problems of aggression. *International Journal of Psychoanalysis* 57:37–44.
Erikson, E. (1963). *Childhood and Society*. 2nd ed. New York: Norton.

Farber, L.H. (1966). *The Ways of the Will*. New York: Basic Books.
Fenichel, O. (1945). *The Psychoanalytic Theory of Neurosis*. New York:
Norton.
French, T.M. (1946). The transference phenomenon. In *Psychoanalytic
Therapy*, ed. F. Alexander and T.M. French, pp. 71–95. New York:
Ronald.

Fromm-Reichmann, F. (1950). *Principles of Intensive Psychotherapy.* Chicago: University of Chicago Press.

Glazer, M.W. (1979). The borderline personality diagnosis: some negative implications. *Psychotherapy: Theory, Research and Practice* 16:376–380.
Grinberg, L. (1979). Projective counteridentification and countertransference. In *Countertransference,* ed. L. Epstein and A.H. Feiner, pp. 169–191. New York: Jason Aronson.

Halleck, S.L. (1967). Hysterical personality traits. *Archives of General Psychiatry* 16:750–757.
Herman, J.L. (1981). *Father–Daughter Incest.* Cambridge, MA: Harvard University Press.
Hollender, M.H. (1971). Hysterical personality. *Comments on Contemporary Psychiatry* 1:17–24.
Horowitz, M.J. (1977). The core characteristics of hysterical personality. In *Hysterical Personality,* ed. M. Horowitz, pp. 3–6. New York: Jason Aronson.

Issacharoff, A. (1979). Barriers to knowing. In *Countertransference,* ed. L. Epstein and A.H. Feiner, pp. 27–43. New York: Jason Aronson.

Janet, P. (1929). *The Major Symptoms of Hysteria.* New York: Macmillan.

Kell, B.L., and Mueller, W.J. (1966). *Impact and Change: A Study of Counseling Relationships.* Englewood Cliffs, NJ: Prentice-Hall.
Krohn, A. (1978). *Hysteria: The Elusive Neurosis.* New York: International Universities Press.

Lazare, A. (1971). The hysterical character in psychoanalytic theory: evolution and confusion. *Archives of General Psychiatry* 25:131–137.
Lazare, A., Klerman, G.L., and Armor, D.J. (1970). Oral, obsessive and hysterical personality patterns. *Journal of Psychiatric Research* 7:272–290.

Leary, T. (1956). *Multilevel Measurement of Interpersonal Behavior.* Berkeley: Psychological Consultation Service.

——. (1957). *Interpersonal Diagnosis of Personality.* New York: Ronald.

Levenson, E.A. (1972). *The Fallacy of Understanding.* New York: Basic Books.

Luisada, P.V., Peele, R., and Pittard, E. (1974). The hysterical personality in men. *American Journal of Psychiatry* 131:518–522.

Marmor, J. (1953). Orality in the hysterical personality. *Journal of the American Psychoanalytic Association* 1:656–671.

Masterson, J.F. (1976). *Psychotherapy of the borderline adult.* New York: Brunner/Mazel.

Mueller, W.J. (1973). *Avenues to Understanding: The Dynamics of Therapeutic Interactions.* Englewood Cliffs, NJ: Prentice-Hall.

Mueller, W.J., and Kell, B.L. (1972). *Coping with Conflict: Supervising Counselors and Psychotherapists.* Englewood Cliffs, NJ: Prentice-Hall.

Murray, H.A. (1943). *Thematic Apperception Test Manual.* Cambridge, MA: Harvard University Press.

Nagera, H. (1975). *Female Sexuality and the Oedipus Complex.* New York: Jason Aronson.

Pruyser, P. (1975). What splits in splitting? *Bulletin of the Menninger Clinic* 39:1–46.

Racker, H. (1974). *Transference and Countertransference.* London: Hogarth Press.

Reich, W. (1949). *Character Analysis.* New York: Orgone Institute Press.

Semmler, K. (1977). Die Bedeutung der Sexualisierung in der Familiendynamik fur die Entstehung der Borderline-Hysterie. Trans. Dora G. West. *Dynamische Psychiatrie* 10:264–274.

Shapiro, D. (1965). *Neurotic Styles.* New York: Basic Books.

Siegman, A. (1954). Emotionality: the hysterical character defense. *Psychoanalytic Quarterly* 23:339–353.

Sperling, M. (1973). Conversion hysteria and conversion symptoms: a revision of classification and concepts. *Journal of the American Psychoanalytic Association* 21:745–772.

Sullivan, H.S. (1953a). *Conceptions of Modern Psychiatry.* New York: Norton.

———. (1953b). *The Interpersonal Theory of Psychiatry.* New York: Norton.

———. (1956). *Clinical Studies in Psychiatry.* New York: Norton.

Tupin, J.P. (1974). Hysterical and cyclothymic personalities. In *Personality Disorders: Diagnosis and Management,* ed. J.R. Lion, pp. 70–84. Baltimore: Williams & Wilkins.

Veith, I. (1965). *Hysteria: The History of a Disease.* Chicago: University of Chicago Press.

———. (1977). Four thousand years of hysteria. In *Hysterical Personality,* ed. M. Horowitz, pp. 7–93. New York: Jason Aronson.

Wolstein, B. (1964). *Transference.* 2nd ed. New York: Grune & Stratton.

Zetzel, E.R. (1968). The so-called good hysteric. *International Journal of Psychoanalysis* 49:256–260.

Index

A

Abse, D. W., 5
Acting-out behaviors
  as countertransference
    reaction, 155-156
  containing, 221-223
  insubstantiality and, 107-108
Adolescence, client emergence
  into, 238-239. *See also*
  Puberty
Adult relationships. *See* Female
  adult relationships; Male
  adult relationships
Adult relationship themes, 39-
  62. *See also* Displacement(s)
  commitment, 49
  control, 49, 57
  feelings, 58-62
  insubstantiality, 49, 51-56
  irresponsibility, 57
  mastery, 49
  performance, 49

responsibility, 49-51
sexuality, 49
victimization, 49
Adult relationship themes,
  analytic elements of, 49-51
  behavioral manifestations, 50
  contents, 49
  dynamic functions, 50
  form, 49-50
  psychogenic base, 50-51
  structures, 49
Affect
  control of, 60-61
  fear of, 58-62
  in identity crisis, 236-237
  isolation of, displacement
    and, 43-46, 56, 272-273
  as key to inner experience,
    162
  magnification of, as
    countertransference
    phenomenon, 141, 146-147
  sexualization of, 12, 16-17, 29

The Authors

William J. Mueller received his B.S. from Marquette University and his Ph.D. from the University of Wisconsin. He is Professor, Counseling Center and Department of Psychology, Michigan State University, a Diplomate in Counseling Psychology of the American Board of Professional Psychology, and a Fellow of the American Psychological Association. Dr. Mueller is the author or co-author of over a dozen books and articles in the areas of counseling and psychotherapy, personality, and supervision.

Albert S. Aniskiewicz received his B.A. from Rutgers University and his Ph.D. from Purdue University. He is Professor, Counseling Center and Department of Psychology, Michigan State University. Dr. Aniskiewicz is a Diplomate in Clinical Psychology, American Board of Professional Psychology, and a Fellow of the Society for Personality Assessment. He is the author of a number of journal articles on a broad range of psychological issues.